Ideas, Interests and Forei[gn Aid]

Why do countries give foreign aid? Although many countries have official development assistance programmes, this book argues that no two of them see the purpose of these programmes in the same way. Moreover, the way countries frame that purpose has shaped aid policy choices past and present. The author examines how Belgium long gave aid out of a sense of obligation to its former colonies, the Netherlands was more interested in pursuing international influence, Italy has focused on the reputational payoffs of aid flows, and Norwegian aid has had strong humanitarian motivations since the beginning. But at no time has a single frame shaped any one country's aid policy exclusively. Instead, analysing half a century of legislative debates on aid in these four countries, this book presents a unique picture both of cross-national and over-time patterns in the salience of different aid frames and of varying aid programmes that resulted.

A. MAURITS VAN DER VEEN received his Ph.D. in Government from Harvard University, and is currently an Assistant Professor at the College of William & Mary. He has also taught at the University of Pennsylvania and the University of Georgia. His research focuses on the impact of ideas on the making of foreign policy; in addition to foreign aid, he has written on European integration and human rights policy.

Cambridge Studies in International Relations: 120

Ideas, Interests and Foreign Aid

EDITORS
Christian Reus-Smit
Nicholas J. Wheeler

EDITORIAL BOARD
Stuart Croft, James Der Derian, Martha Finnemore, Lene Hansen, Robert Keohane, Rachel Kerr, Jan Aart Scholte, Peter Vale, Kees Van Der Pijl, Jutta Weldes, Jennifer Welsh, William Wohlforth

Cambridge Studies in International Relations is a joint initiative of Cambridge University Press and the British International Studies Association (BISA). The series will include a wide range of material, from undergraduate textbooks and surveys to research-based monographs and collaborative volumes. The aim of the series is to publish the best new scholarship in International Studies from Europe, North America and the rest of the world.

Cambridge Studies in International Relations

119 Emanuel Adler and Vincent Pouliot
   International Practices
118 Ayşe Zarakol
   After defeat
   How the East learned to live with the West
117 Andrew Phillips
   War, religion and empire
   The transformation of international orders
116 Joshua Busby
   Moral movements and foreign policy
115 Séverine Autesserre
   The trouble with the Congo
   Local violence and the failure of international peacebuilding
114 Deborah D. Avant, Martha Finnemore *and*
   Susan K. Sell
   Who governs the globe?
113 Vincent Pouliot
   International security in practice
   The politics of NATO–Russia diplomacy
112 Columba Peoples
   Justifying ballistic missile defence
   Technology, security and culture
111 Paul Sharp
   Diplomatic theory of international relations
110 John A. Vasquez
   The war puzzle revisited
109 Rodney Bruce Hall
   Central banking as global governance
   Constructing financial credibility
108 Milja Kurki
   Causation in international relations
   Reclaiming causal analysis
107 Richard M. Price
   Moral limit and possibility in world politics
106 Emma Haddad
   The refugee in international society
   Between sovereigns

Series list continues after index

Ideas, Interests and Foreign Aid

A. MAURITS VAN DER VEEN

CAMBRIDGE UNIVERSITY PRESS

CAMBRIDGE UNIVERSITY PRESS
Cambridge, New York, Melbourne, Madrid, Cape Town,
Singapore, São Paulo, Delhi, Tokyo, Mexico City

Cambridge University Press
The Edinburgh Building, Cambridge CB2 8RU, UK

Published in the United States of America by Cambridge University Press, New York

www.cambridge.org
Information on this title: www.cambridge.org/9780521264099

© A. Maurits van der Veen 2011

This publication is in copyright. Subject to statutory exception
and to the provisions of relevant collective licensing agreements,
no reproduction of any part may take place without the written
permission of Cambridge University Press.

First published 2011

Printed in the United Kingdom at the University Press, Cambridge

A catalogue record for this publication is available from the British Library

Library of Congress Cataloging in Publication data
Veen, A. Maurits van der.
  Ideas, interests and foreign aid / A. Maurits van der Veen.
    p. cm. – (Cambridge studies in international relations)
  Includes bibliographical references and index.
  ISBN 978-1-107-00974-5 (hardback) – ISBN 978-0-521-26409-9 (paperback)
  1. Economic assistance. 2. Economic assistance, European. I. Title.
  HC60.V397 2011
  338.91–dc23   2011018862

ISBN 978-1-107-00974-5 Hardback
ISBN 978-0-521-26409-9 Paperback

Cambridge University Press has no responsibility for the persistence or
accuracy of URLs for external or third-party internet websites referred to in
this publication, and does not guarantee that any content on such websites is,
or will remain, accurate or appropriate.

Contents

List of figures		*page* viii
List of tables		ix
Preface		xi
1	The many uses of foreign aid	1
2	One policy, multiple goals: framing and foreign aid	23
3	Debates about aid: contents and patterns	48
4	Aid frames: origins and evolution	77
5	The administration of aid policy	110
6	The generosity contest: determinants of aid volume	139
7	The popularity contest: selecting the recipients of aid	171
8	Conclusion: frames and policy	210
Appendix A: Legislative debates coded		235
Appendix B: Debate coding examples		247
Appendix C: Aid distribution: data and sources		259
Bibliography		264
Index		283

Figures

3.1 Relative weight of different aid frames, averaged over all four countries *page* 61
3.2 Relative weight of different aid frames, Belgium 65
3.3 Relative weight of different aid frames, Italy 68
3.4 Relative weight of different aid frames, the Netherlands 70
3.5 Relative weight of different aid frames, Norway 73
6.1 Aggregate ODA performance of DAC member states 143
6.2 Official development assistance of Belgium, Italy, the Netherlands and Norway, expressed as a percentage of each country's gross national product 144

Tables

1.1	The seven broad frames relevant to aid policy	*page* 10
2.1	Basic hypotheses about the relationship between frames and aid policy	45
3.1	Arguments for aid and their allocation to different frames	57
3.2	Relative weight of general frames over time	60
3.3	Relative weight of general frames over time, relative to dataset average	62
3.4	Average weight of each frame, for the entire period 1955–2000, per country	64
3.5	Strength of general frames over time in Belgium, relative to dataset average	66
3.6	Strength of general frames over time in Italy, relative to dataset average	69
3.7	Strength of general frames over time in the Netherlands, relative to dataset average	71
3.8	Strength of general frames over time in Norway, relative to dataset average	74
3.9	Frequency with which the salience of a frame exceeded the dataset average by at least 25 per cent	75
5.1	Hypotheses about the relationship between frames and tied aid	128
5.2	Hypotheses about the relationship between frames and multilateral aid	132
6.1	Hypotheses about the relationship between frames and aid volume	151
6.2	Summary statistics for dependent and explanatory variables	164
6.3	Determinants of aid volume, *uninteracted*, panel-specific autocorrelation	165

6.4	Determinants of aid volume, *interacted*, panel-specific autocorrelation	166
6.5	Determinants of aid volume, *uninteracted*, no autocorrelation	167
6.6	Determinants of aid volume, *interacted*, no autocorrelation	168
7.1	Top aid recipients over time, all DAC donors	174
7.2a	Top aid recipients over time: Belgium	176
7.2b	Top aid recipients over time: Italy	177
7.2c	Top aid recipients over time: The Netherlands	178
7.2d	Top aid recipients over time: Norway	179
7.3	Hypotheses about the relationship between frames and aid distribution	181
7.4	Independent variables that may affect the selection of aid recipients, with associated frames	199
7.5a	Selection: interacted regressions, all countries combined and each country separately	201
7.5b	Aid share: interacted regressions, all countries combined and each country separately	203
7.5c	Additional data: interacted regressions, all countries combined and each country separately	205
A.1	Debates coded for Belgium	236
A.2	Debates coded for Italy	240
A.3	Debates coded for the Netherlands	243
A.4	Debates coded for Norway	245
B.1	Motivations for aid, with sample quotations, by general frame	248
C.1	Data used to generate Communist-border variable	261
C.2	Summary statistics for non-donor-specific explanatory variables, after processing	262
C.3a	Summary statistics for explanatory variables: Belgium	263
C.3b	Summary statistics for explanatory variables: Italy	263
C.3c	Summary statistics for explanatory variables: the Netherlands	263
C.3d	Summary statistics for explanatory variables: Norway	263

Preface

I have been interested in foreign aid for almost as long as I can remember. Growing up in the Netherlands, I read the free monthly magazine *Sam Sam* (Working Together), published by the Dutch government to educate children about development assistance and distributed to every student in the upper grades of elementary school. When I began to pay attention to national politics some years later, I took for granted that although specific features of the development aid programme were frequently debated in the legislature and in the media, the need to have a large and generous aid programme was rarely questioned. Indeed, it was not until I moved to the United States for college that I encountered arguments against foreign aid per se.

If Americans had a different view of the practice of development assistance policy, they also appeared to have a different view of the theory that might explain it. Rational choice theory, rather more popular in the United States than in Europe, seemed to suggest that government policies must always pursue material interests, which made aid policy – with its ostensibly altruistic goals – hard to explain. I began to wonder how aid policy could be perceived so differently in the Netherlands and the United States, even though the policy instruments were essentially the same; I also wondered whether these differing perceptions might explain how widely aid programmes varied across donor states; and I wondered how the logic of rationality might account for a policy that seemed to have so many different possible motivations.

It quickly became clear that the best way to turn these puzzles into a manageable research project was to look in more detail at the aid policies of countries that were broadly similar on most key dimensions, but whose aid programmes differed considerably. Accordingly, I decided to focus on small- and medium-sized European countries (even though my argument generalizes to all aid donors, as I explain in the conclusion). As I researched aid policy and elaborated my ideas over the ensuing years, I found that different perceptions of the purpose of aid policy – i.e. aid 'frames' – have a tremendous impact on the shape of a country's aid programme. On the other hand, it proved unnecessary to look for non-rational motivations: while policy-makers often pursue non-material goals – such as meeting an obligation or establishing a reputation – they do so quite rationally. In fact, the key to understanding aid policy lies not in explaining away aid frames that highlight non-material goals, but rather in obtaining reliable measures of the strength of different frames. Here I found legislative debates to be invaluable, and I spent many months combing through the parliamentary records of Belgium, Italy, the Netherlands and Norway to learn how legislators had framed aid from the inception of national aid programmes to the present.

Over the life of this project I have been fortunate to receive support from more people and organizations than I can ever properly thank. A Mellon Foundation Dissertation Research Grant through the Department of Government at Harvard University supported my initial investigations into the topic. Krupp Foundation Grants through Harvard's Center for European Studies made possible extensive field research in 1995 and 1996 in the Netherlands, Belgium, Italy and Norway, as well as the initial phase of dissertation writing during the 1996–1997 academic year. Further field research during the summer of 1997 was supported by a Jens Aubrey Westengard Summer Research Grant, and the processing of that research was facilitated by a Mellon Foundation writing grant through Harvard's Government Department. Without the generous support of these different foundations, it is unlikely that I would have been able to tackle a project of this scope or bring it to successful completion.

My field research would not have been possible without the assistance and accessibility of a number of libraries and research institutes, many of which I have visited repeatedly over the years. In all four countries studied, the libraries and the librarians of the national aid administrations – DGIS in The Hague, ABOS in Brussels, DGCS in Rome and NORAD in Oslo – were extremely helpful. In addition, several research institutes graciously let me use their libraries and offered me space to work. In particular, in Italy, the Istituto Affari Internazionali

Preface

(IAI) offered me the use of their library as an ersatz office for a number of weeks. Similarly, in Oslo, the Norsk Utenrikspolitisk Institutt (NUPI) generously provided office space during the summer of 1996, and its library and librarians were invaluable during my research there. In addition, stimulating lunch conversations at NUPI greatly added to my understanding of Norwegian politics. A subsequent stay at the ARENA research institute in Oslo some years later proved equally worthwhile and productive.

At Harvard University, I enjoyed affiliations with the Center for International Affairs and the Center for European Studies. After receiving my PhD, I was able to develop the dissertation's argument further during a post-doctoral fellowship at the Christopher H. Browne Center for International Politics at the University of Pennsylvania. I updated the study with data throughout the year 2000 during my first years at the University of Georgia, while the final revisions were undertaken at my current institutional home, the College of William & Mary. I owe a considerable debt of gratitude to all these institutions for the supportive and stimulating intellectual environments they offered.

My greatest debts, of course, are to the people whose support, insights and feedback have made this book much better than it otherwise would have been. In particular, I would like to thank (in no particular order) Brad Mann, Pepper Culpepper, Erik Bleich, Mark Duckenfield, David Leal, Javier Astudillo, Marga Gomez-Reino, Wendy Franz, Andrew Moravcsik, Lucy Goodhart, Milada Vachudová, Robert Putnam, Marc Busch, Jeffrey Checkel, Ian Lustick, Tom Callaghy, Avery Goldstein, Dan Miodownik, Markus Crepaz, Chris Allen, Jaroslav Tir and Mike Tierney, and many more whose omission is due only to my faulty memory, not to any lack of appreciation. Special thanks are owed to the members of my dissertation committee, Lisa Martin, Robert Keohane, Stanley Hoffmann and Peter Hall.

On a more personal note, I cannot thank enough the friends who hosted me in different countries: Roel Mulder in The Hague, Gesa and Bernd Haarpaintner in Brussels, and Cille Skaarberg and Olav Storli Ulvund in Oslo. In addition, I owe some of my most memorable experiences in each country (and, quite possibly, my sanity) to the many running friends I made along the way, including Patrick Aris, Mark van Maaren, Frank Staal, Massimiliano Monteforte, Roberto

Fazzari, Bob Sevene, Rusty Snow, Mark Mayall, Jamahl Prince, Darin Shearer, Mary-Louise Culpepper, Joanna Veltri, Eric Stabb, Kirk Smith and Brock Tessman. Last, but not least, I would like to thank Hilda, Bruno, Janny, Gerlof, and above all my wife, Helen Murphy, who has made not only this book but also my life far better.

1 *The many uses of foreign aid*

Of the seeming and real innovations which the modern age has introduced into the practice of foreign policy, none has proven more baffling to both understanding and action than foreign aid.

– Hans J. Morgenthau, 1960[1]

Take up the White Man's burden –
The savage wars of peace –
Fill full the mouth of Famine,
And bid the sickness cease.

– Rudyard Kipling, 1899

I can handle whatever you put your mind to.
– Leatherman multitools website[2]

Why do countries give foreign aid? Some earnest idealists see aid as a modern form of Kipling's 'White Man's burden': a worthy, noble enterprise, aimed at lifting those worse off than ourselves out of poverty. More critical observers point to the poem's call for expansionism and Western control, and condemn aid as simply a modern form of imperialism. Others, still, note that Kipling may have intended his poem as satire, criticizing foolish notions about both the value and the feasibility of assisting those allegedly in need of superior Western beliefs, skills and products; aid, they suggest, is a similarly misguided and often counterproductive policy. There may be kernels of truth in each of these characterizations, but even taken together they offer at best an incomplete picture of the multifaceted policy area that is

[1] Morgenthau, foreword to G. Liska, *The new statecraft: Foreign aid in American foreign policy*, vii.
[2] Sales text on the front page of www.leatherman.com, accessed 7 August 2007.

contemporary foreign aid. Aid programmes can handle whatever policy-makers put their minds to, making them the foreign policy version of a multitool or Swiss army knife.

Every advanced industrialized nation has a foreign aid programme, and each of these programmes officially aims to foster the development of denizens of the poorest countries. The sums involved are considerable. In recent years, annual transfers have exceeded $100 billion, which translates to over $100 per donor state citizen per year. In some donor states the aid programme accounts for 5 per cent or more of the government budget. On the recipient side, official development assistance (ODA)[3] accounts for a large share of international capital flowing into less developed countries (LDCs). Nevertheless, the factors shaping foreign aid remain ill-understood, more than half a century after Morgenthau first described the policy as 'baffling'. Aid levels rise and fall without obvious causes. Explanatory factors that appear important in one case are insignificant in another. And case studies of different aid programmes frequently explain similar empirical patterns using incompatible models. One of the best recent studies on foreign aid frankly concludes that 'There are too many interacting variables to justify a model that would be both parsimonious and insightful'.[4]

I argue that the central factor overlooked in the literature on aid is ideational: ideas about the goals and purposes of aid policy shape its formulation and implementation. Different goals for aid result in different policy choices. Aid policy is puzzling in part because it is not obvious *ex ante* what the goal of official development assistance ought to be: aid can serve goals from security (e.g. fighting terrorism), to financial gain (promoting exports), to humanitarianism. Apparent contradictions in the literature result in part from a tendency to assume the dominance of one particular category of goals over all others. As Snyder, Bruck and Sapin already pointed out five decades ago, 'To assume motivation begs many of the most significant questions which arise in the study of international politics'.[5] A key goal of

---

[3] In order to avoid repetitiveness, I use the terms aid, foreign aid, development aid, development assistance and development cooperation interchangeably throughout the remainder of the study. A formal definition of aid as an instrument of government policy is provided below.
[4] C. Lancaster, *Foreign aid: Diplomacy, development, domestic politics*, 9.
[5] R. C. Snyder, H. W. Bruck and B. Sapin, *Foreign policy decision-making: An approach to the study of international politics*, 137.

this book, then, is to show that it is possible to measure, rather than assume, motivation, and that doing so can improve our understanding of foreign policy decision-making considerably. As such, though the focus of the study is on foreign aid, its implications extend well beyond this particular issue area. Indeed, the question 'Why do countries give aid?' could easily be rephrased as 'How does (foreign) policy get made?' The model I develop can be applied to the more general question too.

The twenty-first century has brought a renewed interest in the politics of foreign aid, among policy-makers as well as observers. Bono, the lead singer of U2, has made headlines worldwide with his advocacy of debt relief.[6] Economist Jeffrey Sachs argues, in his bestseller *The end of poverty*,[7] for a considerable increase in foreign aid, targeted at proven life-saving and poverty-reducing measures. Significantly, governments have got in on the act as well. In September 2000, the United Nations member states committed themselves to meeting a series of ambitious Millennium Development Goals by the year 2015, among others by increasing official development assistance considerably. This commitment has since been reaffirmed at regular intervals. Thus, in March 2002, participants at the International Conference on Financing for Development in Monterrey, Mexico, recognized that 'a substantial increase in ODA will be required';[8] at the Gleneagles summit in 2005, the G-8 claimed that official development assistance (ODA) by 2010 would be $50 billion greater than it had been in 2004 (an increase by about half);[9] and the closing declaration of the 2008 Doha International Conference on Financing for Development called upon countries to maintain their commitment to devote 0.7 per cent of GNP to ODA.[10]

Yet despite all this enthusiasm, actual progress has been disappointing. The Millennium Development Goals, which include such targets as universal primary education, reducing child and maternal mortality, and reversing the spread of malaria, are ambitious and resist easy intervention. More generous aid has flowed to some countries, such

[6] J. Tyrangiel, 'Bono's mission'.
[7] J. Sachs, *The end of poverty: Economic possibilities of our time*.
[8] M. G. Wabl, 'A "Monterrey consensus" might replace the Washington consensus'.
[9] G-8, 'The Gleneagles Communiqué', 26.
[10] United Nations, *Doha Declaration on financing for development*, 18.

as Mali. However, others, such as Guinea, are rather less popular among aid donors. In addition, much of the increase in aid in recent years has come in the form of debt relief, rather than as additional new funds. Indeed, at the aforementioned Monterrey conference, the United States blocked a joint commitment to raise ODA spending to 0.7 per cent of gross national income (GNI), a decades-old target of the United Nations.[11] US ODA in 2005 was just 0.22 per cent of GNP, less than one-third of this official target.[12] Moreover, scepticism about the value of ODA has become increasingly prominent. In 2006, economist William Easterly tellingly borrowed the title of Kipling's classic poem for a book highlighting the failures of aid policy over the past few decades: *The white man's burden: Why the West's efforts to aid the rest have done so much ill and so little good.*[13]

In light of such developments, the question that opened this chapter – why do countries give foreign aid? – needs to be sharpened somewhat. Better questions might be: why do some countries consistently fall short of their commitments to increase foreign aid? Why do countries persist in funding aid projects that are likely to fail? And why are some recipient states so much more successful at attracting aid than others? These are among the central questions addressed in this book. As the subsequent chapters demonstrate, the answer to these and other questions can be found at least in part in the different goals associated with official development assistance in different donor states.

In making this case, I present an in-depth analysis of the first half-century of official development assistance, from 1950 until 2000 (the year the Millennium Development Goals were adopted). The analysis focuses on four European countries: Belgium, Italy, the Netherlands and Norway. The aid programmes of these four countries over the course of the second half of the twentieth century present a broad range of empirical variation in terms of the generosity of aid, the distribution of funds across recipient nations, and the types of projects funded. To help explain these programmes, I measure the ideas of policy-makers about the goals of development assistance in each of these countries at different points in time, through an in-depth

---

[11] Wabl, 'A "Monterrey consensus"'.
[12] OECD, *Development co-operation report 2006: Summary.*
[13] W. Easterly, *The white man's burden: Why the West's efforts to aid the rest have done so much ill and so little good*; cf. also D. Moyo, *Dead aid: Why aid is not working and how there is a better way for Africa.*

content analysis of legislative debates about foreign aid. As we shall see, legislators are remarkably candid about the goals they consider relevant and significant in the context of aid. Hence these debates provide us with invaluable insights into the prominence of different ideas about aid cross-nationally and over time. Moreover, it is easy to show that the measure of aid ideas that we can derive from the debates is causally prior to aid policy outcomes, and can thus not be discounted as mere 'cheap talk'.

The information derived from analysing legislative debates can be categorized into broad 'frames' policy-makers use to think about this issue area. Frames, in this context, are organizing units that serve to make sense out of incoming data. They help interpret, prioritize and classify information. To simplify matters somewhat, we can think of frames in terms of word associations: mention a policy instrument to a decision-maker, and ask her for the first broad political concepts that come to mind. Does 'aid' evoke 'security', or 'trade', or 'humanitarianism', for example? Returning to the metaphor of the Swiss army knife, frames are like the individual tools that can found in such a knife. It is often said that 'When all you have is a hammer, everything looks like a nail'. But what if you have a Swiss army knife? Some may view it as a hammer, and still see nails everywhere; others may see a screwdriver, and discern only screws. Others, still, may see a set of pliers, mini scissors, or even a weak nail file. It is important to note, too, that different Swiss army knives incorporate different sets of tools. In the same way, the set of goals envisioned for foreign aid varies from one country to the next, as well as over time.

A key feature of frames is that they both specify goals and suggest particular policy choices, just as a hammer suggests both a goal (hammering something into something else) and a particular target (a nail). Frames thus shape the overall organization and quality of aid programmes, but they also affect specific features, such as the total size of the aid budget, or the geographical allocation of aid. In other words, what Morgenthau saw as the 'baffling' nature of aid policy is explained by the fact that different ideas about aid have been dominant at different times and in different donor states. Nor is aid policy unique in this respect: a variety of policy instruments can be conceived of as Swiss army knives for their particular issue area. For example, the United States Department of Agriculture noted in a 1996 bulletin: 'It may be tempting to view [revolving loan funds] as the "Swiss army knife" of development policy.'[14] The broader implications of this approach for the study of policy-making in general will be taken up briefly in the concluding chapter.

The remainder of this chapter is divided into four sections. First, I present some background information on development assistance. Next, I introduce the seven broad frames that categorize how decision-makers think about aid. Following this, I lay out the core features of the theoretical model. Finally, I briefly preview the empirical evidence supporting the model, as presented in the subsequent chapters of the book.

Development assistance past and present

Development economist Peter Bauer once argued that '[t]he one common characteristic of the Third World is not poverty, stagnation, exploitation, brotherhood or skin colour. It is the receipt of foreign aid'.[15] Indeed, many less developed countries would face serious political, economic and social upheaval if aid flows were to dry up, as aid often contributes significantly to the national income of recipient states. For example, aid to the tiny island nation of São Tomé and Principe exceeded its gross national product by 16 per cent in 1998, and even a medium-sized state such as Nicaragua received aid flows exceeding 50 per cent of its GNP that year.[16]

Development cooperation as we know it today has its origins in the immediate post-Second World War period. International institutions were among the first to pursue the goal of development explicitly. For example, the 1945 United Nations Charter called upon member states to 'employ international machinery for the promotion of the economic and social advancement of all peoples'. The $13 billion economic recovery programme known as the Marshall Plan was another important early initiative, and is widely seen as an inspiration for later aid programmes. In many ways, however, the colonial powers took the lead in giving shape to aid policy, in the spirit of Kipling's poem.

---

[14] United States Department of Agriculture, 'Are revolving loan funds a better way to finance rural development?', 1.
[15] P. T. Bauer, *Reality and rhetoric: Studies in the economics of development*, 40.
[16] OECD, *Geographical distribution of financial flows to aid recipients. 1998 report*, Table 25.

Development assistance past and present 7

Already in 1945, the United Kingdom passed a 'Colonial Development and Welfare Act' reorganizing British development aid. Aid flows to Dutch colonies from 1946–51 totalled $1.46 billion, and a Belgian ten-year plan for the Congo made available $500 million during the 1950s.[17]

During the 1960s, these colonial programmes were gradually transformed into development assistance programmes. Around the same time, other industrialized states such as Denmark and Norway began to establish their own programmes from scratch. Moreover, the United Nations designated the 1960s the 'Development Decade', symbolizing the reigning optimism about the possibility of accelerating economic growth rates in the Third World so as to allow them to 'catch up' to the rich states. A major feature of the Development Decade was the introduction of commonly accepted volume targets for aid flows. In addition, the 1960s saw the creation of a central coordinating agency for the aid policies of OECD states: the Development Assistance Committee (DAC). One of its first challenges was to produce agreement on official requirements for financial flows to be considered foreign aid. By 1969 the standardization of terminology was largely complete, including a formal definition of 'official development assistance':

[ODA consists of] those flows to developing countries and multilateral institutions provided by official agencies, including state and local governments or by their executive agencies, each transaction of which meets the following tests: a) it is administered with the promotion of the economic development and welfare of developing countries as its main objective, and b) it is concessional in character and contains a grant element of at least 25 per cent.[18]

The 1970s brought a growing concern with the quality of aid. An international group of experts, headed by former Canadian Prime Minister Lester Pearson, worried that '[a] good deal of bilateral aid

---

[17] J. Van Soest, *The start of international development cooperation in the United Nations, 1945–1952*, 31.
[18] OECD, *Twenty-five years of development co-operation, a review: Efforts and policies of the members of the Development Assistance Committee, 1984 report*, 171. The grant element of aid is the degree to which loan or credit terms are less demanding than market terms, through longer grace periods or lower interest rates, for example.

has ... been dispensed in order to achieve short-term political favors, gain strategic advantages, or promote exports from the donor'.[19] Their conclusion both illustrated that aid can be used to pursue a range of different goals, and alarmed those who felt aid ought to be primarily humanitarian in nature. Accordingly, major aid donors began to study how best to direct aid at specific, poorer subgroups within LDCs, and how better to meet 'basic human needs'. The drought in the Sahel put humanitarian relief on the agenda for good from the mid 1970s.

The 1980s and 1990s were a period of consolidation and stagnation in many donor states. Budget constraints, together with a perceived 'aid fatigue', generated pressures for reduced aid budgets and for the restructuring of aid programmes to reflect domestic economic interests more closely.[20] In 2000, when the Millennium Development Goals were adopted, the DAC states gave a combined total of $53.7 billion in official development assistance, accounting for 0.22% of their collective gross national income. This represented an increase in real terms of about 10%, following an aggregate decline of about 25% in real terms that took place from 1992 to 1997. In absolute terms, Japan was the largest donor in 2000, with $13.5 billion (or more than 25% of total OECD aid flows), followed by the United States ($10 billion) and Germany ($5 billion). Measured relative to the donor's economic size, aid flows ranged from a low of 0.1% of GNI for the United States to 1.06% of GNI for Denmark.[21]

Six years later, the Millennium Development Goals appeared to have had at least somewhat of an impact. In 2006, the United States was the largest aid donor by far, with $23.5 billion.[22] Japan had become only the third-largest donor, with $11.2 billion, exceeded also by the United Kingdom's $12.5 billion. Moreover, France and Germany, too, had increased their aid levels to over $10 billion. As a result, total DAC ODA had increased to $104.4 billion. Nevertheless,

---

[19] L. B. Pearson and the Commission on International Development, *Partners in development*, 5.
[20] It should be noted that aid 'fatigue' or weariness is a concept that dates back at least to the 1960s. *Ibid.*, 4; F. Van Dam, *Onbehagen rond de ontwikkelingshulp*. Since then, it has been trotted out at regular intervals to defend reductions in government expenditures on ODA, but its credibility as a causal factor determining aid levels is obviously questionable.
[21] OECD, *ODA steady in 2000; other flows decline*.
[22] Of course, this increase in US aid was driven more by the wars in Iraq and Afghanistan than by the Millennium Development Goals.

only five countries exceeded the official UN goal of 0.7% of GNI in aid: Sweden, Norway, the Netherlands, Luxembourg and Denmark. With an aid level that had risen to 0.18% of GNI, the United States stood out less than it had five years earlier; nevertheless, only one OECD donor was less generous in comparative terms: Greece, one of the poorest of the DAC donors. As noted above, a large share of the increase in ODA was due to debt relief. Since debt relief is a one-time-only charge – a particular debt can only be forgiven once – aid levels were expected to decline again in subsequent years.[23] That they did not do so – in 2008 and 2009 total DAC ODA was about $120 billion – suggests that the increased political visibility of foreign aid may be making countries more reluctant to cut their programmes.[24]

The goals of foreign aid

Students of aid policy tend to polarize into two camps: those who think humanitarian considerations dominate and those who feel that the self-interest of donor states (or actors within those states) prevails. Some observers maintain that 'aid [is] a response to world poverty which arose mainly from ethical and humane concern'.[25] Others, however, argue that 'foreign aid programs are shaped with the interests of the aid-giving countries primarily in mind'.[26] Still others try to reconcile the opposing claims by arguing that aid policy itself serves as an arena for this struggle between humanitarianism and direct self-interest: 'despite many changes over the years, there has been one constant in the history of aid, namely that the development objectives of aid programmes have been distorted by the use of aid for donor commercial and political advantage'.[27]

In part as a result of this Manichean distinction between self-interest and humanitarianism, much of the literature on aid has been 'trapped in something of an intellectual vacuum'.[28] Casting our net

[23] OECD, *Development co-operation report 2007*.
[24] OECD, *Development co-operation report 2010*.
[25] D. H. Lumsdaine, *Moral vision in international politics: The foreign aid regime, 1949–1989*, 3.
[26] E. S. Mason, *Foreign aid and foreign policy*, 3.
[27] P. Hjertholm and H. White, 'Foreign aid in historical perspective', 80.
[28] P. J. Schraeder, S. W. Hook and B. Taylor, 'Clarifying the foreign aid puzzle: A comparison of American, Japanese, French, and Swedish aid flows', 295.

Table 1.1 *The seven broad frames relevant to aid policy*

Frame	Goals for aid
Security	Increase donor's physical security: support allies, oppose Communism, etc.
Power/influence	Pursue power: increase leverage over others, win allies and positions of influence in international fora
Wealth/economic self-interest	Further economic interests of donor economy; support export industries
Enlightened self-interest	Pursue global public goods: peace, stability, environmental health, population control, etc.
Reputation/self-affirmation	Establish and express a certain identity in international relations; improve international status and reputation
Obligation/duty	Fulfil obligations, whether historical or associated with position in international system
Humanitarianism	Promote the well-being of the poorest groups worldwide; provide humanitarian relief

wider so as to include the full range of possible goals helps transcend this problem. Overall, goals for aid can be classified into seven general categories: security, power and influence, economic self-interest (wealth), enlightened self-interest, self-affirmation and reputation, obligation and duty, and humanitarianism, as shown in Table 1.1.

Each of these general frames has been used by policy-makers to explain and defend aid policy. Moreover, all of these frames appear in the literature, though they are not always explicitly delineated. In fact, many authors simply emphasize the general self-interest of states, and the 'Swiss army knife' nature of aid: 'Foreign aid has served as a microcosm of donor states' foreign policies; for every donor, a different story can be told about the use of aid as an agent of national interest.'[29] Unfortunately, scholars have found it impossible to specify *ex ante* 'which of many potential self-interests are at play in the execution of aid policy'.[30] Most authors, nevertheless, explicitly emphasize one or more of the frames listed in the table, while some refer to almost all of them.

The security and power frames have long been prominent in studies of aid that draw on *realpolitik* insights. Five decades ago, Morgenthau already contended that 'Much of what goes by the name of foreign aid today is in the nature of … bribes … [It] performs … the function of a price paid by the [donor] to the [recipient] for political services rendered or to be rendered by the latter to the former'.[31] Thus a number of authors point to security interests,[32] whereas others emphasize strategic or power-political considerations.[33] Nevertheless, the most common interest-based explanation for aid has been that of economic self-interest, with the interests served ranging from developing or securing export markets, to safeguarding

---

[29] S. W. Hook, *National interest and foreign aid*, 16.
[30] Schraeder *et al.*, 'Clarifying the foreign aid puzzle', 296.
[31] H. J. Morgenthau, 'Preface to a political theory of foreign aid', 302. Along the same lines, Banfield argues that 'From the standpoint both of morality and American national interest we ought to prefer to give aid on a *quid pro quo* basis' (E. C. Banfield, 'American foreign aid doctrines', 20). A modern version of this same argument is made in B. Bueno de Mesquita and A. Smith, 'Foreign aid and policy concessions'; see also B. Bueno de Mesquita and A. Smith, 'A political economy of aid'.
[32] For example, K. B. Griffin and J. L. Enos, 'Foreign assistance: Objectives and consequences'; K. B. Griffin, 'Foreign aid after the Cold War'; R. F. Hopkins, 'Political economy of foreign aid'; M. Kato, 'A model of U.S. foreign aid allocation: An application of a rational decision-making scheme'; R. D. McKinlay and A. Mughan, *Aid and arms to the Third World: An analysis of the distribution and impact of U.S. official transfers*; D. Porter, *U.S. economic foreign aid: A case study of the United States Agency for International Development*; L. Schoultz, 'U.S. foreign policy and human rights violations in Latin America: A comparative analysis of foreign aid distribution'; E. R. Wittkopf, *Western bilateral aid allocations: A comparative study of recipient state attributes and aid received*.
[33] A. Alesina and D. Dollar, 'Who gives foreign aid to whom and why?'; J. S. Hoadley, 'Small states as aid donors'; R. O. Keohane, 'Political influence in the General Assembly'; J. H. Lebovic, 'National interest and U.S. foreign aid: The Carter and Reagan years', 125; P. Mosley, *Overseas aid: Its defence and reform*, 34–7; E.R. Wittkopf, 'Foreign aid and the United Nations votes'; World Bank, *World development report 1990: Poverty*, 4.

the supply of valuable imports, to providing employment for donor state nationals.[34]

While an emphasis on material goals characterizes much of the study of international relations, the literature on foreign aid has, at times, seemed somewhat insulated from trends in the broader discipline. This helps account for the fact that, despite being largely ignored by the latter, altruism and humanitarianism have been prominent in the aid literature.[35] The remaining three frames in Table 1.1, in contrast, do not fit comfortably within either the international relations or the aid literature, and tend to crop up in a more ad hoc fashion. For example, a notion of enlightened self-interest is evident in the argument that aid 'has always had an economic dimension, namely, an attempt to create a strong, expanding, global capitalist economy'.[36] Similarly, the Brandt Commission reports of the early 1980s highlighted the potential impact of international crises and instability on living standards worldwide.[37]

---

[34] E.g. Banfield, 'American foreign aid'; Y. De Schaetzen, 'L'Italie et l'Afrique: La volonté politique conjuguée avec le dynamisme des entrepreneurs'; C. R. Frank, Jr and M. Baird, 'Foreign aid: Its speckled past and future prospects'; Griffin, 'Foreign aid'; K. A. Hagen, '"Poenget er at dette skal være utviklingshjelp." En analyse av ordningen med "statsgaranti på særlige vilkår ved eksport til og ved investeringer i utviklingsland", og denne ordningens tilknytning til Norsk utviklingshjelp i perioden 1963–1984'; G. Hancock, *Lords of poverty: The power, prestige, and corruption of the international aid business*; P. Hoebink, 'Geven is nemen: De Nederlandse ontwikkelingshulp aan Tanzania en Sri Lanka'; Kato, 'A model of U.S.'; E. S. Kirschen, 'Objectifs et determination de l'aide aux pays sous-développés'; A. Maizels and M. K. Nissanke, 'Motivations for aid to developing countries'; G. Mureddu, 'Obiettivi espliciti e impliciti degli aiuti allo sviluppo'; S. C. Poe, 'United States aid allocation: The quest for cumulation'.

[35] E.g. R. Gounder, *Overseas aid motivations: The economics of Australia's bilateral aid*; S. Holdar, 'The study of foreign aid: Unbroken ground in geography'; Lumsdaine, *Moral vision*; Mosley, *Overseas aid*; A. Noël and J.-P. Thérien, 'From domestic to international justice: The welfare state and foreign aid'; G. Ohlin, *Foreign aid policies reconsidered*; O. Stokke, 'The determinants of aid policies: Some propositions emerging from a comparative analysis'; J. Verloren van Themaat, 'Waarom geven landen hulp?'; Wittkopf, *Western bilateral aid*.

[36] Griffin, 'Foreign aid', 647; see also Hopkins, 'Political economy'.

[37] W. Brandt and the Independent Commission on International Development Issues, *North-South: A programme for survival*; W. Brandt and the Independent Commission on International Development Issues, *Common crisis North–South: Cooperation for world recovery*.

Turning to reputation, Morgenthau already emphasized the importance of 'prestige aid', reflected in a preference for large, very visible projects: 'It follows ... from the very political orientation of foreign aid that its effect upon the prestige of the giving nation must always be in the minds of the formulators and executors of foreign aid policies.'[38] Finally, several authors have suggested that states may provide aid because doing so is seen as an obligation incumbent upon the state.[39] This obligation may derive from factors such as the gap in living standards between rich and poor countries,[40] feelings of guilt over former colonial exploitation,[41] or the presence of 'a climate of opinion which accepts as universally valid the proposition that the highly developed industrial nations have an obligation to transfer money and services to underdeveloped nations for the purpose of economic development'.[42] It is in this last frame that echoes of Kipling's 'White Man's burden' are most clearly heard.

Frames and foreign aid policy: the model

The sheer volume of aid makes development assistance a topic of considerable importance in its own right. In addition, it also presents a uniquely interesting issue area for testing competing international relations theories. In other areas of international relations, the scope for different beliefs about the goals of a particular policy is often narrower. Though other policies can likewise have a Swiss army knife aspect, they often incorporate fewer distinct 'tools' (i.e. frames or goals). This makes it harder to test theories such as the one I develop here. After all, some Swiss army knives, too, are little more than just knives, with perhaps a flimsy screwdriver thrown in as a bonus. In such cases, a theory that simply assumes away the screwdriver may

---

[38] Morgenthau, 'Preface to a political theory', 308; see also J. L. Rhi-Sausi *et al.*, 'Italian bilateral aid policy, 1983–1993'; O. Stokke, 'Norwegian development-cooperation policy: Altruism and international solidarity'.
[39] C. Pratt, *Internationalism under strain: The North–South policies of Canada, the Netherlands, Norway, and Sweden*; O. Stokke, *Western middle powers and global poverty. The determinants of the aid policies of Canada, Denmark, the Netherlands, Norway and Sweden*.
[40] Lumsdaine, *Moral vision*.
[41] Mureddu, 'Obiettivi espliciti'.
[42] Morgenthau, 'Preface to a political theory', 303; see also Lancaster, *Foreign aid*, 5.

well make predictions that are just as accurate as one that insists on recognizing the multitool nature of the instrument.

Compared to some other foreign policy instruments, foreign aid is like a top-of-the-line Swiss army knife: as we have seen, there is a wide range of plausible goals for aid. This makes it easier to demonstrate that it is not only a knife, or only a screwdriver. More importantly, this makes it possible to show that foreign aid is not the same tool at all times: in some countries or at some points in time it may not have included a screwdriver at all, but instead a set of pliers. In other words, studying foreign aid allows us to formulate and test richer models than would be possible if the scope for relevant goals were narrower and the structural constraints on its use greater.

How can we use information about different frames for aid policy to explain policy choices? Why should these frames – mere 'intangible' ideas and beliefs – even matter? After all, much of the international relations literature privileges the material – somehow more 'tangible' – interests of state and sub-state actors, along with the structural constraints facing them. Other goals might be present in the discourse of leaders and publics, but most realist and liberal models of international relations predict that such goals will not have major policy implications when it comes time to make real choices with material costs and benefits. Those models assign the same basic interests (security, power, wealth) to all actors, and explain differences in outcome by looking for variation in capabilities or constraints. In contrast, I argue that different outcomes are often determined by differences in what state actors see as the goals of a particular policy, and, moreover, that these goals need not be exclusively, nor even primarily, material in nature.

The next chapter discusses the theoretical foundations of the model in some detail. I situate frames at an intermediate level in a hierarchy of policy-relevant ideas, connecting core beliefs about national identity to issue-specific beliefs about the relationship between choices and outcomes. Core beliefs encompass the broad identity of the nation, its purposes and its 'type', i.e. the kind of nation it represents or would like to represent. They derive from broad cultural traditions as well as from the specific historical background of the state. Beliefs about identity are the touchstone for the various frames through which decision-makers perceive different issue areas. Frames must be compatible with these beliefs in order to become widely accepted.

Frames and foreign aid policy: the model 15

Frames, in turn, are general ways of thinking about a particular policy. They specify the goals that are relevant to that policy, and suggest particular policy choices. A growing literature on frames and framing has demonstrated that they can have a significant impact on policy choice.[43] This is not to suggest that a reliance on frames implies irrational behaviour. On the contrary, given the limitations of human rationality, people – and hence decision-makers – have no choice but to rely on frames to impose order on the world around them. In other words, the true test of rational choice theories is not whether a state pursues its material interests, as is often suggested, but rather whether the state pursues the interests suggested by the frame(s) dominant in a particular issue area.[44]

As noted earlier, the key challenge for such a model is measuring the strength of the relevant frames in a way that does not depend on the observed policy outcomes. Since frames are mental constructs, their relative strength is not directly measurable. However, frames also build shared understandings of an issue area, and serve to communicate and coordinate general attitudes towards policy. This implies that the contents of public discourse can serve as an acceptable – albeit imperfect – proxy for the frames that are salient in the minds of decision-makers.[45]

My approach is to analyse the contents of legislative debates on aid policy. These debates feature contributions from a politically representative subset of the elite. In addition, since the immediate audience consists of other legislators, the debates are less likely to feature 'cheap' posturing than are speeches aimed directly at constituents. I measure the relative strength of different frames for aid by counting the number of times legislators refer to a specific reason for giving aid. To return to the Swiss army knife metaphor for a moment: if a legislator refers to it as a knife six times, and as a screwdriver just once, this tells us something important about that legislator's perceptions

---

[43] E.g. W. A. Gamson, *Talking politics*; D. Schön and M. Rein, *Frame reflection: Toward the resolution of intractable policy controversies*; D. A. Snow and R. D. Benford, 'Ideology, frame resonance, and participant mobilization'.

[44] Cf. P. Sabatier, 'The advocacy coalition framework: Revisions and relevance for Europe'.

[45] Cf. V. A. Schmidt, 'Democracy and discourse in an integrating Europe and a globalising world'.

of the tool in question. As we shall see, such tallying produces an unrivalled picture of the variation of frame strength over time and across donors.

How can that picture, in turn, help us explain policy choices? As the dominant frames in the legislative discourse change, we should expect policy to change accordingly. For instance, if aid is seen by decision-makers primarily as an instrument to support export industries, we can expect a correlation between aid flows and commercial ties, with important export partners receiving more aid. On the other hand, if the purpose of aid is seen to be primarily humanitarian, we can expect a correlation with indices of relative need in recipient countries, not with trade. If, instead, obligation is a dominant frame – perhaps because policy-makers feel called upon to assume Kipling's 'White Man's burden' – aid is likely to be focused on those recipients to whom an obligation is felt.

Frames thus not only specify goals, they also operate as selectors of the conventional explanatory variables that will shape policy choice. This suggests why conventional models of aid policy fight a losing battle: the factors that shape aid policy vary both over time and from one donor state to the next. It is futile, therefore, to try to explain aid policy with just one or two variables, and indeed empirical evidence underscores the inadequacy of models that attempt to explain foreign policy by referring only to the security, power-political or material interests of state actors. Conversely, but for similar reasons, single-country case studies, especially those covering a limited time period, are unlikely to provide us with useful generalizable findings.

This discussion raises two important questions: where do dominant frames come from, and how do they change? I argued above that frames must be compatible with deeper beliefs about a nation's identity and values. In Chapter 4, I show that when development assistance was introduced as a new policy, the most salient frames derived organically from a state's historical experiences in international relations. They were often the same frames that had been prominent in the context of related foreign policies, such as colonial or missionary activities. After all, if one needs to design a new Swiss army knife for a novel issue area, chances are the result will look similar to a tool that worked well in a related context.

Contrary to expectations common in the literature, the prominence of particular frames is not usually greatly affected by shifts in political power. This should not come as a surprise, in view of the model presented here. The empirical chapters show that the dominant frames in the national discourse are, more often than not, shared across the political spectrum. Moreover, foreign aid is like a Swiss army knife designed by a committee composed of representatives of different parts of the policy-making elite. As a result, just who wields the instrument in the end turns out to matter comparatively little. Instead, changes over time in the salience of different frames usually result from the particular experiences of donor states with the policy in question – the Swiss army knife gets redesigned, so to speak. For example, economic self-interest became less prominent as a frame for aid in Italy primarily because it became clear that the aid programme had failed to promote economic growth in the Italian economy.

When international norms play a role, it is only because they happen to be congruent with the existing aid discourse in a particular country. Thus, the Dutch and Norwegian governments have been noticeably more receptive than the Belgian and the Italian governments to new humanitarian initiatives promoted by international aid agencies, because the humanitarian frame is far more salient in the former than in the latter countries. Finally, changes in beliefs about the goals of aid are to some degree endogenous. The Dutch and Norwegian governments, in particular, have expended considerable resources trying to shape the overall public discourse on aid, emphasizing the frames of humanitarianism and enlightened self-interest. In Italy and Belgium, on the other hand, governments systematically attempted to minimize the visibility and salience of aid policy, in order to obscure the conflict between the main themes in the aid discourse and the empirical realities of aid policy.

Frames and foreign aid policy: the evidence

The choice of Belgium, Italy, the Netherlands and Norway as case study countries offers the widest possible variation in official development assistance past and present, while simultaneously controlling for a number of potential causal factors. Italy has long been one of the least generous donors, whereas the Netherlands and Norway are among the most generous, with Belgium somewhere in-between. Belgium and the Netherlands have a significant colonial background, whereas Norway does not, with Italy somewhere in-between. Norway and Belgium have tended to concentrate their aid on fewer recipient states than have Italy and the Netherlands. At the same time, all four are small- to medium-sized European powers with similar economic interests and political standing within the international community. Most international relations theories would thus expect them to have similar aid policies. Including larger powers or non-European donors in the sample would introduce additional factors that would make testing the specific theoretical model presented here more difficult. However, in the concluding chapter I present anecdotal evidence suggesting that the model applies equally to other donor states, large and small.

Chapter 3 presents the dataset generated by coding legislative debates on development assistance in the four case study countries over the course of five decades. This dataset uncovers considerable variation both over time and across donor states in terms of the frames that are most salient. For example, the security frame was of some importance in all four countries during the 1950s and 1960s, but its presence has been negligible since. Conversely, humanitarianism was comparatively unimportant at the start, but has grown in salience over time to account for over a third of all arguments for aid in recent years. The reputation and obligation frames turn out to be surprisingly important too.

Even more interesting are the systematic and enduring cross-national differences that emerge. Belgians emphasize the obligation aspects of aid, together with its value for promoting the country's economic self-interest. The latter frame has been dominant in Italy as well, but the second most prominent general frame in that country has been self-affirmation and prestige (i.e. reputation), rather than obligation. The reputation frame has been relatively salient in Norway too. However, its implications have been strikingly different, since in Norway this frame has been coupled not with the wealth frame but rather with humanitarianism. In addition, the obligation and influence frames have also been prominent in Norway at different times. In the Netherlands, finally, influence has been a dominant consideration throughout. As in Norway, the second most prominent frame has been humanitarianism. However, whereas this frame stood out from the beginning in Norway, it came to the fore in the Netherlands only during the 1970s.

Chapters 5 to 7 apply these measures of frame strength to the explanation of aid policy. Chapter 5 discusses the overall organization of aid programmes as well as the quality of the aid provided through these programmes. The findings show that aid administrations are significantly shaped by the dominant frames in the aid discourse. For example, the strength of the wealth frame in Belgium helps explain why the development administration was initially associated with the Department of Commerce, instead of Foreign Affairs. The Netherlands has tried to obtain international influence by playing a leading role in international development fora, and by setting an example in introducing new humanitarian priorities into its aid programme. In all donor states, policy reform has remained superficial and symbolic unless preceded by a real shift in the aid discourse. The evidence also demonstrates that the form aid takes is related in a fairly straightforward manner to the relative strength of particular frames, in particular the wealth and humanitarian frames. For example, a salient wealth frame has produced an emphasis on conditioning aid upon purchases in the donor state ('tied aid') in both Belgium and in Italy.

The evidence regarding patterns in multilateral aid donations is less straightforward. In the aid literature, multilateral aid is generally seen as more humanitarian in nature than is bilateral aid, since multilateral agencies are considered more likely to privilege the interests of recipient states. However, multilateral aid is open to a number of different interpretations, and as a result multilateral aid figures vary not only with the salience of different frames, but also with particular causal beliefs about the nature of multilateral aid. For example, Dutch and Norwegian aid officials have been suspicious about the effectiveness of some multilateral organizations, and have used humanitarian arguments to explain their decisions to channel less – rather than more – of their aid budget through such agencies. In addition, the European Union (EU) is a prominent multilateral aid donor, and both the Belgian and Italian governments have portrayed aid channelled through EU agencies as an obligation associated with their EU membership, rather than as especially humanitarian in nature.

Chapter 6 deals with the most concise measure of an aid programme: its overall size. The evidence presented helps explain many of the puzzles associated with the dramatically divergent aid volume of different donor states. Belgium's performance reflects the sense that Belgium has an obligation not to fall too far behind in generosity compared to its peer states. The absence of such a sense of obligation helps explain why Italy's aid levels (and, for that matter, those of the United States) have consistently been near the bottom of all DAC donors. In the Netherlands and Norway, the obligation frame drove the initial impetus for a growing aid effort. Subsequent extensions of the scope of activity were shaped by the salient position of the influence frame in the Netherlands and the reputation frame in Norway. In Norway's case, the pursuit of prestige has resulted in efforts to match or outperform the country's peers, most notably Denmark and Sweden. A statistical analysis of the factors determining aid volume confirms the role of frames as selectors of conventional variables. Interacting a measure of frame strength with the associated explanatory variables both increases our explanatory leverage and uncovers patterns in the determinants of aid volume that would otherwise fail to be noticed.

Chapter 7 presents similar results for a quantitative analysis of the distribution of aid flows across recipient states. A sophisticated statistical model demonstrates the relevance of aid frames both to the initial selection of recipients and to the subsequent decision regarding the amount of aid each recipient is to receive. As is the case with aid volume, coupling measures of frame strength with the appropriate explanatory variables uncovers numerous patterns as well as increases our overall explanatory leverage. Moreover, the statistical analysis allows us to identify patterns associated with the frames that are less prominent but nevertheless can be shown to have a certain impact in the aid distribution process.

Case studies of the aid distribution process in each donor state also show that frames are at the root of the striking empirical differences in recipient choice. In Belgium, the conception of aid as an obligation has implied a disproportionate focus on the former colonies. In the Netherlands, in contrast, a weaker sense of obligation explains the wide dispersion of aid beyond the country's former possessions. In Italy, the strength of the reputation frame results in a heavy emphasis on the visibility and grandeur of Italy's aid involvements. The focus has been on large, visible projects, preferably in target countries where other donor states will be able to see (and hopefully admire) them. In Norway, finally, a focus on aid effectiveness associated with the humanitarian frame resulted in a preference for English-speaking recipients, with whom it would be easier to discuss the implementation of aid projects. In addition, a prominent reputation frame was reflected in aid flows to recipient states whose political goals the

Norwegian state wished to align itself with. Among the most visible manifestations of this approach was the distribution of aid funds to several liberation movements in Africa.

The concluding chapter of the study ties together the empirical findings and discusses potential extensions and generalizations. I briefly review the value of the theoretical model in explaining additional features of aid policy, such as the allocation of funds across different types of projects. In addition, I present findings from other studies illustrating the importance of frames in shaping the aid policies of other donor states. In light of the demonstrated power of the theoretical approach developed here, I also discuss its applicability to other issue areas in foreign as well as domestic policy-making. Finally, I consider the promises and pitfalls of alternative methods of measuring the importance of different frames in a particular issue area.

Conclusion

Five decades ago, Morgenthau argued that 'As military policy is too important a matter to be left to the generals, so is foreign aid too important a matter to be left to the economists'.[46] This study highlights the non-economic determinants of official development assistance, by emphasizing the ideas and politics that inform aid policy, and by underscoring the need to take into account a much wider range of preferences than most economists – and many political scientists – have traditionally done. Official development assistance presents us with a wealth of intriguing empirical variation in policy, not only across donor states, but also over time. This variation is greater than can be explained with most conventional models of foreign aid, which privilege the diametrically opposed motivations of self-interest and altruism. It is also greater than any of the conventional international relations theories would predict. The range of empirical variation provides a nearly ideal testing ground for the frame-based theory of foreign policy choice introduced here.

I argue that frames have a powerful causal impact on policy choice, by clarifying and defining goals and interests. The frames relevant to foreign aid can be classified into seven broad categories: security, power or influence, wealth, enlightened self-interest, reputation or

---

[46] Morgenthau, 'Preface to a political theory'.

self-affirmation, obligation, and humanitarianism. Measures of the relative strength of different frames can be combined with conventional explanatory variables to generate empirical predictions for aid policy. The empirical chapters of the study test these predictions and support the argument that policy frames shape policy choices.

However, the significance of this book extends beyond the study of foreign aid to international relations theory more generally. In identifying frames as determinants of foreign policy outcomes, I add to the growing constructivist literature in international relations theory. Frames as an explanatory concept have only recently been adopted by political scientists, and then primarily by those studying framing effects in the media. The strength of this study is that it measures the variation in the distribution of frames over time and in different states in systematic fashion, which has rarely been done. Moreover, these measures are then linked to policy outcomes through qualitative as well as quantitative analyses, helping overcome the problems of overdetermination and the use of anecdotal evidence that often bedevil analyses of the impact of ideas on foreign policy.

In addition, my findings regarding the policy implications of considerations of reputation and obligation highlight the importance of non-material goals and interests in policy-making, at a time when such goals are often ignored or downplayed because of their uncomfortable fit within simple rational choice models. Finally, the analysis of the elite discourse on foreign aid that lies at the heart of this study sheds new light on the dynamics of policy-making across advanced industrial states more generally, not just in the issue area of aid policy.

2 | *One policy, multiple goals: framing and foreign aid*

Development aid is a political and composite instrument.
— Norwegian Development Minister
Sydnes, 2000

Simply put, the number of objectives we are trying to pursue has become rather large ... several of these objectives primarily satisfy the conceptions we ourselves in the Netherlands have regarding the goals of our policy.
— Dutch legislator De Haan, 1997[1]

What explains foreign policy choice? States with similar structural positions in the international system, and facing similar constraints, often implement strikingly different foreign policies. It would appear that such similar states have different conceptions of their national goals and interests, and that these differences, in turn, shape policy choices. In this chapter, I discuss the nature and origin of ideas about the purpose(s) of different policies. Specifically, I argue that the relative strength of different frames – ways of thinking about a particular issue – has a major impact on policy outcomes.

I develop the theoretical model in three stages. The first part of the chapter briefly reviews the role of preferences and ideas in the international relations literature. Much of the conventional literature has tended to emphasize structures and constraints, while paying

---

[1] *Stortingstidende*, 16 May 2000, and *Handelingen*, 9 December 1997, respectively. Unless otherwise noted, all translations are by the author. To avoid excessively long citations for legislative debates, references to the parliamentary record of the four case study countries are given by date and page number, preceded by the abbreviated title of the record: *Parlementaire Handelingen* (Belgium), *Atti Parlamentari* (Italy), *Handelingen* (Netherlands) or *Stortingstidende* (Norway). Additional information on the debates coded is provided in Appendix A.

insufficient attention to the preferences of actors, and to the origins of those preferences. Next, I develop a model of frames and their implications for the definition of interests and policy goals, and argue that the constraints and structures emphasized in realist and liberal models can be understood as restrictions on the salience of different frames. The third part of the chapter applies the model to foreign aid policy. It derives predictions regarding the origins of frames for aid and their evolution over time, and discusses how the theoretical model allows us to overcome the problems of overdetermination and inconsistent findings that have plagued the literature. Finally, I generate some general hypotheses connecting different frames to predictions about the quality, volume and distribution of official development assistance.

International relations theory: constraints, preferences, ideas

Assuming that foreign policy is made by rational actors, we can think of it as the outcome of a process in which the preferences of those actors are subjected to a set of constraints. This suggests that we need to model three key variables: actors, their preferences, and the constraints they face.[2] In the international relations literature of recent decades, the emphasis has been on the first and third of these variables. For example, neorealism assumes that states are rational actors, sub-state actors do not matter, and that state preferences are fully determined by the constraints of an anarchic international system and its distribution of power and capabilities. To put it somewhat differently, the constraints are such that states have little or no room for choice.[3] Hence we need not concern ourselves with what state preferences might be in the absence of those constraints.

Realists thus tend to assume the existence of 'a national interest as an objective datum'.[4] Unfortunately, such an 'objective' national interest is, of course, a chimera.[5] Indeed, it is common to find realists

---

[2] See M. Finnemore and K. Sikkink, 'Taking stock: The constructivist research program in international relations and comparative politics', 393.
[3] Cf. K. N. Waltz, *Theory of international politics*.
[4] H. J. Morgenthau and N. Chomsky, 'The national interest and the Pentagon papers', 362.
[5] Cf. C. V. Crabb, Jr and J. Savoy, 'Hans J. Morgenthau's version of realpolitik', 226; S. Hoffmann, *Primacy or world order? American foreign policy since the Cold War*, 133; K. N. Waltz, 'Reflections on *Theory of international politics*: A response to my critics', 331.

passionately arguing both for and against a policy such as foreign aid, each appealing to the same 'national interest', and each arguing that the other fails to understand correctly the national interest as it applies to aid.[6]

Classical realism allows a wider scope for the interests and preferences of states as actors, by taking into account the domestic qualities of the state as well as the nature of the international system. The obvious problem with expanding the possible scope of state preferences in this manner is that it is not as systematic as we might like. Given a range of possible interests (glory, security, wealth, etc.), how can we determine their relative importance independently from observed state action? Attempts to take into account preferences that go beyond security and power almost invariably lose realism's defining focus on fixed, limited preferences, making their identification as 'realist' models problematic.[7]

A key advantage of liberal models is that preferences are taken seriously.[8] The strategic interaction of sub-state actors within society and with the state shapes state preferences, and thus policy choice. The international constraints privileged by realist models take on secondary importance. However, moving the analysis down one level does not resolve the problem of identifying the relative importance of preferences and constraints, nor does it shed new light on the source of the former. As with realism, therefore, determining the preferences of actors independently from their choices remains the central challenge.

Realist and liberal models alike tend to assume that the preferences of actors (be they states, groups or individuals) are exogenous and stable. Moreover, it is usually assumed that these preferences can be reduced to material goals such as security, wealth or power. Neither of these assumptions are empirically tenable and many authors, accordingly, are forced to introduce changing beliefs and perceptions into their models in an ad hoc fashion, weakening the power of their analysis.[9]

---

[6] Banfield, 'American foreign aid'; Liska, *The new statecraft*; see e.g. M. F. Millikan, 'The political case for development aid'.
[7] A. Moravcsik and J. W. Legro, 'Is anybody still a realist?'.
[8] A. Moravcsik, 'Taking preferences seriously: A liberal theory of international politics'.
[9] Cf. Moravcsik and Legro, 'Is anybody still a realist?'.

Approaches where this step is taken explicitly and deliberately, on the other hand, are usually classified as constructivist.

Constructivist models often retain most of the features of one of the conventional approaches to international relations theory at the same time. For example, some constructivists choose to accept most realist assumptions except for the limitations on the ideational nature of preferences,[10] while others align themselves more with idea-oriented versions of liberalism.[11] All, however, explicitly focus on the changing preferences of actors, constructed in the process of interacting with others in the context of domestic and international structures.

Moreover, whereas realism and liberalism tend to conceive of ideas as instruments used by actors to achieve their actual material goals, constructivism argues for the possibility that ideas determine those goals, or even become goals themselves.[12] For example, as Lumsdaine argues in the context of foreign aid, membership in institutions can lead to an internalization of the goals and values of those institutions.[13] In addition, constructivism emphasizes the importance of norms and ideas that reside in the nation's collective consciousness, associated with conceptions of national identity. The main challenge for constructivism is providing a coherent framework for explaining the role of ideas in the formation and evolution of preferences.[14]

Though many realist and liberal models prefer to ignore it, preferences are, by their very nature, ideas. In order to prefer one thing over another, we have to have beliefs about what makes that one thing more preferable. Such beliefs are variable, even at the most fundamental levels. For example, the existence of a system of independent sovereign states does not automatically determine how those states define their most basic national interests.[15] Even behaviour apparently in line with realist expectations is often driven by realist beliefs, rather than

---

[10] E.g. A. Wendt, *Social theory of international politics*.
[11] E.g. M. E. Keck and K. Sikkink, *Activists beyond borders: Advocacy networks in international politics*.
[12] P. J. Katzenstein, 'Introduction: Alternative perspectives on national security', 5.
[13] Lumsdaine, *Moral vision*.
[14] See also Y. Vertzberger, *The world in their minds: Information processing, cognition, and perception in foreign policy decision-making*.
[15] C. Reus-Smit, *The moral purpose of the state: Culture, social identity, and institutional rationality in international relations*.

International relations theory: constraints, preferences, ideas 27

by the inescapable constraints realists assume.[16] If preferences are not determined exclusively by the pressures of survival, nor by the structure of the system of independent sovereign states, then where do they come from? Some authors attempt to solve this conundrum by borrowing the notion of revealed preferences from economics. Unfortunately, this rapidly leads to circular reasoning: preferences are derived from behaviour, and are then argued to explain that same behaviour.

A more useful approach is to proceed by organizing and categorizing ideas first. Most models divide ideas into three groups: core values or beliefs, general cognitive and normative attitudes or frames, and issue-specific ideas about particular policy options.[17] The third layer of ideas is mostly causal in nature, including ideas about expected connections between choices or actions and outcomes. Causal ideas help policy-makers decide which actions to choose, given certain interests and preferences. Of the three categories of ideas, this is where the implications for empirical outcomes are most straightforward, but nonetheless often striking.[18]

At the other extreme we find core values or beliefs. In the foreign policy context, these are best thought of in terms of national identity: 'Foreign policy is about national identity itself: about the core elements of sovereignty it seeks to defend, the values it stands for and seeks to promote abroad.'[19] As a result, '[f]or most of the major states, identity has become a subject of considerable political controversy'.[20] An extensive sociological literature on (national) identity provides a fruitful source of insights for understanding national identity better. For example, Anderson traces images of national identity to the historical and cultural background of each nation, including religious and dynastic traditions,[21] and others point to national symbols and values as the core around which a nation is formed.[22]

---

[16] A. I. Johnston, 'Realism(s) and Chinese security policy in the post-Cold War period'.
[17] For example, J. Goldstein and R. O. Keohane, *Ideas and foreign policy: Beliefs, institutions, and political change*; J. Hurwitz and M. Peffley, 'How are foreign policy attitudes structured? A hierarchical model'.
[18] E.g. R. Jervis, *Perception and misperception in international politics*.
[19] W. Wallace, 'Foreign policy and national identity in the United Kingdom', 65.
[20] Katzenstein, 'Introduction: Alternative perspectives', 19.
[21] E.g. B. Anderson, *Imagined communities: Reflections on the origin and spread of nationalism*, 19.
[22] W. Bloom, *Personal identity, national identity, and international relations*, 52.

Nations are often very concerned with the image of themselves they convey in their international actions. Moreover, empirical evidence suggests that these images matter for their interactions with other states.[23] In addition, nations often emulate others whose image or status they aspire to.[24] In sum, national identity can be conceptualized as a basic worldview, combined with ideas about the type of national image a nation aspires to, as well as a sense of the values represented by the nation. Even these basic features provide valuable information for explaining policy choice: 'Knowing about a state's perception of its own identity (both type and role) should help us to understand how the state will act.'[25]

The intermediate category of ideas that I focus on here – general attitudes and frames – connects the core values of national identity to the causal ideas that shape policy choices. As Lancaster puts it in her analysis of foreign aid, 'while [shared values and world views] are slow to change, the way political elites frame aid-giving in terms of those values can have a visible impact on public support for aid'.[26] Frames, then, represent ways of thinking about relatively broad issues, such as development cooperation. They provide a context within which more specific policy questions can be interpreted. Among others, they indicate why a particular policy might be valuable or desirable – in other words, which interests are involved – and suggest which additional considerations might be relevant to that policy. The next section of the chapter elaborates on the nature of frames in more detail.

Frames and discourse in policy-making

The concept of a frame originated in the cognitive sciences,[27] but it has by now accumulated a considerable pedigree in the social sciences.[28] An extensive literature on frames has established that the way people think about an issue – how they frame the issue in

---

[23] R. Jervis, *The logic of images in international relations*; Jervis, *Perception and misperception*.
[24] Anderson, *Imagined communities*, 90–92.
[25] Finnemore and Sikkink, 'Taking stock', 399.
[26] Lancaster, *Foreign aid*, 6.
[27] E. Goffman, *Frame analysis: An essay on the organization of experience*.
[28] E.g. M. Rein and D. Schön, 'Reframing policy discourse'; Y. Surel, 'The role of cognitive and normative frames in policy-making'.

their minds – has a considerable impact on their policy attitudes and choices.[29] Frames are affected by, but cannot be reduced to underlying material interests; among others, they are also significantly influenced by national discourses. As a result, one often finds striking differences from one country to the next – or over time within a single country – in the way a particular issue is framed.[30]

The main function of frames is to organize different pieces of information in a coherent fashion. In addition, they may include default values or assumptions to be used when certain data are not available. In this way they help actors understand the world around them.[31] Most importantly for our purposes, frames can also specify goals, and thereby determine (or activate) interests. The study of framing effects in the media has been quite fertile in recent years. A recent overview of the field by Chong and Druckman highlights a key foundation that this literature and my approach here share: the premise that 'an issue can be viewed from a variety of perspectives and can be construed as having implications for multiple values or considerations'.[32]

The set of different considerations that together enter into a person's evaluation of an issue constitute a 'frame in thought'.[33] Individual components of this frame have been called, at various times, perspectives (in the formulation cited above), dimensions,[34] considerations,[35] values[36] or beliefs,[37] and of course frames. Though Chong and Druckman tend to reserve the term frame for composite frames only, each individual dimension by itself also frames an issue, and it therefore makes sense to refer to them individually as frames too. Throughout this study, I use the modifiers 'composite' or 'overall' when referring to sets of frames.

---

[29] D. Chong and J. N. Druckman, 'Framing theory'; Goffman, *Frame analysis*.
[30] E. Bleich, *Race politics in Britain and France: Ideas and policy-making since the 1960s*; P. Hall, 'Policy paradigms, social learning and the state: The case of economic policy-making in Britain'.
[31] J. Kingdon, *Agendas, alternatives and public policies*.
[32] Chong and Druckman, 'Framing theory', 104; see also M. N. Barnett, 'Culture, strategy and foreign policy change: Israel's road to Oslo', 25.
[33] Chong and Druckman, 'Framing theory', 105.
[34] W. H. Riker, 'Heresthetic and rhetoric in the spatial model'.
[35] J. R. Zaller, *The nature and origins of mass opinion*.
[36] P. M. Sniderman, 'The new look in public opinion research'.
[37] I. Ajzen and M. Fishbein, *Understanding attitudes and predicting social behavior*.

A frame, then, is an individual perspective on an issue, which specifies a particular goal relevant to that issue, and which likely suggests a metric to use in assessing the different policy options available. To return to the Swiss army knife or multitool metaphor introduced in the previous chapter, frames represent the individual tools, and the composite frame represents the multitool itself. Policy choices, finally, are the tasks performed with the multitool. It is worth noting here the risk of some conceptual slippage. Policy can refer both to a particular approach to an issue area and to actual actions taken. Aid policy is a Swiss army knife in the former sense, a composite frame that serves as the answer to questions such as 'Why should we give foreign aid?' or 'How should we think about foreign aid?'. Throughout the book, I will strive to distinguish clearly between this overall vision of aid and the actual implementation of aid programmes (i.e. policy in the second sense), but given the close connections between the two, occasional ambiguity may be unavoidable.

Measuring frames

A key problem for any study of frames is that 'frames in thought' cannot be measured. 'Frames in communication', on the other hand, do lend themselves to measurement. However, communication inevitably carries with it some uncertainty about the correspondence between the communicated frames and those that the communicator has in his or her head. In other words: how reliable are the former as proxies for the latter? It is impossible to be certain, as game theoretical models make quite clear.[38] Moreover, empirical evidence is ambiguous on this point. It has been well established that people are reluctant to express the reasons for their decisions if they suspect that these reasons violate public norms.[39] On the other hand, some studies suggest that important decision-makers are frequently quite honest about their thinking.[40]

---

[38] E.g. D. Austen-Smith, 'Strategic models of talk in political decision making'; J. Johnson, 'Is talk really cheap? Prompting conversation between critical theory and rational choice'.

[39] E.g. W. M. Epstein, 'Response bias in opinion polls and American social welfare'; see also D. R. Kinder and L. M. Sanders, *Divided by color: Racial politics and democratic ideals*.

[40] For example, T. Risse, '"Let's argue!" Communicative actions in world politics'; see also F. V. Kratochwil, *Rules, norms, and decisions: On the conditions of practical and legal reasoning in international relations and domestic affairs*.

Frames and discourse in policy-making

Public discourse inevitably plays an important role in the struggle among different frames. Indeed, a major focus of the extensive literature on media framing effects is on the communication of different frames. Frames may be refined or reinforced, and repeated appeal to a particular frame may serve to introduce it as a relevant frame into the minds of other decision-makers. Finally, public discourse can serve to 'entrap' decision-makers by forcing them to implement policies consistent with their own rhetoric at least on the surface, unless they wish to bear the political cost of apparently hypocritical behaviour.[41] Non-negligible audience costs may thus be associated with a divergence between communication and action, or even between communications at different points in time.

Of course, we expect politicians to put forward arguments that they expect to appeal to their audience. But it does not follow that these arguments are disingenuous. It is interesting to note that most studies of the purposive use of frames to promote particular ways of thinking about an issue evince little or no interest in the convergence (or lack thereof) between the 'frames in thought' and 'frames in communication' of political elites. For the present study, however, this is a key issue. Fortunately, we need not rely simply on wishful thinking in this respect, for two reasons. First, as already noted, communication leaves a record and dishonest communication may be punished. Second, ways of thinking about a particular issue are often widely shared across a society, as we shall see in the empirical chapters. As a result, members of the political elite – who themselves form part of society – are likely to share frames with their audience.[42] In the end, however, this remains an empirical question: if communicated frames do not provide us any explanatory leverage over policy, it is likely that they do not, in fact, correspond to the frames used by the political elite in making policy decisions.

There are, of course, ways to minimize the problem. In this study, I do so by focusing on a particular type of public communication:

---

[41] F. Schimmelfennig, 'The community trap: Liberal norms, rhetorical action, and the Eastern enlargement of the European Union'.

[42] Cf. D. A. Scheufele, 'Framing as a theory of media effects'; R. Ball, 'Cultural values and public policy: The case of international development aid'; see also J. N. Druckman, L. R. Jacobs and E. Ostermeier, 'Candidate strategies to prime issues and image'; R. M. Entman, *Projects of power: Framing news, public opinion, and U.S. foreign policy*.

speeches in the legislature. Legislatures elected by proportional representation, as is the case in each of the case study countries, contain a representative sample of the overall political elite.[43] As a result, legislative debates stand as perhaps the best single source for measuring the relative strength of different frames across the entire policy-making elite. They will contain a distribution of frames we can use as an accurate proxy for the comparable measure we would get from an analysis of the communications of *all* members of the policy-making elite (i.e. bureaucrats, leaders of non-governmental organizations, etc.), if it were possible to obtain a representative sample of such communications.[44]

Legislatures generally have the final say on appropriations, so studying legislative debates might also be valuable for offering insight into the actual decision-making process. Note, however, that this is *not* what I am arguing; I am interested in legislative debates for the insights they offer into how legislators *think* and *argue* about a particular policy area, not for how they actually *vote*. After all, legislatures often do little more than rubber-stamp policy proposals put forward by the executive branch, and party whips can induce legislators to vote against their preferred outcomes. On the other hand, such discipline rarely extends to the conscious or unconscious framing of a policy issue by speakers in legislative debates. More importantly, I argue that even in contexts where it may appear that the government is exerting a strong influence over an aid programme, final policy choices generally take place within aid bureaucracies, and these are staffed by a cross-section of the political elite. Empirically, political appointments never penetrate very far into aid bureaucracies. We cannot systematically measure the frames used by these bureaucrats, but

---

[43] At first glance, this might appear to imply that my approach is not generalizable to majoritarian or even presidential systems. However, recent research suggests that governments, and to a lesser degree legislatures, in majoritarian democracies are in fact quite 'representative', and display what Mansbridge has labelled 'gyroscopic' representation, in which policy-makers draw on their own values and principles rather than making strategic, possibly party-based, calculations. M. Golder and J. Stramski, 'Ideological congruence and electoral institutions'; J. Mansbridge, 'Rethinking representation'. I return to this issue in the concluding chapter.

[44] Cf. J. Milliken, 'The study of discourse in international relations: A critique of research and methods'; see also P. Muller, 'Les politiques publiques comme construction d'un rapport au monde'.

given the representative quality of legislatures, there is good reason to think that measuring the frames used by legislators provides a useful proxy. Once again, this is ultimately an empirical question.

Taking legislative debates as raw material has additional advantages. First, budget allocations require that most policies be debated at least annually, and thus we can sample the contents of this discourse at regular intervals in relatively similar conditions. Second, legislative debates on spending include an implicit budget constraint, forcing participants to weigh the importance of particular policy proposals relative to all other government spending initiatives. Third, since legislators are better informed than the general public, contributions will often be of higher quality than public speeches addressed to the latter. Compared to other possible sources for content analysis, legislative debates probably minimize the risk of disingenuous framing.[45]

The next issue to address is whether we can measure frames in ways that allow us to assess their relative strength across cases. Although the literature on media framing has focused more on single case studies, broad cross-national and over-time measurements along these lines do have a strong pedigree in sociological institutionalism.[46] In the present study I combine such a broad, quantitative approach, which allows me to demonstrate correlations between frames and policy, with qualitative case studies and process tracing, in order to establish the causal nature of these correlations.

The more quantitative approach is particularly valuable in assessing the relative validity of multiple causal explanations. Many outcomes in international relations are overdetermined, in the sense that they could have been caused by several different, possibly independent, causal processes. Quantitative methods allow us to compare alternative causal explanations, reducing the risk of overdetermination. Another common problem with qualitative analyses is the lack of a systematic procedure for obtaining the appropriate evidence. This problem is particularly acute in some constructivist work, because of its reliance on the statements (oral or written) of actors as measures

---

[45] Cf. D. W. Larson, 'Problems of content analysis in foreign-policy research: Notes from the study of the origins of Cold War belief systems', 248.
[46] For example, F.O. Ramirez, Y. Soysal and S. Shanahan, 'The changing logic of political citizenship: Crossnational acquisition of women's suffrage rights, 1890–1990'; G. Thomas et al., *Institutional structure: Constituting state, society and the individual.*

of their ideas and beliefs. It is almost always possible to find a quotation from a policy-maker to support a particular argument. It is more difficult to establish that this quotation is representative, and accurately reflects the relevant ideas and beliefs of that policy-maker and her peers.[47] For this reason, I place a particular emphasis on using systematic measures of different ideas even in the qualitative parts of the study.

Origins and evolution of frames

Where do competing frames come from, and how can we explain differences in their strength and persuasive power? Generally speaking, a frame is more easily accepted if it is compatible with other frames that are already associated with a given issue, if an analogous frame is associated with a different but comparable issue, and if the frame meshes with the underlying set of core values that constitute national identity.[48] As Schmidt has argued, 'deeper structures of national values and identity' and '[c]ulturally and historically specific conceptions ... set the limits to the transferability of new ideas'.[49] Indeed, as I show in Chapter 4, differences in national experience and background have clear and identifiable implications for the salience of different frames and thereby for policy choice.

When new policy initiatives are introduced, frames can be derived from a variety of sources. Since new issues 'are distinguished by the absence of general agreement about how to construe them',[50] policy-makers commonly look to comparable initiatives in their own national past for candidate frames. This explains why both colonial

---

[47] This is a problem in Lumsdaine's work on development assistance (Lumsdaine, *Moral vision*). His argument that humanitarianism was a dominant motivation from the start, although supportable by quotations from numerous actors, simply does not match the systematic empirical evidence regarding the motivations that mattered in the 1950s and 1960s, as I show in the next chapter.
[48] M. Finnemore and K. Sikkink, 'International norm dynamics and political change'; B. Jobert, 'Europe and the reshaping of national forums: The French case'; E. A. Nadelmann, 'Global prohibition regimes: The evolution of norms in international society'; R. Price, 'Reversing the gun sights: Transnational civil society targets land mines'.
[49] Schmidt, 'Democracy and discourse', 287; see also P. Hall, 'Conclusion'.
[50] Chong and Druckman, 'Framing theory', 108.

and missionary activities in the nineteenth and early twentieth centuries were important sources for ideas about the purpose of aid. In addition, policy-makers may look to states with similar national identities or experiences to see how they have dealt with comparable issues.[51]

Explaining the origins of different frames and their initial appeal does not explain their long-term success, however. In fact, we know surprisingly little about the dynamics of framing in context where multiple frames compete for salience.[52] Nevertheless, some basic regularities are well established. At the simplest level, frames that are communicated more frequently or more insistently are likely to become more widely accepted.[53] In addition, studies have shown that frames that suggest costly policies can expect more resistance, while frames whose proponents also offer material benefits may be more readily accepted.[54] Structural factors also affect the persuasiveness of different frames. As Hall points out, the political and administrative viability of competing ideas may vary according to the ease with which the policies they suggest can be implemented by the government bureaucracy.[55]

Finally, if we are trying to explain changes in the relative strength of different frames over time, it is crucial to take into account the available information about the state's recent experiences with a particular policy. In particular, if a decision-maker believes a policy to have been unsuccessful at pursuing a certain purpose, the frame associated with that purpose is likely to lose prominence. For example, the widespread perception among Italians by the early 1990s that foreign aid had hurt, rather than helped, their reputation made it less likely that policy-makers would think of aid as a policy whose goal was reputational. Given the importance of policy feedback in this context, it follows that governments can play an important role in helping certain frames – by disseminating information about the successful

---

[51] E.g. Bleich, *Race politics in Britain*.
[52] Chong and Druckman, 'Framing theory', 113.
[53] D. Chong and J. N. Druckman, 'Framing public opinion in competitive democracies'.
[54] Keck and Sikkink, *Activists beyond borders*, 201; S. Marullo, R. Pagnucco and J. Smith, 'Frame changes and social movement contraction: U.S. peace movement framing after the Cold War'.
[55] Hall, 'Conclusion'.

pursuit of the broad goal associated with a frame, or by withholding information about failures. Chapter 4 provides several examples of such initiatives on the part of government administrators.

Establishing frames as causal factors

Much of the literature on framing effects has focused on policy issues with straightforward binary choices: respondents can be either for or against a particular initiative, and only one or at most two competing frames apply.[56] Unfortunately, the study of foreign aid is rather more complex: as discussed in the previous chapter, there are at least seven broad perspectives that must be taken into account, and each has different implications for policy choice. After all, almost nobody opposes foreign aid altogether: most people support some aid initiatives while opposing others.[57] This also means that linking the salience of particular frames to policy outcomes becomes rather less straightforward.

The discussion in the first part of this chapter made it clear that frames – and ideas more generally – cannot be considered a residual, third category next to realist and liberal explanatory factors. Instead, as noted earlier, realism and liberalism highlight important constraints in the policy-making process: international and domestic structures,[58] and the organization and material capabilities of different actors. However, the relevance (and thus influence) of these constraints will vary along with the salience of different frames. When domestic or international constraints are tight, liberal or realist variables can predict policy outcomes quite accurately. However, this is not always the case, and in the context of development assistance it is only rarely so.

---

[56] See P. M. Sniderman and S. M. Theriault, 'The structure of political argument and the logic of issue framing', for a critique of this tendency from within the literature.

[57] Even Easterly's *The white man's burden*, a book that appears at first glance aggressively anti-aid, is actually quite positive about certain types of development assistance, especially initiatives aimed at public health such as provision of deworming drugs, or efforts to control malaria.

[58] Cf. D. Dessler and J. Owen, 'Constructivism and the problem of explanation: A review article'.

To ignore the role of frames would imply not just excluding potentially crucial variables, but also misunderstanding the process by which these realist and liberal variables affect policy outcomes. To restate my earlier claim: security, power and wealth matter, but only because policy-makers believe they do. Just how – and how much – they affect policy depends not just on the degree to which they are favoured by the various constraints those decision-makers face, but also, and a priori, on their salience among the frames salient in the minds of decision-makers.

Goals other than security, power and wealth are likely to figure in the policy-making process too. In particular, goals related to core beliefs and national identity are likely to be prominent. So are considerations of prestige and status, which are emphasized in some contemporary realist accounts.[59] It is perfectly rational to hold such non-material preferences, as I pointed out in the previous chapter. Not only does rational choice theory not require making any assumptions about the nature of the goals of actors, it also does not require that the audience for a policy be coterminous with the apparent targets of that policy. Thus, if the public values a particular policy as a symbol of national identity, *it* can be seen as the real audience of aid policy, and it makes sense even from a limited, materialist standpoint for governments to implement that policy. A quotation from the first Norwegian debate on development aid provides an illustration: '[We want] an effort on the part our nation which can be meaningful, and which will show that the Norwegian people understand the seriousness of the problem.'[60] The real goal here is not development in the Third World, but rather expressing something about Norway's national identity.

The frames we are concerned with in this study are those that suggest a particular way of thinking about development cooperation. They answer the question: 'What is the goal of foreign aid, to us?' One can easily find answers that appeal to realist or commercial ways of approaching foreign policy: aid might strengthen a state's international position, or it might serve to strengthen its export industries. However, image and status might equally well serve as

---

[59] E.g. R. L. Schweller, 'Realism and the present great power system: Growth and positional conflict over scarce resources'.
[60] Representative Pedersen, *Stortingstidende*, 5 May 1952: 1223.

justifications, as might obligation and responsibility, or humanitarianism. How, then, can we test a model in which composite frames – composed of the seven frames listed here, but with varying levels of relative salience – are argued to govern policy choices? How does one show that ideas have an identifiable causal impact, and that they are neither epiphenomenal, nor ad hoc rationalizations of policy chosen for other reasons?

Arguments that ideas are simply epiphenomenal imply either that social actors are hardwired to have certain interests, or that the constraints they face are such that any differences in their interests cannot find expression. Although there is a kernel of truth in each of these arguments – certain human motives do seem to have biological origins, and constraints do put some limits on choice, as we discussed earlier – it is impossible to take such claims as complete explanations of policy choices. The argument that frames communicated by policy-makers are mere rationalizations or convenient 'hooks' is more difficult to deal with.[61] Reasoning straightforwardly from the strength of specific frames to policy outcomes is problematic. After all, decision-makers may appeal to particular normative frames merely to hide their pursuit of their own material self-interest, as we have discussed.

Sceptics argue that since reliable measurement of the ideas that *really* matter – the frames in the minds of decision-makers – is impossible, we are better off assuming the strength of particular ideas rather than trying to measure them. Just which ideas we ought to assume is not always clear, however. As Khong noted in response to similar challenges to his theory of analogies: 'Skeptics doubt that the policymakers' analogies tell us much about their decisions, but they (the skeptics) fail to identify the other grounds that supposedly tell us more.'[62] Moreover, rejecting attempts at measurement altogether is only defensible if there is a risk that measurements may point us systematically in the wrong direction. This seems implausible, since it is unlikely that rationalizations and 'true' underlying beliefs could be completely incompatible and yet still each call for the same policy choice.

---

[61] K. A. Shepsle, 'Comment'.
[62] Y. F. Khong, *Analogies at war: Korea, Munich, Dien Bien Phu, and the Vietnam decisions of 1965*, 17.

In the end, this challenge is fundamentally empirical, as noted earlier: if my measures of frames fail to help us explain aid policy, then we must reject them, and perhaps even the model they inform. In fact, there is an even better test: if the model presented here is correct, the explanatory power of imperfectly measured goals for aid should exceed that of assumed goals. For this reason, I consistently compare the power of my model to that of potential alternatives, in particular those appealing to assumed geopolitical or economic self-interest, as well as those that rely exclusively on structural constraints to explain policy outcomes.

A frame model of foreign aid policy

As I argued in Chapter 1, frames for thinking about aid policy can be divided into seven broad categories: security, power and influence, wealth and commercial interests, indirect or enlightened self-interest, self-affirmation and prestige, obligation and duty, and humanitarianism. Each of these frames can be associated with one or more different explanatory variables. For example, if aid is framed in security terms, we would expect the international security environment to have an impact on policy. During the Cold War, until 1989, a recipient's proximity to a Communist state might have been relevant too. On the other hand, if aid is framed in purely economic terms, none of those considerations ought to matter; instead, trade and investment relations will shape aid policy. Hence we can model the policy-making process as one in which different frames select the relevant variables that will determine the shape of aid policy.

Unfortunately, a number of explanatory variables may be associated with more than one particular frame or goal, producing overdetermined outcomes. This problem has been most evident in explanations of the preference of donor states for channelling aid to their former colonies. Does such aid contribute to a donor's geo-strategic presence,[63] does it simply reflect existing economic ties,[64] or does it indicate that donors feel a sense of collective guilt for colonial exploitation, or a sense of shared cultural experiences and traditions?[65] Or,

---

[63] Schraeder *et al.*, 'Clarifying the foreign aid puzzle'.
[64] T. Hayter, *Aid as imperialism*; Hoebink, 'Geven is nemen'.
[65] Mureddu, 'Obiettivi espliciti'.

finally, is it a spurious correlation resulting from the fact that aid targets the poorest and many ex-colonies are disproportionately poor?

Interacting measures of frame strength with the appropriate associated variables allows us to address this issue. The policy features predicted for each of the different frames ought to be reflected in policy outcomes in proportion to the relative salience of each frame within the elite's policy discourse. Hence, if we explicitly link frames to variables, only the interaction variable representing the appropriate frame(s) ought to be significant. The same interaction process will also help account for the fluctuating influence of particular variables that has often been noticed in the literature: their impact should vary along with the strength of the associated frame. Finally, frame-variable interactions may well bring out empirical patterns that remained unidentified in standard tests that identify constant effects only.

Unfortunately, it is not always possible to find appropriate variables to serve as proxies for the concepts we wish to measure. For example, when a security frame is prominent, we would expect a tense international situation to result in an increased reliance on aid. But how can we measure the quality of the international situation a state faces? We can test this hypothesis anecdotally, but it is difficult to come up with a systematic measure of international security tensions.

Given that we will have to rely on imperfect proxies for different concepts, it is important to try to generate testable hypotheses for as many different features of a state's aid policy as possible.[66] The dependent variables most useful for our purposes are the general administration of an aid programme, the quality of aid, its total volume, and its distribution across recipient states. The first two are analysed in Chapter 5, using process tracing and parallel case studies to investigate the importance of frames. In reasoning from aid frames to the overall administration of an aid programme, I am interested in implications for the original administrative set-up as well as for subsequent reorganizations. The analysis of aid quality focuses on two common measures: the degree to which aid disbursements are tied to purchases in the donor state, and the share of total aid that is allocated through multilateral organizations. The other two variables of interest – aid volume and geographical distribution – lend

[66] G. King, R. O. Keohane and S. Verba, *Designing social inquiry: Scientific inference in qualitative research*.

themselves well to statistical analysis, and are treated in Chapters 6 and 7, respectively.

Basic hypotheses

In this section, I outline general hypotheses for the quality, volume and distribution of aid, categorized by frame. The discussion here focuses on general predictions; case-specific predictions are derived in the empirical chapters, after taking into account the measures of frame strength presented in Chapter 3. Most of the hypotheses are fairly straightforward and logical; moreover, they are in line with predictions found in the aid literature. A few may seem less obvious at the moment, but their relevance will become clear in the individual empirical chapters.

A security-oriented frame can be expected to produce a correlation of aid volume with military expenditures, as well as with levels of international tension. The standard assumption in the literature is that overall aid will go up if military spending increases or international tensions sharpen, and down if either falls. Thus, military spending is used as a proxy for the salience of security considerations in the overall policy outlook of leaders; international tension serves as an exogenous indicator of the same idea. As for the recipients of security-oriented aid efforts, we expect them to be states whose allegiance is valued for security reasons, such as friendly regimes or states abutting enemy nations. Since security is a state-level goal, aid is more likely to be aimed at states and governments than at subgroups within those states. For this same reason, multilateral aid is likely to be less important, unless elites believe that international organizations such as the UN are important in fostering international stability and security.

The predictions deriving from a power-political frame are similar to those for the security frame. We expect the volume of aid disbursed to be inversely related to the other strategies for the pursuit of power that are open to the state. For example, foreign aid might be one of the few means available for a small state to increase its influence over another state, or to raise its international influence in general. A major power, on the other hand, is likely to have several other instruments at its disposal. The recipient states selected by donors motivated by power are likely to be states that have strategic value in some sense, such as countries with military or economic potential. In addition, continuing ties with former colonies may increase the political value of having an influence over those states. There will also be a payoff to obtaining the allegiance of countries that have high international visibility. Among others, such countries might offer a way to influence other, less important, LDCs indirectly. Since aid can be expected to have a greater impact the more concentrated it is, a concern for power and influence also suggests that donors will concentrate their aid disbursements on a limited number of recipient countries. As for the quality of aid, influence – especially within international institutions – might be hampered if the donor violates international standards, so we may expect underperforming states to converge to such standards when interested in influence. Donors are also likely to participate in all multilateral initiatives perceived to help extend their influence more widely.

A wealth-oriented frame ought to result in a preference for recipient states of economic importance: those offering large export or investment markets, as well as those that already are important trading partners. In addition, if a lot of the donor's trade is with LDCs, then we would also expect a fairly high overall aid volume. Furthermore, aid is expected to be widely dispersed: many LDCs should receive small sums as donors sponsor individual projects of interest to their national firms throughout the developing world, rather than pursue an integrated aid programme with a few specific recipients. We can expect aid quality to be low: most aid should be tied to purchases in the donor country, and it is likely that levels of multilateral aid (which is less easily controlled by domestic economic interests) will be low.

Where enlightened self-interest is a prominent frame, we expect the overall international exposure of the donor to influence its aid policy. Trade with LDCs will again be important, as an indicator of a donor's vulnerability to international economic shocks. Also important is the extent to which international instability is likely to affect the donor – for example, if it is a popular destination for refugees. As far as target countries are concerned, a relatively large number of states should receive aid, since international public goods such as stability and justice are at stake nearly everywhere. Particularly prominent recipients may be states with large populations, as well as those that are unstable or appear likely to become so. Such states may affect the overall health of the world economy as well as produce large streams of refugees. In addition, as the salience of international environmental issues grows over time, we would expect countries with a sizable environmental patrimony to become prominent targets of aid. Finally, we expect high levels of multilateral aid, since multilateral organizations tend to emphasize the preferred types of projects – those addressing population control and the environment, for example. No specific prediction follows for levels of tied aid.

Donor states where aid is seen in terms of self-affirmation and status will attempt to stand out among their peer group. Thus, they ought to meet or exceed international norms regarding aid volume as well as quality. In addition, they are likely to pursue recognition for generosity towards states with high international visibility. These may be internationally prominent states, but also those that are favoured recipients of peer states, since this is where the actions of our prestige-oriented donor will be most readily noticed. Aid flows are also likely to be concentrated on friendly regimes, since those are more likely to be grateful and appreciative. It is difficult to make a prediction for multilateral aid, as our expectations depend on the way multilateral aid is viewed: if status within an institution is considered to be of value, we expect high multilateral aid. If overall status within the aid community and among recipients is more important, we expect multilateral levels to be lower, as bilateral aid makes the donor state more visible. Finally, donors interested in prestige ought to favour large, high-profile aid projects.

States that view aid as an instrument to fulfil obligations and duties will be concerned with a similar set of variables. However, here we expect donors merely to match the average effort of their peers, or even just to stay above some minimal expected level of performance. In addition, the volume of aid will be more of a side effect than a goal in itself. For example, if aid is perceived as an obligation associated with being an industrialized state, the minimum acceptable expenditures may be expressed as a share of overall government expenditures. Aid flows to specific recipients are likely to be correlated with aid disbursements by peers, for visibility reasons. Moreover, since a sense of obligation is relatively independent of recipient state characteristics, we will expect aid flows to be relatively consistent from year to year even as those characteristics change. We also expect governments to want to get the maximum benefit out of fulfilling their obligation, and thus tied aid levels will be high, unless the issue of tied aid is politically very salient. Predictions regarding multilateral aid are more difficult: mandatory contributions to international organizations will be made faithfully, but we should expect little more. Whether or not that results in a high share of multilateral aid in the overall budget will depend on the total size of that budget.

The last category is that of humanitarian frames. Here, aid volume is likely to be correlated with wealth – richer countries have fewer humanitarian needs at home – and may well be correlated with welfare spending, under the assumption that both are informed by the same humanitarian norms.[67] Recipients will be disproportionately selected from among the neediest states, where need may be measured by per capita income levels as well as by other indicators that measure standards of living more directly, such as mortality and literacy rates. We would also expect a preference for those states most likely to put their receipts to good use, i.e. states with good governance.[68] Furthermore, since needs are great throughout the developing world, we can expect the number of recipients to be relatively large. We should also expect low levels of tied aid. The prediction for multilateral aid is, once again, equivocal. If multilateral aid is seen as higher in quality because it is less likely to be captured by domestic economic interests, we expect high levels of multilateral aid. If, on the other hand, there are doubts about the quality or efficiency of multilateral institutions (as there have been about a number of the UN organizations), we would expect lower levels.

Each of these hypotheses will be elaborated further in the empirical chapters. By way of summary, Table 2.1 provides an overview of the interactive predictions, showing hypotheses for aid volume (V) and geographical distribution (D) for each frame, and matching each with the variables that are expected to correlate with aid policy if that frame is salient in the aid discourse.

Conclusion

Although most observers agree that ideas are important in international relations, our understanding of *how*, *why* and *when* they

---

[67] Lumsdaine, *Moral vision*.
[68] However, good governance is a relatively recent preoccupation for most donor states.

Conclusion

Table 2.1 *Basic hypotheses about the relationship between frames and aid policy*

V = volume (size of aid programme); D = distribution (selection of recipients).

Category	Predictions	Relevant variables
Security	**V** Correlated with defence effort, international tension	Military expenditures, international tension
	D Friendly regimes, states encircling enemies	UN voting agreement, regime-type and location
Influence	**V** Inversely related to other ways to obtain power	Relative GDP
	D Allied states, countries with military or economic potential, ex-colonies Aid concentrated on a few target states	GDP, UN voting agreement, population, colonial status
Wealth	**V** Correlated with economic importance of LDCs to donor state	Trade with and investment in LDCs
	D Trading partners Countries with economic potential	Trade with recipient, GDP
Enlightened self-interest	**V** Correlated with international vulnerability, international tension	Trade with LDCs, international tension
	D Unstable, high-population states States with great environmental patrimony Aid relatively dispersed among recipients	Population, stability, area
Reputation	**V** Exceed peer group	Peer aid volume
	D Friendly regimes, visible (popular) recipients	UN voting agreement, share of world aid receipts
Obligation	**V** Match peer group, correlated with size of government	Peer aid volume, government expenditures

Table 2.1 (*cont.*)

Category	Predictions	Relevant variables
	D Visible recipients, ex-colonies, trading partners; aid relatively constant from year to year	Total aid receipts, colonial status, trade with recipient
Humanitarianism	V High, correlated with welfare spending and wealth	Wealth, welfare spending
	D Poorest states, most basic human needs, states with good rights records; aid dispersed across many recipients	GDP/capita, mortality, literacy, political and civil rights

matter remains incomplete. The model introduced in this chapter provides one way of taking into account ideas in a systematic fashion, centred around frames. Given the limited cognitive capabilities of humans, frames are an inescapable heuristic device for dealing with the world around us. More importantly, the distribution and relative strength of competing frames has important policy implications that have neither been generally acknowledged, nor widely studied.

Policy debates on particular issues are suffused with a variety of competing frames, whose relative strength, I argue, will be reflected in policy outcomes. The range of possible frames, as well as their relative strength, is hardly infinite. Constraints arise from national experiences, political and administrative structures, the material strength of particular domestic groups, and the geopolitical context. For example, the imperative of state survival puts certain limits on the type of frame that is likely to be persuasive. Similarly, the weight of commercial interests will make it difficult to ignore wealth-oriented frames entirely. In other words, most realist and liberal models of international relations highlight some important truths, but tend to obscure the processes determining outcomes: the importance of security or of wealth as a determinant of policy depends on the relative strength of the associated frames.

Conclusion

Once we accept the frame model, it also becomes easier to understand why non-material, often identity-related, concerns so often come to the fore in qualitative or anecdotal accounts of international relations. An important goal of this study is to demonstrate their importance in a more systematic and quantitative fashion. Accordingly, the last part of this chapter introduced a number of testable hypotheses associated with such non-material goals. In the empirical chapters, I show that prestige- and obligation-oriented frames have often been just as important in shaping foreign aid policy as have power- or wealth-oriented frames. First, however, we need to investigate patterns and trends in the salience of different frames for aid over time in different countries. Chapter 3 introduces this evidence, while Chapter 4 discusses the sources of the observed differences, as well as the factors that cause them to change over time.

3 | Debates about aid: contents and patterns

I must say that I have rarely been involved in an issue, an initiative, where there are so many motivations for becoming involved as is the case here.

– Norwegian legislator Moe, 1952[1]

Development assistance can serve a wide range of possible goals. Which goals matter most will depend on the way policy-makers frame the issue. This chapter presents measures of the relative prominence of different frames for aid, illustrating variation across both time and space. Although numerous patterns are shared across all four countries studied, their national aid discourses display enduring differences, dating from the early years of development assistance and lasting until the present day.

In Belgium, the frames of obligation and economic self-interest have dominated the aid discourse. Economic self-interest has also been central to Italian discussions of aid policy, but in that country this frame has been accompanied by an interest in the reputational aspects of aid. In turn, reputation has been an important secondary frame in Norway as well. However, in that country it has been coupled with a dominant emphasis on humanitarianism. In the Netherlands, finally, the two most prominent frames in relative terms have been humanitarianism and power.

The chapter proceeds in three steps. First, I discuss the coding methodology used in measuring the relative strength of different frames. Next, I introduce the overall dataset. In the third section, finally, I present information on the relative strength of different frames on a country-by-country basis. These data will be central to the discussion in the subsequent chapters.

---

[1] *Stortingstidende*, 5 May 1952: 1229.

Methodology

As discussed in Chapter 2, I expect legislative debates on official development assistance to provide us with information about the frames used by the political elite in decision-making. Though not all decision-makers are legislators, and not all legislators are decision-makers – those from fringe parties rarely have much real influence – legislative debates nevertheless are extremely valuable because they provide us with a window into an elite discourse that is, by definition, representative. Moreover, the quality of debate is higher than is often the case in public fora, so the level of 'noise' and disingenuousness is kept to a minimum. In other words, though legislative debates are at best an imperfect proxy for the actual thoughts of decision-makers, they are likely the best proxy available, and there are reasons to believe their shortcomings will not introduce so much distortion as to make them of little value.

The key challenge facing us here is converting the raw debate material into useful measures of the relative strength of different frames for aid. The main issues to be decided are: 1) which debates to code, and how to code them; 2) how to aggregate the codes from one speaker to the next within a debate; and 3) how to combine individual codes into the seven broad frames identified in the previous chapter. Before discussing each of these issues further, it is worth examining briefly how other authors have resolved similar questions in their studies of legislative debates on aid.

Several other studies have used legislative debates to gain insights into elite thinking on foreign aid. As early as 1964, Ruge investigated the legislative debates on technical assistance – an early form of foreign aid – in Norway, the United Kingdom and the United States.[2] Her rationale for relying on legislative debates resembles mine: she emphasized that 'the representative belongs to a nation … With his fellow countrymen he shares a set of values, a national history, etc.'. Moreover, she argued that legislative debates illustrate 'the way in which the offering of technical assistance is presented and possibly "sold" to the public' and thus

---

[2] The study covering the earliest aid debates, albeit published later than Ruge's, is probably G. R. Winham, 'Developing theories of foreign policy making: A case study of foreign aid', which analysed debates on the Marshall Plan in the US Congress.

go beyond 'stereotyped' government publications showing 'only what the governments want others to think their motives were'.[3]

Ruge coded debates by counting arguments for or against aid in each separate contribution by a legislator. About 30 per cent of all such speaking turns in her dataset contained arguments about aid. Interestingly, many of these referred to the self-image of the donor state.[4] She concluded that 'in starting concrete bilateral projects ... a country is also trying to create an image of itself in the international sphere in general, not only in relation to the receiving country. Bilateral [technical assistance] programs are a way of gaining international prestige'.[5] In other words, she found the reputation frame to be quite salient in these early debates.

Most subsequent studies of legislative aid discourses have concentrated on a single donor country. For example, Balsvik studied Norwegian aid debates from 1952 to 1966, hoping to find differences between political parties.[6] Although she found some variation in the types of goals that were emphasized – i.e. the frames that were salient – the differences between parties were small and not statistically significant.[7] A similar study for Belgium also found that arguments for aid were largely consistent across different political parties, despite small differences in emphasis.[8] Interestingly, though these early studies found that political parties within a country tend to share the same frames, the dominant frames in the two countries were quite different. In Norway the salient goal was the promotion of international peace and stability, whereas in Belgium economic objectives were paramount.[9]

In a more recent study, Breuning studied debates in the Netherlands, Belgium, and the United Kingdom, using role theory to link her findings to policy outcomes.[10] She defined four distinct roles: good neighbour,

[3] M. H. Ruge, 'Technical assistance and parliamentary debates', 77.
[4] Ibid., 78, 85.
[5] Ibid., 81.
[6] R. Balsvik, 'U-landsdebatt i det Norske Storting, 1952–1966'. Her study was extended in 1974 in S. E. Trygstad, 'U-hjelpsdebatten i Stortinget, 1965–74'.
[7] Balsvik, 'U-landsdebatt', 89, 118.
[8] M. Gedopt, 'Belgisch buitenlands beleid inzake ontwikkelingssamenwerking. Houding regering – parlement', 113.
[9] Balsvik, 'U-landsdebatt', 83; Gedopt, 'Belgisch buitenlands beleid', 29–39.
[10] M. Breuning, 'Words and deeds: Foreign assistance rhetoric and policy behavior in the Netherlands, Belgium, and the United Kingdom'; cf. K. J. Holsti, 'National role conceptions in the study of foreign policy'.

Methodology 51

activist, merchant and power broker. These roles roughly correspond to the humanitarian, enlightened self-interest, economic self-interest, and power-political frames as used in this study. Unfortunately, Breuning did not explain why she picked just these four frames, nor did she say much about her method for attributing specific reasons for giving aid to these general roles. Moreover, although she predicted – and largely found – that British legislators would emphasize the power broker, the Dutch the activist, and the Belgians the merchant roles, she provided no clear explanation for those predictions.[11]

In all of these studies, year-to-year changes in the contents of the legislative aid discourse were minor at best. This suggests that we need not sample debates at annual intervals. All studies also found that it is common for legislators to express several reasons for giving aid within a single speaking turn. It will be important, therefore, to keep track of multiple arguments for each speaker. The literature also suggests it is important to make the coding categories as specific as possible, so as to avoid prejudging the aggregation into overarching categories. Finally, the substantive findings of each study provide intriguing support for my overall model: ideas about aid varied more across countries than within them, remained comparatively constant over time, and appeared to have a bearing on the aid policies implemented in each country.

Debates and codes

The first decision to be made for the present project is that regarding the debates selected for coding. My source material is legislative debates on development assistance. I focus, as much as possible, on annual debates regarding the foreign aid budget. For reasons discussed earlier – these debates are repeated annually in essentially the same format, and the budget constraint makes cheap talk more difficult – these debates offer the most useful raw material for our purposes. Sometimes the aid budget is debated alongside other foreign policy issues; in those situations, I analyse only those sections of each

---

[11] Breuning's explanation was somewhat ad hoc and not fully consistent. For example, she emphasized the UK's heritage of empire, even though both the Netherlands and Belgium are also former imperial powers. Similarly, Belgium was cited for its dependence on international trade, even though trade with LDCs is no less important for the Netherlands or the UK.

legislator's contribution that deal explicitly with foreign aid and relations with developing countries.

Though budget debates account for the bulk of the raw material, a few more general aid debates were included as well. This was done when major policy debates took place, or when additional material was helpful to provide a minimum quantity of debate text in a given year. Since we do not expect ideas about aid to change rapidly, debates were sampled at 2–3 year intervals, with a focus on budget debates for years ending in 0, 2, 5 or 8. A full list of the debates coded in each country appears in Appendix A. Debates were coded in a pseudo-random order, in order to avoid biasing results by treating observations from the same year or from the same country in immediate succession.[12]

Next we need to decide how to code these debates. My approach here is one of content analysis rather than of discourse analysis. These two approaches represent closely related techniques each based on the general assumption that our beliefs are both reflected in our statements and of causal importance to our actions. However, discourse analysis is more postmodern in nature, and is often associated with a rejection of conventional methodological and research design criteria.[13] More importantly for the present discussion, discourse analysis also tends to focus on different features of a discourse than does content analysis. Inspired by the work of Saussure, Foucault and Derrida,[14] it focuses most often on the conscious or unconscious use of particular words, and on the way that these not only affect action, but also construct perceptions of reality.[15]

---

[12] Full randomness would imply the possibility of randomly selecting all the debates from a single country in chronological order. This was explicitly prevented by ensuring that year and country changed from one debate to the next. All the coding was done by the author, but for each country one debate was also coded by a separate coder with facility in the appropriate language(s), in order to test the reliability of the coding. In each case, intercoder differences were minor.

[13] J. George, *Discourses of global politics: A critical (re)introduction to international relations*; R. Price and C. Reus-Smit, 'Dangerous liaisons? Critical international relations theory and constructivism'.

[14] J. Derrida, *Positions*; M. Foucault and C. Gordon, *Power/knowledge*; F. de Saussure *et al.*, *Cours de linguistique générale*.

[15] See e.g. J. Weldes, *Constructing national interests: The U.S. and the Cuban missile crisis*; Milliken, 'The study of discourse'.

Methodology 53

In contrast, content analysis is more interested in specific policy-related concepts and goals expressed in a discourse, such as roles,[16] beliefs about other actors in international relations,[17] and, of course, frames.[18] I shall pay little attention to legislators' specific choice of words or phrases in referring to issues of development assistance. Nor am I particularly interested in references to aid goals without an explicit motivation. Statements such as 'my party has long been of the opinion that the Netherlands must give at least 1 per cent of its national income in aid'[19] may be interesting, but they tell us nothing about the frames informing the proposed policy. For the same reasons I exclude vague appeals to the importance of giving aid or to the many reasons for doing so, as in Moe's quotation opening this chapter.

Instead, I code arguments that refer to specific reasons for giving aid. For example: '[My party] issues a strong call for aid by the free and rich Atlantic world, based upon Christian moral prescriptions.'[20] Or: 'A new form of expansion and export opportunity is to be found in the provision of technical assistance to the less developed countries ... Trade will follow the technical experts.'[21] In order to prevent introducing too much interpretation, I tallied all explicit reasons for aid without performing any aggregation at the coding stage. In all, I coded forty-four different reasons for giving aid, ranging from the Christian duty cited above to statements suggesting merely that aid needs to be given for the sake of continuity. The full list of different arguments appears in Table 3.1 towards the end of this section of the chapter, as well as in Appendix B, where each argument is illustrated with one or two quotations from the coded debates.

The focus on explicit statements about a legislator's own motivations for aid implies that two types of argument were not counted, although they were noted and will occasionally be cited in the empirical chapters. First are arguments referring to particular motivations

---

[16] Holsti, 'National role conceptions'.
[17] Larson, 'Problems of content analysis'.
[18] Chong and Druckman, 'Framing theory', 107.
[19] Ruygers, *Handelingen*, 2 November 1962: 161.
[20] Biesheuvel, *Handelingen*, 3 February 1960: 661.
[21] Major, *Parlementaire Handelingen*, 10 February 1954: 12.

evident in current aid policy but not necessarily shared by the speaker:

> If we examine the activities of Belgian development policy, we reach the conclusion that [it] ... is strongly shaped by 1) historically determined orientations, 2) interest groups connecting our Belgian industry and certain firms or activities in particular 'resource-rich' developing countries.[22]

Often the speaker implies a negative assessment regarding these motivations. Cases where such a judgment is made explicit constitute the second type of argument excluded. For example, Belgian representative Saintraint argued against export promotion as a reason for providing aid in the 1962 budget debate: 'financial assistance will not be truly useful' if provided with the goal of 'opening markets and allowing the industrialized nations new outlets for their excess production'.[23] Since our interest here is in the frames people actually use in determining their approach to aid policy, it was judged best simply to ignore their claims about the frames used by others and about frames they reject.

Speaking turns and aggregation across speakers

As is standard practice, my coding unit was the speaking turn, i.e. a speech by a single speaker that is uninterrupted except for brief, non-substantive interruptions. Interruptions that did introduce new information, be it ideational, factual or otherwise, were treated as speaking turns themselves. Non-substantive interruptions may be heckles, quick questions of clarification, etc. For each speaking turn, I tallied all references to specific arguments for providing development assistance. Moreover, I counted multiple appeals to the same argument when separated by at least two intervening paragraphs of discussion. This allowed for a proper relative weighting in cases where different motivations were clearly not of the same importance to a speaker.

Combining expressed arguments for aid across different speakers raises some difficult issues, as there are several different ways to aggregate the data. The simplest is just to note each argument that

---

[22] Vanvelthoven, *Parlementaire Handelingen*, 17 May 1978: 2053.
[23] *Parlementaire Handelingen*, 21 February 1962: 19.

is used in a particular speaking turn. This implies ignoring repeated references to the same frame by a speaker. However, it may give an inaccurate representation of the speaker's overall frame for aid, for example where the overall frame is almost entirely security-oriented, with only a small humanitarian modification. Counting different frames may make the two frames appear equally important. A better approach, then, is to tally every argument made for aid, taking into account multiple references to the same frame.

The next issue arises when we compare the length of different speaking turns. Neither of the two methods mentioned so far takes length into account. However, we should like to avoid overweighting those who speak only briefly yet mention ten different reasons for giving aid, as compared to those who speak for two pages on a single frame for aid. The most straightforward technique for doing so is to allot one point to each speaking turn, to be divided among the different (and possibly repeated) motivations expressed by that speaker. This addresses the problem of over-representing those who rapidly make many superficial arguments, but not the issue of very brief versus very long speaking turns. The final modification, then, is to weight each speaking turn by its length in the printed record. Such weighting is only accurate within a given debate, since printing formats vary over time as well as from one country to the next. However, since the goal is to aggregate only to the level of country-year data, this is not a problem.[24]

From arguments to broad frames

The final issue to discuss is the aggregation of the forty-four different arguments for giving aid into the seven general frames introduced in the previous chapter. The explicit reasons for aid were not imposed a priori but rather derived from the aid literature, as well as by close reading of an initial sample, including debates from all four countries and five decades under consideration. The inductive derivation

---

[24] It is worth noting that the implications of choosing one of the four modes of aggregation discussed here are comparatively small. The correlation between the first and last methods discussed, for the individual arguments coded (i.e. before aggregation into the seven broader frames) is 0.84 for Belgium, 0.78 for Italy, 0.79 for the Netherlands and 0.92 for Norway. At the aggregated frame level, correlations are higher still.

of arguments for aid made it possible to avoid forcing statements into categories that seemed only an impartial match.[25]

After coding, the individual arguments for aid were aggregated into the seven frames introduced in the previous chapters. Inevitably the attribution process is not entirely straightforward, since some arguments for aid could be argued to fit more than one general frame. Whenever this was the case, the individual tallies for each argument were evenly distributed across the relevant frames, as indicated in Table 3.1. The table shows the forty-four individual arguments for aid, sorted by the general frame (or frames) they were attributed to.

The most obvious example of an argument that appears to be compatible with multiple frames is the claim that aid is in the national interest of the donor state. Such an argument seemed equally likely to refer to the security, power-political, economic or enlightened interests of the state, and accordingly its score was divided over those four frames. More common were cases where an argument seemed to fit into just two different frames. For example, should we interpret a desire to set an example or to achieve a position of leadership as an expression of power-political goals or of the pursuit of status? Another potentially power-political goal, that of establishing a presence, may simultaneously reflect a wealth-oriented frame. After all, presence may imply not only influence but also trade flows, construction contracts, and other economic connections.

The category of enlightened self-interest includes several potentially ambiguous arguments. An interest in promoting democracy, international justice or international distributive justice might follow from a desire to promote international stability or worldwide economic growth. At the same time, it might also reflect a humanitarian concern with human rights and basic human needs. Rather than assume one or the other, the tallies for these arguments were split across the two potential frames. The final ambiguous argument is the assertion that development cooperation is a 'noble task'. This may reflect a feeling of state obligation – with the emphasis on the task – but it may also be an expression of reputational considerations – with the emphasis on its nobility.

---

[25] Cf. Larson, 'Problems of content analysis'.

Methodology

Table 3.1 *Arguments for aid and their allocation to different frames*

Security – security, military, and geopolitical interests
Struggle against Communism
Geopolitics more generally
Burden-sharing
An alternative to military expenditures
Supporting allied regimes
(1/4) Self-interest

Power – power and influence
Influence
(1/2) Assuming a leadership position
(1/4) Self-interest
Obtaining a voice in international institutions
(1/2) Presenting an example for others to follow
(1/2) Establishing an international presence

Wealth – economic benefits
Economic self-interest
Job creation
(1/4) Self-interest
Promote exports
Secure valuable imports
(1/2) Establishing an international presence

Enlightened self-interest – global peace, stability, justice
Prevent global instability
Prevent environmental degradation
Mutual dependence of North and South
(1/4) Self-interest
Strengthening the United Nations
(1/2) International justice
(1/2) International distributive justice
(1/2) Support democratization and democracy

Reputation – identity, reputation, status
Express national identity
Prestige and status

Others do less
Symbolic significance of aid
(1/2) Assuming a leadership position
(1/2) Presenting an example for others to follow
(1/2) A noble and glorious task

Obligation – duty, responsibility, peer pressure
Responsibility as rich nation
Guilt over colonial exploitation
Shared history with recipients
Adhere to international standards
Importance of continuity
(1/2) A noble and glorious task
Role in international system
Repayment for own aid receipts
Others do more
Public support
Support structural adjustment

Humanitarianism – norms, morals
Humanitarianism
Because there is a gap between rich and poor

Table 3.1 *(cont.)*

Christian charity	International solidarity
Morally right	(1/2) Support democratization and democracy
Support admired regimes	(1/2) International justice
Promote human rights	(1/2) International distributive justice

Fortunately, for the vast majority of the arguments coded the allocation process is straightforward. Moreover, those arguments for which there is some question about the best allocation are not particularly common. As a result, minor changes in allocating them to one frame or another have little impact on the overall salience of different frames.

The dataset

A total of 3,017 arguments for giving aid were tallied, uttered in some 1,400 speaking turns over the course of half a century and spread across four countries. The total number of speaking turns examined was closer to 3,000, but most did not contain explicit statements about the arguments for aid policy, concentrating instead on issues of administration or implementation. The share of speaking turns without explicit arguments increased noticeably over time, as aid changed from a new policy to an established one and legislators increasingly deemed it unnecessary to defend aid per se. For example, the 1962 aid debate in Belgium featured an average of nearly three explicit reasons for aid per speaking turn. In contrast, a 1997 discussion about the future of Belgium's aid policy averaged just over one argument every four speaking turns.

The total number of arguments coded varied considerably from year to year. In most years, ten to fifty reasons for aid were coded, but outliers in either direction were not uncommon. For example, the figure for Norway in 1968 was 127, whereas a few cases offered just seven or eight explicit arguments to be coded.[26] We can think of each debate as providing a sample of the actual underlying distribution of frames.

---

[26] Moreover, there are two years where only two Italian legislators proffered explicit motivations, although each of them mentioned several arguments. A complete breakdown of all the individual arguments coded, per year and by country, is available from the author upon request.

The dataset 59

Since we are interested in a measure of the relative strength of seven different frames, a sample of just seven or eight arguments is likely to present a rather unrepresentative – i.e. 'noisy' and distorted – impression of the underlying distribution. Fortunately, since the relative strength of different frames is unlikely to change dramatically even over the course of five years, we can combine multiple observations to provide us with a better sense of the actual values. Accordingly, I use a trailing three-period moving average when referring to the relative levels of importance of different frames most of the time, including in the tables and figures in this chapter. This means, for example, that the data point used for 1960 is actually the average of the individual measures for 1955, 1958 and 1960.[27]

In Italy and the Netherlands, discussion of development assistance began as early as the 1950 budget debates, although in the Dutch case there was but a single mention of aid. In Norway, the first – and immediately quite extensive – aid debate was held in 1952, providing an excellent overview of the strength of different frames at the inception of the Norwegian aid programme. In Belgium, finally, the earliest relevant statements occurred in 1954, so the first time-point coded was 1955. The figures below show data for the period 1955–2000. This implies that the first data point for Belgium is based on a single observation, and for Norway and the Netherlands on just two observations. (The single argument coded for the Netherlands in 1950 does not provide a useful overall picture.) Only in Italy do we have a three-period trailing average already by 1955. By 1960, however, we have at least three observations for each country. Since most comparative aid policy data only dates back to 1960, this works out well for the empirical analyses in the later chapters.

The three individual arguments mentioned most often framed aid as a humanitarian policy (302 occurrences), a measure to improve the donor's reputation or standing (245), and an instrument for preventing global instability (240).[28] Table 3.2 gives information on the relative strength of different frames for the entire dataset, derived by averaging

---

[27] The data for individual years used in generating these averages are available from the author.
[28] In contrast, a few codes were used fewer than a dozen times. Arguments for the support of countries undergoing structural adjustment policies (three occurrences) and for supporting the United Nations (five) were the least common.

Table 3.2 *Relative weight of general frames over time. ESI = enlightened self-interest.*

Year	Security	Power	Wealth	ESI	Reputation	Obligation	Humanitarianism
1952	0.05	0.06	0.14	0.05	0.39	0.17	0.14
1955	0.06	0.06	0.19	0.07	0.32	0.19	0.12
1958	0.11	0.07	0.18	0.07	0.26	0.18	0.14
1960	0.13	0.07	0.18	0.07	0.22	0.20	0.13
1962	0.15	0.06	0.16	0.08	0.19	0.18	0.18
1965	0.10	0.05	0.14	0.09	0.23	0.21	0.19
1968	0.06	0.05	0.15	0.12	0.21	0.20	0.20
1970	0.04	0.06	0.13	0.13	0.20	0.26	0.18
1972	0.03	0.05	0.11	0.14	0.16	0.28	0.23
1975	0.04	0.07	0.11	0.12	0.16	0.28	0.22
1978	0.04	0.08	0.12	0.12	0.15	0.22	0.27
1980	0.04	0.08	0.13	0.13	0.17	0.19	0.26
1982	0.04	0.08	0.13	0.15	0.14	0.16	0.31
1985	0.06	0.07	0.15	0.15	0.15	0.17	0.26
1988	0.06	0.07	0.14	0.15	0.15	0.14	0.29
1990	0.05	0.06	0.11	0.12	0.19	0.16	0.30
1992	0.04	0.07	0.04	0.16	0.19	0.18	0.33
1995	0.03	0.08	0.08	0.19	0.21	0.15	0.26
1998	0.03	0.09	0.08	0.22	0.18	0.13	0.27
2000	0.03	0.10	0.08	0.20	0.18	0.10	0.32
Average	*0.06*	*0.07*	*0.13*	*0.13*	*0.20*	*0.19*	*0.23*

data points for a given year (moving averages) across the case study countries. The numbers represent the relative weight of each frame compared to the others in that year (so the rows sum to 1).

Averaged over the entire dataset, the security and power frames have been least prominent, with relative weights of 0.06 and 0.07 respectively. Economic self-interest and enlightened self-interest come next, with 0.13. Given the prominence of the former in the aid literature, this is less than might have been expected.[29] One the other hand, enlightened self-interest is ignored as a relevant frame in much of the literature. This is true even more of the next two frames: reputation (0.20) and obligation

---

[29] As we shall see below, however, the picture in individual countries is sometimes more in line with the expectations of the literature.

The dataset

Aid frames 1955–2000

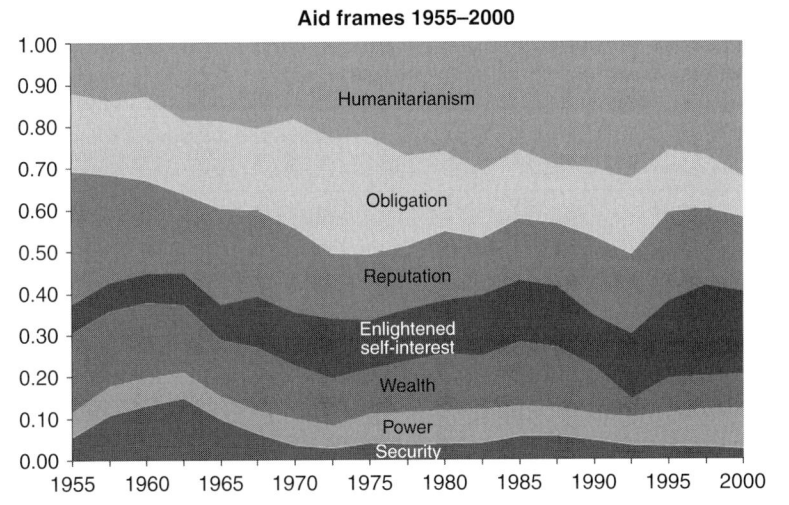

Figure 3.1 Relative weight of different aid frames, averaged over all four countries

(0.19), which together constitute nearly 40 per cent of the composite frame for aid we observe in any given year. Humanitarianism, finally, has been the most prominent frame overall, with a relative weight of 0.23. Overall, security and power were about half as prominent as one might have expected if all general frames were equally important, whereas humanitarianism was nearly twice as salient.

Not surprisingly, the relative salience of different frames does vary over time. Figure 3.1 gives a graphical picture of the data in Table 3.2. The figure shows that wealth, reputation and obligation each were more important than humanitarianism during the first half of the 1960s. This finding strongly contradicts claims that humanitarianism was the dominant frame from the beginning, *pace* Lumsdaine.[30] As the figure indicates, humanitarianism was merely one among a number of competing frames at the start, and far from the most important one. The figure also puts to rest concerns that representatives will tend to defend aid only in the most appealing, humanitarian terms, even if they have different frames in mind themselves. Instead, representatives clearly feel – and publicly argue – that a number of different frames are relevant to the aid issue area.

[30] Lumsdaine, *Moral vision*.

Table 3.3 *Relative weight of general frames over time, relative to dataset average. ESI = enlightened self-interest.*

Year	Security	Power	Wealth	ESI	Reputation	Obligation	Humanitarianism
1955			0.47		0.59		
1958	0.86		0.39		0.29		
1960	1.24		0.41				
1962	1.54		0.26				
1965	0.68						
1968							
1970						0.39	
1972						0.49	
1975						0.51	
1978							
1980							
1982							0.33
1985							
1988							0.27
1990							0.30
1992							0.42
1995				0.46			
1998		0.30		0.72			
2000		0.39		0.57			0.39
Count	4	2	4	3	2	3	5

A somewhat sharper picture of differences over time can be obtained by comparing the relative salience of each frame in a given year to its average weight in the entire dataset. Accordingly, Table 3.3 shows only those instances where the relative salience exceeded this average by more than 25%. For example, the first row in the table shows that in 1955, the wealth frame was 47% more salient than the average over the half century of data, and the reputation frame was 59% more salient. The bottom row of the table gives a count of the number of entries in each column. Here we see that humanitarianism has been disproportionately salient most often, but only since the early 1980s, and even then not consistently so. In contrast, security and economic self-interest have not been disproportionately prominent since the mid

National patterns 63

1960s. The obligation frame was unusually salient during the 1970s, at a time when strident rhetoric about the obligations of the North towards the South, and about the importance of creating a New International Economic Order, were also at their peak.

While the data presented so far will be of some help in elucidating general trends in development assistance over time, they do little for our understanding of cross-national differences. The next section of the chapter discusses the national patterns that emerge from the data.

National patterns

The most straightforward way to highlight the differences across the four countries is to show the overall averages in relative frame strength for the entire period in each country. This information appears in Table 3.4. Reading down each column, the striking differences in national aid frames become immediately obvious. For example, the wealth frame for aid is several times more important in Belgium and Italy than it is in either the Netherlands or Norway. In contrast, the humanitarianism frame is rather more salient in those two countries than it is in Belgium and, especially, in Italy. In the Netherlands, the relative salience of the power frame stands out quite strongly, whereas the same can be said for the obligation frame in Belgium. In Italy and Norway, finally, reputation is more important, though the differences are not as striking. The remainder of this section describes the patterns for each country in more detail.

Belgium

Belgium's status as a colonial power ended with Congo's independence in 1960. Its official bilateral aid activities began two years later, in 1962. Multilateral efforts, however, were already well underway during the 1950s, and several frames for foreign aid can already be discerned in debates over Belgium's contributions to these efforts. The top ten individual arguments for aid expressed by legislators from 1955 to 2000 were economic self-interest (8.8% of the 534 coded arguments), solidarity with the Third World (8.6%), a shared history with aid recipients, especially Congo/Zaire (8.4%), prestige and status (8.1%), international stability (6.4%), humanitarianism (6.0%), a

Table 3.4 *Average weight of each frame, for the entire period 1955–2000, per country. ESI = enlightened self-interest.*

Country	Security	Power	Wealth	ESI	Reputation	Obligation	Humanitarianism
Belgium	0.07	0.04	0.17	0.11	0.15	0.26	0.20
Italy	0.08	0.07	0.22	0.13	0.20	0.15	0.15
Netherlands	0.05	0.11	0.08	0.13	0.18	0.17	0.28
Norway	0.04	0.06	0.04	0.15	0.22	0.18	0.31

sense of responsibility as a rich nation (3.9%), the feeling that others do more in this issue area (3.7%), general self-interest (3.4%) and export interests (3.2%).

Given the importance in the overall dataset of humanitarianism, the second place for international solidarity is not, perhaps, all that surprising. Rather more interesting, however, are the first- and third-place arguments, which belong to the frames of economic self-interest and obligation, respectively.[31] Several additional arguments in the top ten refer to these two frames: general self-interest and export interests for the former, and a sense of responsibility plus the feeling that Belgium falls short compared to other donor states for the latter. This impression of the importance of obligation and economic self-interest as frames for aid is reinforced when we look at broad patterns in the relative strength of all seven different frames, shown in Figure 3.2. The figure also indicates that reputation was a significant frame for aid in Belgium from the mid 1960s until about 1980, and again in the latter half of the 1990s.

Table 3.5 highlights these patterns in the same way Table 3.3 did for the entire dataset. As was the case for that table, the only entries shown are those where the relative salience of a particular frame

---

[31] Interestingly, the idea of aid as inspired by international solidarity became *less* important during the 1980s, supplanted by more general humanitarian concerns as well as specific interests in democracy and human rights. Quite often, solidarity has been perceived by Belgians as a norm imposed from the outside – as early as 1962, van Bilsen portrayed aid as an international solidarity tax (*Belgisch Staatsblad*, 18 January 1962) – whereas humanitarianism is felt to be more internally motivated. In this sense, the salience of solidarity as a humanitarian motivation for aid throughout the 1970s can be seen as additional support for the importance of a sense of obligation.

National patterns 65

Aid frames in Belgium 1955–2000

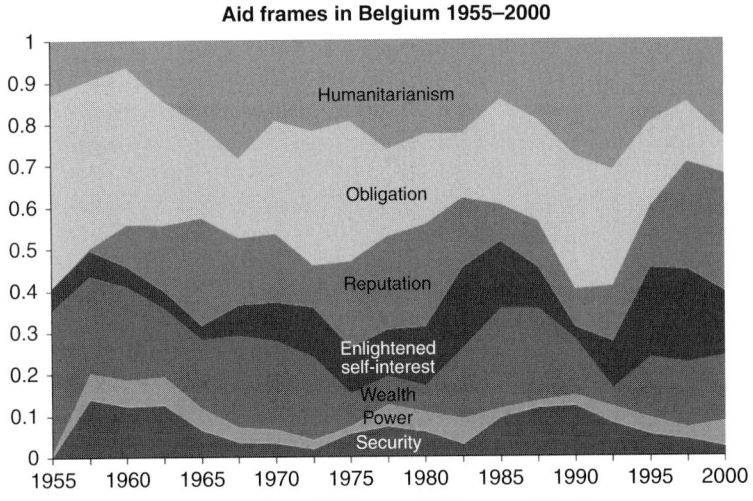

Figure 3.2 Relative weight of different aid frames, Belgium

exceeds the overall dataset average by 25% or more. The first row in the table shows that in 1955, the wealth frame was 167% more salient than in the dataset average, whereas obligation was 147% more salient. Indeed, each of these two frames continues to be unusually important during nearly the entire period under consideration, showing up in the table eleven times. Also salient, albeit at a much lower level, is the security frame. This is observable not only in the early years of the aid programme, when it was an important frame for almost every aid donor, but also from the mid 1980s to the early 1990s. The other frames stand out less in the table. Strikingly, the humanitarianism frame exceeded the overall dataset average only at a single data point, in the early 1990s. This illustrates legislators' willingness to offer arguments for aid that are not necessarily idealistic or altruistic in nature.

With the gradual decline in importance of economic self-interest and obligation after the early 1990s, two new frames appear to have taken over in the Belgian aid discourse: enlightened self-interest and reputation. As we shall see in the next chapter, the importance of the former frame is due in large part to concerns over instability and conflict in the former colonies, and hence the term 'enlightened' may not be entirely appropriate: although the problems in Congo have had a major impact throughout Africa, Belgian concerns appear to have

Table 3.5 *Strength of general frames over time in Belgium, relative to dataset average. ESI = enlightened self-interest.*

Year	Security	Power	Wealth	ESI	Reputation	Obligation	Humanitarianism
1955			1.67			1.47	
1958	1.39		0.82			1.16	
1960	1.10		0.75			1.02	
1962	1.15		0.28			0.60	
1965			0.30		0.29		
1968			0.73				
1970			0.67			0.45	
1972			0.57			0.72	
1975						0.80	
1978	0.25						
1980							
1982			0.32	0.54			
1985	0.61		0.87	0.27		0.36	
1988	1.00		0.73			0.31	
1990	1.08					0.71	
1992	0.37					0.48	0.36
1995				0.69			
1998				0.77	0.28		
2000					0.41		
Count	8	0	11	4	3	11	1

been governed mostly by their own economic and political interests. Be that as it may, concerns with instability, refugee populations, etc. clearly became more salient in the 1990s.

Italy

Legislative debates on the aid budget have not usually been very visible in Italy. Development assistance is rarely discussed separately from the foreign affairs budget, and usually takes up only a small part of the budget deliberations.[32] Moreover, few legislators are interested

---

[32] In Norway, where foreign affairs and development cooperation are also generally debated together, aid policy often accounts for as much as 90 per cent of the budget discussion (and of the budget!).

in aid. The same two or three speakers raise the issue year after year, and their contributions do not vary much over time. Throughout the 1950s, most of the legislative interest in development issues focused on Italy's relations with its protectorate, Somalia. Multilateral aid was discussed on a case-by-case basis only, as individual appropriations came up for approval.

Many early multilateral aid contributions were motivated with the argument that Italy actually received more funds from those multilateral institutions than it contributed. Italy was in the process of rebuilding after the Second World War, and the economically lagging Mezzogiorno region was a prominent target of Marshall Plan aid and related initiatives.[33] A general debate on reasons for giving foreign aid first took place in 1962, when a law on Technical Cooperation was approved. Technical cooperation evolved into development cooperation a decade later, in 1971. Nevertheless, many Italian observers date the beginning of Italy's aid policy only to 1979, when the first integrated law on development cooperation (law 38/79) was passed.[34] Still, since discussions and expenditures date back to the 1950s, there is no reason to ignore the first few decades of Italian activity in this field.[35]

The ten most frequently mentioned individual arguments for aid from 1950 to 2000 were prestige and status (fully 17% of the 530 coded arguments), economic interests (10.4%), international instability (8.5%), humanitarianism and international solidarity (6.2% each), general self-interest (5.7%), the sense that others do more (4.2%), export interests (3.8%), Cold War considerations (3.6%) and a desire to increase Italy's presence in the developing countries (3.4%). It is rather striking that more than one in six arguments for aid were related to its potential contribution to Italy's international prestige. In second place, economic self-interest was mentioned more than 10 per cent of the time, more even than was the case in Belgium. Humanitarian arguments appear only in a shared fourth place, noticeably lower than in Belgium.

---

[33] In addition, in the early years the legislators' interest was often aimed at supporting projects to aid Italian colonists in Libya, an effort whose 'foreign aid' qualifications are dubious.
[34] E.g. E. Grilli and F. Daveri, 'Italia e terzo mondo', 61.
[35] One suspects that the tendency of Italian observers to ignore the earlier periods implicitly concedes that Italy's performance through the 1970s left a lot to be desired.

Aid frames in Italy 1955–2000

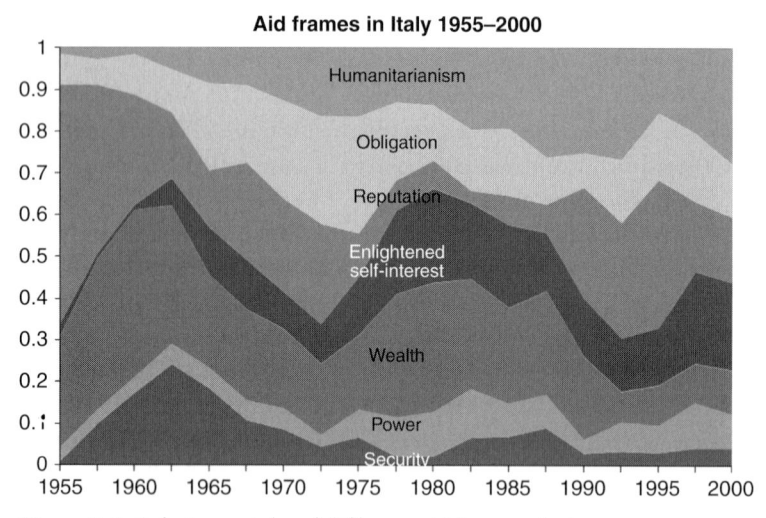

Figure 3.3 Relative weight of different aid frames, Italy

The patterns suggested by the relative strength of these individual arguments also emerge at the aggregate level, as shown in Figure 3.3 and Table 3.6. Perhaps most important to note is the low relative salience of the humanitarian frame. Humanitarianism is only the third-ranked frame, on average, after reputation and economic self-interest. Indeed, each of the latter two accounted for 40 per cent or more of the composite aid frame at least once, whereas the salience of humanitarianism never exceeded 30 per cent. It is not surprising, then, to find fifteen entries for the wealth frame in Table 3.6, six for the reputation frame, and none at all for the humanitarianism frame.

Indeed, the table makes even more obvious than the figure the dominance of economic self-interest throughout the 1980s. Reputation was salient throughout the 1950s (concentrated on Italy's performance in Somalia) and again in the 1990s. The third-ranked motivation, on average, was obligation. Figure 3.3 shows that a steady concern with obligation has characterized legislative debates. However, the table suggests that this concern was not all that large compared to that evident in the dataset as a whole, with appearances only during the 1970s. This may explain why Italy's sense of obligation has been enough to convince Italy to maintain an aid programme, but not to do much more than that, as we shall see in the empirical chapters.

Fifth in overall importance, but of particular relevance from the late 1970s to the mid 1980s, and again in the late 1990s, is enlightened

Table 3.6 *Strength of general frames over time in Italy, relative to dataset average. ESI = enlightened self-interest.*

Year	Security	Power	Wealth	ESI	Reputation	Obligation	Humanitarianism
1955			1.09		1.86		
1958	0.70		1.81		1.02		
1960	1.95		2.11		0.32		
1962	3.10		1.58				
1965	2.14		0.73				
1968	0.85		0.70				
1970	0.48		0.47			0.27	
1972			0.32			0.38	
1975			0.39			0.50	
1978		0.37	1.30	0.56			
1980		0.56	1.41	0.77			
1982		0.71	1.05	0.42			
1985			0.79	0.55			
1988	0.56		0.94				
1990			0.55		0.32		
1992					0.38		
1995					0.77		
1998		0.58		0.73			
2000				0.66			
Count	7	4	15	6	6	3	0

self-interest. Together with the obligation frame, it appears to serve on occasion as an alternative to the reputation frame. Finally, although security has not been an important frame in absolute terms, it was more noticeable in Italy than in the other three countries during the 1960s – after all, Italy shared a border with a socialist state, Yugoslavia.

The Netherlands

Where economic self-interest, obligation and reputation have been the dominant frames for aid in both Belgium and Italy, none of these stands out in the Dutch case. Instead, pride of place goes to power and humanitarianism. The difference is immediately evident when we look at the frequencies of individual arguments for aid. The ten specific arguments coded most often in aid debates are

Aid frames in the Netherlands 1955–2000

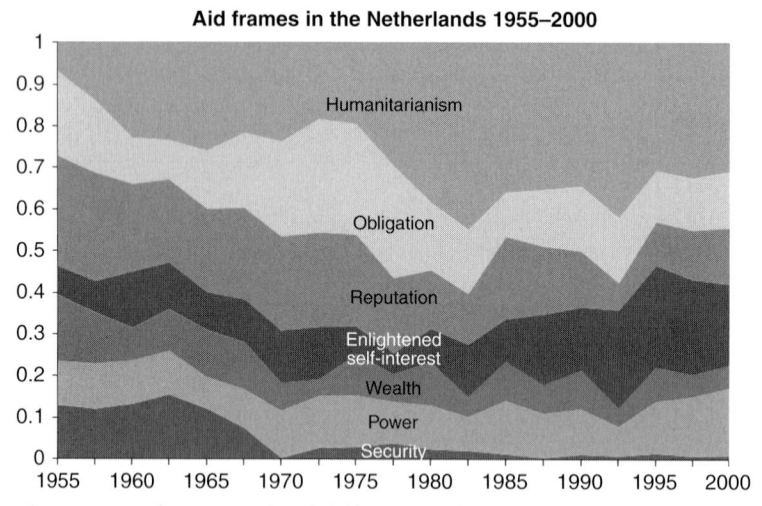

Figure 3.4 Relative weight of different aid frames, the Netherlands

general humanitarianism (10.5% of 898 arguments coded), leadership (6.3%), international stability (6.0%), international solidarity and Christian principles (5.6% each), responsibility (4.8%), setting an example (4.5%), favourable public opinion (4.1%), general economic interests (3.9%) and prestige and status (3.7%). The humanitarian frame accounts for the most popular argument as well as for those in positions four and five; the power-political frame corresponds to the second and seventh most common arguments.

The impression given by the frequencies of individual arguments is reinforced in Figure 3.4 and Table 3.7. First, the increasing dominance of humanitarianism, especially since the mid 1970s, stands out. Although it has declined somewhat in importance after peaking in the mid 1990s, its relative salience still exceeded the dataset average by more than a third in 2000. Even more striking in relative terms, power has remained steadily important since the very beginning, appearing sixteen times in Table 3.7, with only three brief gaps. Moreover, its importance was at its height at the end of the century, demonstrating an ability to coexist easily with the humanitarian frame.

Obligation has been more important than power in absolute terms, but compared to the other countries it stood out only during the 1970s, as Table 3.7 shows. Similarly, legislators' interest in the reputational aspects of aid has been fairly consistent throughout, but at

National patterns

Table 3.7 *Strength of general frames over time in the Netherlands, relative to dataset average. ESI = enlightened self-interest.*

Year	Security	Power	Wealth	ESI	Reputation	Obligation	Humanitarianism
1955	1.21	0.53			0.33		
1958	1.05	0.57			0.30		
1960	1.25	0.51					
1962	1.64	0.52					
1965	1.06						
1968	0.29	0.33					
1970		0.63					
1972		0.80				0.46	
1975		0.79				0.42	
1978		0.43				0.44	0.28
1980		0.52					0.66
1982							0.94
1985		0.85					0.56
1988		0.54		0.33			0.53
1990		0.58					0.49
1992				0.85			0.82
1995		0.80		0.92			0.33
1998		1.06		0.79			0.40
2000		1.34		0.54			0.34
Count	6	16	0	5	2	3	10

levels that do not diverge much from the dataset average. Enlightened self-interest has gradually become more important, first showing up in Table 3.7 in 1988, and then again throughout the 1990s. On the other hand, the wealth frame does not rate a single appearance in the table, and Figure 3.4 graphically underscores its comparative insignificance.

Norway

Norway differs from the other three states in that it lacks a colonial past.[36] As a result, it did not have an existing policy apparatus

---

[36] If anything, one might argue that Norway was long a colony itself, first of Denmark and later of Sweden.

to be redirected towards development assistance. Instead, Norway's first foray into bilateral development assistance came in the form of a fisheries project in Kerala, India. This represented a completely new endeavour for the Norwegian government, and the initiative was preceded by an extensive debate in the Norwegian legislature in May 1952. Far more legislators participated than was the case in early debates on aid in other states, and the resulting data provide an unusually rich picture of Norwegians' views on aid at the outset.

In the years since, the Norwegian parliament has continued to pay more attention to development issues than have its counterparts in most other countries. Foreign aid is frequently debated twice a year: once for the budget and once in reviewing the development administration's annual report or the minister's annual policy speech. Discussions of aid policy often account for more than 90 per cent of the annual debate on the foreign affairs budget, and many legislators participate. Political parties are often represented by three or four different speakers, and as many as two-thirds of the participants are neither members of the Storting's Committee on Foreign Affairs, nor the official spokespeople for their party on this issue.

As in the Netherlands, humanitarianism has been the strongest overall frame, although in Norway it stands out even more, both in absolute terms and compared to the dataset average. On the other hand, both reputation and obligation are more important than power in Norway's case. The ten individual arguments for aid most frequently mentioned by Norwegian legislators are humanitarianism (13.6% of 1,055 arguments coded), international stability (10.1%), international solidarity (7.8%), prestige and status (7.5%), responsibility (6.3%), supporting democracy (5.5%), aid as an instrument promoting international leadership (3.8%), public support for aid and international distributive justice (3.4% each), and finally the fact that others are more active in development policy (3.0%). The first and third arguments belong to the general humanitarian frame; after that the distribution across different frames is fairly even.

Figure 3.5 shows that in Norway's case the two dominant frames are humanitarianism and reputation. The figure also illustrates the comparative unimportance of the security, power and wealth frames to Norwegian legislators. As noted in Chapter 2, much of the international relations literature assumes that these three together constitute the only relevant goals and interests of states. For development

National patterns

Aid frames in Norway 1955–2000

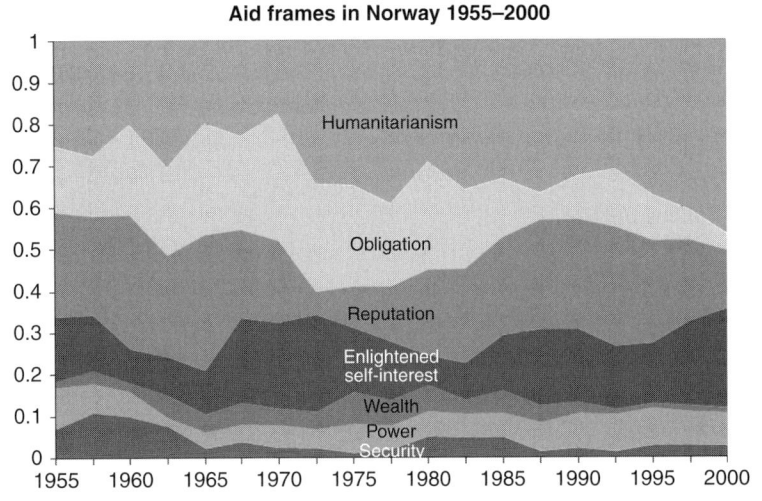

Figure 3.5 Relative weight of different aid frames, Norway

assistance policy in Norway, however, Figure 3.5 shows that this could not be further from the truth. Even combined, they never account for more than one-fifth of the composite frame for aid in that country.

The importance of humanitarianism is also clear in Table 3.8, where it has thirteen entries. After that, as suggested already by the top individual arguments coded, there is no clear secondary frame. Overall, patterns in Norway most closely resemble those in the Netherlands. Nevertheless, reputation is almost continuously more significant than was the case in the Netherlands, as are, to a lesser degree, obligation and enlightened self-interest. On the other hand, the power frame is never particularly noticeable in Norway. Economic self-interest, finally, is as unimportant here as in the Netherlands.

Using the data to generate predictions

We can derive predictions about the aid policies of Belgium, Italy, the Netherlands and Norway by combining the information about the relative strength of different frames presented here with the general hypotheses laid out in Chapter 2. Since the predictions will vary depending on the dependent variable of interest, I shall defer the derivation of hypotheses until the relevant chapters. However, it is useful to discuss briefly the relative advantages of the two measures of frame

Table 3.8 *Strength of general frames over time in Norway, relative to dataset average. ESI = enlightened self-interest.*

Year	Security	Power	Wealth	ESI	Reputation	Obligation	Humanitarianism
1955		0.43			0.25		
1958	0.83						
1960	0.67				0.61		
1962	0.28						0.31
1965					0.63	0.44	
1968				0.59			
1970				0.62		0.63	
1972				0.83		0.38	0.49
1975						0.29	0.51
1978							0.70
1980						0.38	0.26
1982							0.55
1985							0.44
1988				0.43	0.32		0.59
1990				0.37	0.32		0.41
1992		0.30			0.43		0.34
1995		0.29					0.61
1998				0.59			0.77
2000				0.87			1.02
Count	3	3	0	7	6	5	13

salience presented in this chapter: the strength of a frame relative to the others at a particular point in time, and the strength of a frame relative to its average strength across the entire dataset. Each needs to be taken into account in order to generate optimal predictions.

The measure of relative strength at a particular point in time is the more intuitive of the two. After all, if the humanitarian frame is five times as salient as the security frame, we would expect to see this reflected in aid policy. However, if the relative weight of humanitarianism does not vary at all across our observations, we will be hard put to measure its effect. In order to connect variation in aid policy across time and space to variation in frame strength, therefore, comparisons to average levels of frame salience for the entire dataset will be crucial. Nevertheless, it will be important to keep in mind the fact that, on the whole, security and power are not particularly

Table 3.9 *Frequency with which the salience of a frame exceeded the dataset average by at least 25 per cent*

Frame	Dataset avg.	Belgium	Italy	Netherlands	Norway
Security	0.06	8	7	6	3
Power	0.07		4	16	3
Wealth	0.13	11	15		
Enlightened self-interest	0.13	4	6	5	7
Reputation	0.20	3	6	2	6
Obligation	0.19	11	3	3	5
Humanitarianism	0.23	1		10	13

prominent, whereas humanitarianism accounts for about one in four arguments for aid overall.

Table 3.9 presents a summary overview of the information in Tables 3.5–3.8, showing the number of times the weight of each general frame exceeds the dataset average by at least 25 per cent. The two most salient frames in each country have been underlined. The determination of the top two frames for the Netherlands and Belgium is straightforward; for Norway and Italy the situation is more ambiguous. In each of these two countries three frames appear of roughly equivalent importance in Table 3.9: reputation, enlightened self-interest and security (Italy) or obligation (Norway). However, in each country reputation is unambiguously the second most salient frame overall when compared against the other frames. Moreover, in each country the average weight of reputation is also greater than is the case in either Belgium or the Netherlands, as shown in Table 3.4. This amply justifies highlighting reputation as the second most important frame for Italy and Norway.

Summarizing the implications of Table 3.9 in words, we expect Belgium's aid policy to be governed by economic self-interest and a sense of obligation. In Italy, economic self-interest should dominate, with reputational considerations playing a secondary role. Aid policy in the Netherlands should reflect the importance of the humanitarianism and power frames. Norwegian policy, finally, should be shaped by humanitarianism even more strongly, with reputational considerations secondary.

Conclusion

This chapter introduced measures of the strength of different frames for foreign aid. I argued that legislative debates provide the best available source of information about the strength of these frames. A total of forty-four different individual reasons for aid were coded in these debates, ranging in frequency from just a couple of occurrences to over 250, summed across all four countries. These specific tallies were then aggregated into seven broad frames for aid. Several frames that have not received much attention in the literature turn out to be quite important in the aid discourses of different countries: reputation and obligation stand out in particular. The data also indicate that although the security frame was of some importance in the early years of aid, it was never particularly salient, nor has it been of much significance since the late 1960s. Conversely, humanitarianism was comparatively unimportant at the start, but has grown in salience to account for about a third of all arguments for aid, on average, in recent years. The data also reflected striking cross-national differences in legislative aid discourse, as summarized at the end of the preceding section.

Sceptics may suggest that the direction of the causal arrow is from actual aid policy to the relative strength of different frames measured in these debates, rather than the other way around as I argue in my model. Using trailing moving averages reduces the likelihood that this is the case, as it introduces an implicit lagging process for the connection between frames and policy outcomes. Another possible argument is that the relative strength of different frames directly reflects other, underlying variables – for example, the strength of political parties or the economic context. Such alternative hypotheses can only be addressed by considering the patterns introduced in this chapter in more detail, to see whether they can be reduced to patterns in underlying variables – be they aid policy itself or other, exogenous factors. The next chapter tackles this issue, while also examining the relationship between core beliefs about national identity and frames for aid.

4 | *Aid frames: origins and evolution*

While it would be convenient to believe that the decision to launch large-scale aid programmes was the product of clear and uniform thinking on the part of the industrialised nations in the post-war era, the truth is otherwise. From the outset a number of quite different motivations were at work – and at work side by side.

– Hancock, *Lords of poverty*, 69

Chapter 3 highlighted the striking differences, both across donor states and over time, in the framing of development assistance by decision-makers. This chapter looks into the sources of these differences, and analyses the factors that cause ideas about aid to change. In the next few chapters, I will argue that frames for aid are both prior to and shape aid policy; this makes it all the more important to provide an account of the sources of these frames. I do so by relating them to deeper beliefs about national identity and historical experiences. I shall argue that four broad factors affect the relative strength of different frames: national traditions and experiences, the international political and economic context, the efforts of governments as frame entrepreneurs and information providers, and experiences with past policy successes and failures. International norms, on the other hand, exert a weak influence at best.

The chapter is divided into four sections. First, I examine the connections between national identity and the initial discourse on aid that emerged in the 1950s. Since multiple policy frames may be compatible with a nation's history and identity, it is especially important to examine the early debates on foreign aid, as that is where the initial set of relevant arguments will be identified and tested. The second section discusses in more detail the evolution of aid discourses in the four countries. This allows us to see how international influences as well as national experiences influenced these discourses over time. The third section takes a closer look at the impact of governments as frame entrepreneurs. I show that elites are far from passive participants in the policy discourse. Instead, they actively work to increase the prominence of the frames they consider most important, whereas others are downplayed as much as possible. In the fourth section, finally, I discuss the way governments may control the visibility of aid policy and the availability of information about successes and failures, in attempts to prevent or reinforce shifts in the relative salience of different frames.

The origins of aid frames

Where did frames for aid come from when it was a brand-new policy, shortly after the Second World War? In this section, I show that the initial discourse on development assistance was strongly shaped by national historical experiences and ideas about national identity. Where countries had similar national experiences to draw on, such as a colonial background, initial arguments for aid resembled one another. Nevertheless, in each country the decision-makers' particular sense of their own national history, identity and interests set the tone for the different patterns that were to characterize the aid discourses of these countries during the ensuing decades.

Belgium became independent from the Netherlands only in 1830, but the Flemish merchant tradition dates back much further than that. Indeed, the leading expert on Belgian foreign policy argues that

> Without a doubt, promoting industrial, commercial, and financial interests abroad is at the heart of Belgian foreign policy. Despite all manner of changes in the international environment, this has been the constant concern since Belgium's emergence as a nation, accepted by the entire political, industrial and labour elite. This interest is so dominant that it has at times derailed the country's foreign policy, because short-term commercial profit pushed aside all other facets of diplomacy.[1]

In second and third place as factors shaping foreign policy, this same author highlights the idea of an internationally shared francophone culture, and the expression of Flemish–francophone cultural differences.[2] Certain characteristics often associated with Dutch national

---
[1] R. Coolsaet, *Buitenlandse zaken*, 247.
[2] *Ibid.*, 248.

identity, such as an interest in international influence as well as in law and justice, might have been more prominent had Flemish groups had the upper hand during the decades following Belgium's independence. However, the francophone areas were richer and politically stronger, and it was not until well after the Second World War that Flemish groups began to re-assert themselves. Given this background, it is not surprising that the idea of a shared (francophone) identity with – and a resulting obligation to – Zaire was dominant in the early aid discourse, together with a strong dose of economic self-interest. Indeed, Figure 3.2 showed that these two broad frames accounted for almost the entire discourse at the start.

Representative Le Hodey's contribution to the 1954 budget debate captured in a nutshell the combination of economic self-interest, obligation, and a concern with affirming Belgium's place alongside the major industrialized nations that has been the hallmark of Belgian development policy ever since. He argued in favour of providing technical assistance and scholarships to students from developing countries by pointing out that not only would such students be grateful for the education they received, 'but they would be at the same time the best propagandists for our products'. This would serve the 'long-term interests of the nation' while also 'responding to the moral obligations that are imposed on countries with ancient civilizations and advanced cultures such as ours'.[3]

In Italy, as we have seen, economic interests have been coupled with reputational considerations rather than a sense of obligation. Many authors have noted the importance of these two general frames throughout Italy's political culture. For example, in a 1963 study of Italy's foreign policy, one observer emphasized both the importance of looking good ('fare una bella figura') and the fact that Italians see happiness as a product of wealth.[4] These features date back at least to Italy's unification in the 1870s: a consistent goal of late nineteenth-century governments, for example, was 'the grandezza (grandeur) of the fatherland'.[5] Along the same lines, Romano notes that 'The conviction is deeply rooted in the Italian political culture that Italy is a

---

[3] *Parlementaire Handelingen*, 10 February 1954: 6. See also similar comments by Foreign Minister Spaak, *Parlementaire Handelingen*, 30 November 1955: 17.
[4] N. Kogan, *The politics of Italian foreign policy*, 4–5.
[5] *Ibid.*, 30.

different country, carrier of universal values, and destined to transform by its own example and its own diplomacy the very foundations of the international system'.[6]

In sum, Italians are motivated by visions of grandeur and economic gain. The former is associated with a desire for international influence that will be noticeable whenever Italy tries to behave as a great power in a particular issue area. This basic description is very much in line with the image emerging from the data presented in Chapter 3.[7] Some quotations from aid debates illustrate how economic interest and the pursuit of prestige blended in Italy's early aid discourse: in 1957, representative Vicentini pointed out that: 'An engineer trained in Italy is often the best propagandist and channel for the penetration of Italian products … In this noble and peaceful competition, Italy must maintain and improve its own position.'[8] His colleague Pacciardi even argued that 'this is a purely commercial policy and we have to treat it as such'.[9] However, in commenting on Italy's activities in Somalia, representative Pintus emphasized the reputational aspects:

[T]hat which matters most, morally and for the international prestige of Italy, is the recognition on the part of the free world and the entire African world of the loyalty, the sincerity, and the capability with which she has … completed an enterprise of significance that is exceptional and unique in the history of peoples.[10]

Such hyperbole is rarely found in Dutch foreign policy discussions, although the Dutch share with Italy a certain ambivalence about their identity as a medium or small power, as well as a sense of historical mission. Many facets of Dutch national identity can be traced back to the golden age of the Dutch republic, the seventeenth century. This period cemented the image of the Dutch as merchants, interested in trade and profits, but also in the international stability and peace

---

[6] S. Romano, 'La cultura della politica estera italiana', 33.
[7] In fact, the emergence of power as a comparatively salient frame by the late 1970s is eerily foreshadowed in a statement by a young Italian diplomat around 1960: 'Italy needs twenty years to develop economically and politically; then we shall make our voice heard again in international politics'. Quoted in Kogan, *The politics of Italian*, 145–6.
[8] *Atti Parlamentari*, 15 October 1957: 36493.
[9] *Ibid.*, 36514.
[10] Presentation of 1959–60 budget, *Atti Parlamentari*, 1959, N. 828-A: 161.

The origins of aid frames   81

necessary for successful commerce.[11] Since that era, 'peace, profits and principles' have remained central themes in Dutch foreign policy.[12] In the nineteenth century, for example, 'the Netherlands extolled its pacifism and self-satisfaction as sublime virtues beneficial not only to the Dutch but to the whole of mankind'.[13]

The shock of the Second World War did little to shake the enduring faith of the Dutch in the principles of international trade, cooperation and law. On the contrary, the experience strengthened their interest in taking a leading role and setting an example in these areas. The small size of the Netherlands was not seen to be an insurmountable obstacle in pursuing international influence.[14] However, the Dutch outlook on international relations has not been limited to the power frame. Most experts on Dutch foreign policy also highlight the continuing salience of humanitarian and egalitarian goals, dating back at least to the nineteenth century.[15]

This general portrait of Dutch foreign policy identity matches the ideas expressed in the early legislative debates on foreign aid. Of particular interest is the way in which economic self-interest, which fits well with the Dutch merchant tradition, disappeared quite rapidly as an important frame. This illustrates the degree to which elites have choices regarding which frames to emphasize when a new policy area is introduced. Although the issue of foreign aid was first raised in the context of the wealth frame, in a 1950 legislative debate,[16] by the end of the 1950s that frame had been pushed aside. It was replaced by a

---

[11] The long-standing Dutch tradition of support for international law and universal norms can be traced back at least to Grotius, who was not only a political theorist, but also a sometime employee of the Dutch United East India Company, the pre-eminent trading conglomerate of the day.
[12] J. J. C. Voorhoeve, *Peace, profits and principles: A study of Dutch foreign policy*.
[13] E. H. Kossmann, *In praise of the Dutch republic: Some seventeenth century attitudes*, 17.
[14] In 1945, 43 per cent of Dutch citizens – and 62 per cent of those in leading positions – thought that 'a small power like the Netherlands can exert some real influence on the maintenance of world peace'. As possible methods for doing so, respondents most often mentioned 'encouraging international cooperation' and 'pointing others to international law'. NIPO poll cited in Voorhoeve, *Peace, profits and principles*, 11.
[15] For example, Voorhoeve, *Peace, profits and principles*, 18–22; A. Van Staden et al., 'Role conceptions in the post-war foreign policy of the Netherlands'.
[16] *Handelingen*, 29 November 1949: 684.

belief that aid, as an issue in international relations, presented both a challenge and an opportunity for the Netherlands, allowing it to set an example and to take a leading role. This belief is a close match for the nineteenth-century foreign policy aspirations of the Dutch elites.[17]

The 1951 report of the government's Commission on Technical Assistance provides a good example of the emphasis on the potential for Dutch influence and leadership. It began by pointing out that '1951 confirmed the hope … that the Netherlands could play a significant role in the provision of international technical assistance'. Technical assistance was described as 'a new way to promote Dutch interests abroad' which could 'establish the Dutch name in less developed countries at an early stage' as well as 'increase the respect for the Netherlands, with consequences in many areas'.[18] Although humanitarian arguments for assistance could be connected to Dutch traditions, too, they were not prominent at the start. However, they were given a strong boost in a well-received speech in 1955 by the Queen, which reinforced a vision of aid as a noble task or challenge for the rich nations to respond to, and underscored its humanitarian aspects.[19] The impact of this speech illustrates the potential power of norm entrepreneurs, including those in the government.

Norway differs from the other three states in that it did not have a colonial policy to convert into an aid programme. Nevertheless, Norwegians, too, drew upon their national experiences in framing the initial goals for their aid policy. Norway's foreign policy initiatives 'have often had a moralizing tendency and shown an immodest belief that the rest of the world has much to learn from the Norwegians' example'. The large distance between Norway and the power-political centres of Europe has long allowed Norwegians to 'think in different geopolitical directions than other European nations'.[20] Similarly, Riste argues that 'membership in the League of Nations provided a perfect forum for the development of a philosophy which saw the small state as a paragon of virtue, and European

---

[17] E.g. *Handelingen*, 10 May 1951: 1612 and 20 November 1951: 469, 491.
[18] Netherlands, *Jaarverslag over 1951*, 2–3.
[19] The speech was titled 'The prosperity and welfare of the world as a shared responsibility'; cf. Hoebink, 'Geven is nemen', 254.
[20] T. L. Knutsen, 'Norsk utenrikspolitikk som forskningsfelt', 25.

great power politics as the embodiment of evil'.[21] This helps explain why the power-political frame was far less visible in Norway than in the Netherlands. Instead, both as a historical trading nation and as a relatively young state, Norwegians were much more concerned with general issues of international peace and justice. The experience of membership in the League of Nations reinforced the importance of the enlightened self-interest frame.

Another important factor in shaping the Norwegian outlook was the humanitarian activities of famed explorer Fridtjof Nansen in the 1920s. Both the legacy of his ideas and the memory of the acclaim his work brought to Norway as a country were important in winning Norwegians over to the idea of international development assistance. An issue area in which it was possible to combine doing good and looking good was irresistible. Fuelling the desire to do something were pressures from those involved in missionary activities, who saw aid as a way to obtain state support for activities they felt represented the shared values of all the Norwegian people.[22]

Influenced by all these factors, the Norwegian legislature held an extensive debate on development cooperation as early as 1952, at a time when only scattered references to the issue can be found in most other donor states. The debate featured lengthy discussions about the moral imperative to do something about poverty and starvation in the Third World, as well as nightmare scenarios about the global instability that might result from unchecked population growth. Reputational and humanitarian concerns dominated, coupled with a strong emphasis on enlightened self-interest. All three frames directly drew upon Norwegians' sense of national identity.

In sum, the initial discourse in each of these four countries was strongly shaped by core beliefs about the nation's identity, as well as by lessons drawn from the country's own historical experiences.

---

[21] O. Riste, 'The historical determinants of Norwegian foreign policy', 14.
[22] For example, representative Grytnes found it 'very satisfying that even the circles which previously remained on the sidelines and did not understand this work, now see this as a task and are willing to contribute ... the missionary activists are just happy for the assistance they have received in this way'. *Stortingstidende*, 21 May 1953: 1170. See also Balsvik, 'U-landsdebatt', 121. The official history of Norway's development also highlights the historical importance of missionary activities. J. Simensen, *Norsk utviklingshjelps historie, bind 1: 1952–1975. Norge møter den tredje verden*, 28–32.

However, the experiences of Norway and the Netherlands also make clear the influence of normative entrepreneurs in determining the relative strength of the different candidate frames for a policy. In the Dutch case, humanitarian interests were strengthened by a well-received speech by the Queen. In the Norwegian case, those involved in missionary activities similarly played up the humanitarian frame. In Belgium and Italy, on the other hand, humanitarian arguments proved less of a fit with core beliefs and traditions. Moreover, and perhaps as a result, aid debates in these countries also offer little or no evidence of normative entrepreneurs trying to promote such arguments in the emerging national aid discourse.

Changes over time in aid frames[23]

In his work on Belgian foreign policy, Coolsaet maintains that pressure for international convergence in goals and motivations 'in most cases is far less decisive than is commonly assumed'.[24] He argues that national identity and experiences matter far more in shaping foreign policy than do international influences. In this section, I discuss the evolution of the aid discourse in all four countries. Although considerations of space limit us to discussing only the most important trends and patterns, the evidence shows that Coolsaet's claim holds for countries other than Belgium as well.

The 1960s and 1970s: consolidating aid as a policy area

Belgium's bilateral aid policy officially began with a royal decree on 18 January 1962. The decree emphasized that 'the cooperation that [the developing countries] expect from us is an obligation of international justice'.[25] This sense of obligation would be a dominant frame in the Belgian aid discourse almost uninterruptedly throughout the mid 1970s, as we saw in Figure 3.2. It often found expression in a desire not to look bad relative to other donor states. In 1972, representative

---

[23] For a more detailed discussion of changing aid frames over time in the four case study countries, see Chapters 6–9 in A. M. Van der Veen, 'Ideas and interests in foreign policy: The politics of official development assistance'.
[24] Coolsaet, *Buitenlandse zaken*, 248, 250.
[25] King Boudewijn, official statement on 23 October 1961, cited in Belgium, *Hulp door België verleend aan de ontwikkelingslanden, 1962–1963*, 2.

De Facq characterized the aid budget 'as more or less the minimum we have to do not to get a bad image in the Third World and to maintain good commercial relations', illustrating the way the obligation and wealth frames were often intertwined in the discourse.[26]

From the start, the Belgian public was less interested in aid issues than were the Dutch, largely because the dominant frames in the aid discourse did not involve them at a personal level. A 1972 poll of Belgian attitudes towards aid shows that the public recognized the primacy of obligation and economic concerns as driving factors. When asked to name the reasons behind the aid programme, export and import concerns were strikingly salient, followed closely by several arguments emphasizing Belgium's obligations as a rich state and a former colonial power.[27]

The Flemish community has been rather more interested in aid issues than have the francophones, as a result of their exposure to the development discourse in the Netherlands. The Flemish are, accordingly, disproportionately represented in legislative aid debates. Nonetheless, their exposure to Dutch debates has not had much influence on their frames for aid. Indeed, there is surprisingly little convergence over time in the aid discourses – and policies – of these two closely connected countries.

The first official bilateral aid initiative in Italy came with the passage of law 1594 in 1962.[28] During the legislative debate over this law, the main frames relevant to Italy's aid emerged quite clearly. The government emphasized reputation, claiming that 'there is reason to believe that most of the underdeveloped countries await our initiative with interest'.[29] In contrast, representatives felt that economic goals ought to prevail over reputation: instead of arguing that 'our contribution must be proportional to the demands of our prestige', the government ought to accept that 'the goal of these new initiatives must be above all that of increasing our export opportunities'.[30]

---

[26] *Parlementaire Handelingen*, 31 May 1972: 1345.
[27] UNIOP, *De onderontwikkeling in de Derde Wereld en de geldinzamelingen*, 26–7.
[28] Laws in Italy are numbered consecutively over the course of a calendar year, across all subjects. Nearly every government initiative is couched in legalistic terms and adopted in the form of a law.
[29] *III Commissione*, 12 July 1962: 199.
[30] Representative Bartesaghi, *III Commissione*, 12 July 1962: 200.

The wealth frame continued to dominate the aid discourse for several decades. In the words of representative Pedini: 'Technical assistance affords us an optimal method to participate in the development of a country and in the investments and consumption of its market.'[31] A new law in 1967 tellingly placed export and foreign investment credits ahead of 'assistance to developing countries'.[32] By and large, the public agreed with the emphasis on wealth and self-affirmation as the relevant frames for development assistance. One observer noted that by the early 1970s most people had come to agree that 'a country obtained prestige and weight in the international context in proportion to its activities in the Third World'.[33]

Given the importance of the reputation frame, Italy's growing economic prosperity inspired a feeling by the early 1970s that a more active participation in development cooperation had become no less than an obligation, necessary to cement Italy's status as an advanced industrial state, and to avoid a worsening reputation internationally. Not surprisingly, Figure 3.3 showed a gradual rise in the salience of the obligation frame at this time. In the debate over a new aid law in 1971, now State Secretary Pedini referred to the 'desire ... and duty of Italy as a nation and as a member of the European Community to participate ever more in the struggle against underdevelopment'.[34] However, most policy-makers felt that this new law sufficiently addressed Italy's perceived duty, and the salience of obligation declined again after the mid 1970s.

One frame which had been almost invisible until the mid 1970s, but which gradually started to assert itself in the aid discourse, was that of power and influence. Once leaders felt that Italy was making a good-faith effort in development assistance, the growing self-confidence resulting from the post-war economic miracle increasingly became evident in this issue area too. Ironically, the reputation frame became less prominent at the same time, for two reasons. First, although Italy was seen to meet its obligations, comparisons of donor state programmes published by the DAC made it clear that it would be difficult for the country to derive any real prestige from its current

---

[31] *III Commissione*, 23 February 1968: 261.
[32] Subject headings of law 131 of 1967.
[33] Journalist Italo Pietro, interviewed in F. Tana, 'Terzo Mondo e opinione pubblica: Le responsabilità della stampa – intervista a Italo Pietra', 34.
[34] *III Commissione*, 11 November 1971: 277.

policies. Second, rising raw materials prices (including oil) and an ensuing period of inflation and recession put the focus more squarely on the other basic pillar of Italy's aid policy, economic self-interest. Figure 3.3 showed quite clearly the rising importance of the wealth frame at this time.

The demonstration of international interdependence provided by the oil crisis and the subsequent recession also resulted in a rise in the importance of the enlightened self-interest frame. Its salience was heavily promoted by politicians in the radical party (PRI), most notably Marco Pannella.[35] He and his colleagues worked tirelessly to instil in Italians a sense of the general importance of international peace, stability and justice. Their activities helped give a stronger weight to the evidence confronting policy-makers about Italy's vulnerability to international economic instability.

By the end of the 1970s, then, we observe a definite change in the contents of Italy's aid discourse. Although economic self-interest continued as a dominant frame, reputation became less relevant. Instead, power and enlightened self-interest had become more prominent. Italy's own experiences account for the rise of power as an important frame, just as they explain the preceding brief rise in the importance of obligation. Enlightened self-interest, on the other hand, became prominent in response to a combination of international events and the visible domestic repercussions thereof.

In the Netherlands, the aid discourse during the 1960s and 1970s was characterized by a salient influence frame, coupled with a gradually growing emphasis on aid as an international obligation and a humanitarian initiative. In the previous section, we saw that the influence frame emerged directly from Dutch national identity. The humanitarian frame did so too, albeit more weakly, and was reinforced by the moral entrepreneurship of the government in the 1950s. A sense of obligation began to grow by the mid 1960s. For example, representative Peschar argued in the 1962 budget debate that 'We, as the Netherlands, can not permit ourselves to fall short'.[36] The role of Dutch economist Jan Tinbergen is of particular importance

---

[35] Indeed, Pannella became so associated with the issue that when he broached a different topic during the 1985 foreign affairs debate, representative Petruccioli retorted, 'Is hunger in the world not your fight? ... Why don't you talk about that?', *III Commissione*, N.2105–2106, 10 October 1984: 29.
[36] *Handelingen*, 17 November 1961: 155.

here. Tinbergen was instrumental in developing the programme for the second UN Development Decade. This gave rise to a feeling that the Netherlands was obligated to follow the UN's recommendations, seeing as those recommendations had been drafted by a prominent advisor to the Dutch government.

The mid 1960s also marked the end of the security and wealth frames as a steady presence in the Dutch aid discourse.[37] A new White Paper argued that using aid as a geopolitical weapon had largely failed. Similarly, the idea that helping states develop would benefit the donors' export industries in the long run was called into question: the goal of aid was, after all, 'that the recipient states increasingly become producers themselves, and thus could become competitors of the donor states'.[38] This report once again demonstrated the government's norm entrepreneurship: although the security frame had lost most of its visibility by then, the wealth frame still enjoyed numerous adherents in private industry.[39] The White Paper served notice that it would henceforth be less acceptable to emphasize this frame in calling for particular policy initiatives.

Meanwhile, the emphasis on aid as an issue area where the Netherlands could play an influential international role continued unabated. In the 1968 aid debates, for example, representative Van Mierlo argued that, 'In my opinion, it *is* our task to take the lead in these issues. The important thing is to be out in front and to help produce a change in mentality'.[40] Legislators also frequently connected such power-political goals to an underlying interest in reputation: '[T]he identity and character of a nation are reflected in the volume and the intensity of development assistance and in the people's and the government's involvement in these efforts.'[41] The humanitarian frame was strengthened under the influence of Development Minister Pronk, who continually emphasized that aid was to be provided 'as much and as directly as possible to the poorest'.[42] Not incidentally, an

---

[37] Cf. C. S. I. J. Lagerberg and J. Vingerhoets, 'Ontwikkelingssamenwerking: De moeizame weg naar een nieuw beleid', 695.
[38] Netherlands, *Nota: Hulpverlening aan minder ontwikkelde landen*, 23.
[39] Hoebink, 'Geven is nemen'.
[40] *Handelingen*, Foreign Affairs Commission, 16 November 1967: B15. Emphasis in original.
[41] Representative Van Dam, *Handelingen*, 25 November 1971: 1367.
[42] Netherlands, *Bilaterale ontwikkelingssamenwerking: Om de kwaliteit van de Nederlandse hulp*, 13–14.

emphasis on humanitarianism also helped strengthen the Dutch leadership position in the issue area.

In Norway, finally, we have seen that the initial aid discourse combined the general frames of reputation, humanitarianism and enlightened self-interest more or less equally. The main change throughout the end of the 1970s was a growing role for obligation, starting as early as 1960.[43] The obligation frame was linked, however, to the reputational frame: Norway had an obligation to provide aid, because it was a special state, uncorrupted by the power-political and economic interests that characterized other states. In a parallel to the Dutch situation, Norwegians also felt a particular obligation to follow UN recommendations. After all, a countryman of theirs, Trygve Lie, had been the organization's first Secretary General.[44] The internalization of the UN's goals also supported the enlightened self-interest frame in Norway's aid discourse.[45] As representative Moe argued, 'if one does not do this with a feeling that it is urgent, then peace and stability throughout the world will be in the greatest of dangers'.[46]

Interestingly, Moe simultaneously emphasized that 'the authorities ought to be more concerned with our country's reputation'.[47] Nevertheless, as a concern with international peace and stability grew, the reputation frame became less salient for a while. Many felt that such attitudes were not quite appropriate: 'Development aid is a serious international task, and must not be treated as some form of international competition between nations where the most important consideration is one's rank in a table.'[48] Thus obligation temporarily displaced reputation as a prominent concern. However, the obligation

---

[43] This sense of obligation is reflected, for example, in representative Hambro's claim that 'it has become generally accepted that we, as one of the rich countries in the world, have a responsibility on the state level relative to the poor countries'. *Stortingstidende* 1964–5: 3463–4.

[44] H. Hveem, *International relations and world images. A study of Norwegian foreign policy elites*, 117.

[45] For example, the 1961 White Paper on aid explicitly underscored the importance of aid as 'an important part of the peace policy which the nations of the world have committed themselves to pursue as members of the United Nations'. Norway, *Engen-utvalget: Instilling fra utvalget for utredning av spørsmålet om Norges hjelp til utviklingslandene*, 5.

[46] *Stortingstidende*, 21 May 1968: 3761.

[47] *Ibid.*, 3762.

[48] Representative Stray, *Stortingstidende*, 6 December 1967: 1572. See also representative Thyness, *Stortingstidende*, 15 November 1971: 1023.

frame became gradually less important after the mid 1970s, as the UN became well established. To the extent that the Norwegians' sense of obligation derived from their commitment to the UN, the success of the latter reduced the importance of foreign aid as an instrument to strengthen it.

By the beginning of the 1970s, humanitarian motives became increasingly salient. A net exporter of oil, Norway was much less negatively affected than most other countries by the international economic instability that characterized this era, and hence neither the wealth nor the enlightened self-interest frames received as much of a push as they had in some other countries. Meanwhile, traditional interests in international justice and distributive justice came to the fore in response to the crises faced by developing countries, raising the salience of humanitarianism.[49]

Aid discourse in the 1980s and 1990s: crisis, fatigue, renewal

The main features of Belgium's aid discourse remained more or less constant throughout the late 1980s. By the early 1990s, however, dissatisfaction with the realities of Belgium's aid policy became increasingly prominent. Although there was widespread agreement regarding the significance of the wealth frame, the evidence increasingly suggested that Belgium's policy was doing more for the wealth of individual businesspeople than for the economic health of the country as a whole. A number of serious corruption scandals came to light in the mid 1990s, implicating the administrative top of the development administration.[50] As a result, the significance of the wealth frame remained comparatively low throughout the 1990s.

By the early 1990s, it had also become clear that Belgium's sense of obligation towards Zaire had been exploited by Mobutu Sese Seko, that country's ruler, to line his own pockets, while running his country into the ground. As a result, the sense of obligation Belgians felt towards the Zairean state shrank considerably. The economic self-interest frame and the obligation frame thus became less salient

---

[49] R. Tamnes, *Norsk utenrikspolitikks historie. Bind 6: Oljealder 1965–1995*.
[50] D. De Coninck, *Witte olifanten: De miljardenschandalen van de Belgische ontwikkelingssamenwerking*.

in the Belgian aid discourse in the 1990s. Their decline made room for a renewed focus on enlightened self-interest, inspired by two factors: first, the threats to Belgium's general interests implied by instability in Belgium's former possessions; and second, a growing international concern with issues such as the environment and, more directly, refugees. Finally, worries over corruption scandals and the breakdown of Zaire/Congo made the reputation frame more important in the second half of the 1990s. However, at the turn of the century the staying power of this new focus remained uncertain.

Italy entered the 1980s with wealth, enlightened self-interest and, to a lesser degree, power as the three most salient frames for aid, comparatively. After the mid 1980s, however, the latter two declined in importance once again. By then it had become clear that the ability of developing countries to destabilize the international economic system had been vastly over-estimated during the 1970s, making concerns about international instability seem less relevant. In addition, it appeared that Italy had found other, better avenues to pursue international influence, with its emergence as an active participant in the G-7 summits, for example. This made aid less interesting as a policy, especially since Italy's standing in this area was hardly that of a great power.

Economic self-interest continued to dominate the discourse throughout the 1980s. For example, in debating a new law on aid in 1987, representative Rauti noted somewhat defensively that 'France is not ashamed to say that it is pursuing its own technological, scientific, and productive penetration in eighteen francophone countries in the African continent. Why should Italy not do the same?'.[51] As in Belgium, however, the wealth frame began to decline in importance around 1990. People increasingly suspected that Italy's overall economic well-being was being hurt rather than helped by its aid policy. Although numerous grandiose projects were debated and approved in the parliament, there was often little evidence indicating that these projects were actually executed, or provided the intended contracts for Italian export and construction companies. Instead, much of the money seemed to disappear straight into the pockets of leading politicians, bureaucrats and their supporters.

---

[51] *III Commissione*, 9 December 1986: 12–13.

For some time, policy-makers and elites emphasized instead the reputational benefits of these projects. Even if Italy's overall aid programme was not impressive compared to the other DAC donors, it could still boast of a leading position in individual areas. Thus, Foreign Minister De Michelis argued in 1989 that 'we will be able to confirm that Italy is second to none in Europe'. Such arguments, however, resonated less and less, contradicted as they were by the accumulating evidence. Representative Crippa retorted that Italy's aid policy actually hurt its status: 'what is even worse … is the drop in the international prestige of our country which by now has reached the limits of decency'. Similarly, his colleague Rutelli emphasized the public's increasing disillusionment with the contrast between the grandiose pronouncements and the mediocre results of Italy's foreign aid policy, arguing that average citizens 'simply desire to safeguard the decorum and the image of Italy's foreign aid policy'.[52]

The most important factor affecting the relative strength of different frames for aid in Italy in the 1990s was the country's own experience with its aid programme, in particular the evidence that the results of Italy's aid policy were the opposite of those intended. Economic self-interest and reputation continued to dominate as goals among policy-makers and the public alike. However, accumulating data suggested that the country's economic health as well as its reputation were hurt rather than helped by its aid policy. Growing allegations of corruption and malfeasance led to a bicameral Commission of Inquiry which concluded that 'Among donor countries, Italy … distinguishes itself … by the particular seriousness of malversations'.[53]

These and similar findings seriously undermined the credibility of the wealth and reputation frames as arguments for aid. In their stead, the public's interest in humanitarian actions gradually found some expression, albeit in a very limited fashion. Indeed, the Commission of Inquiry did not refer to humanitarian considerations at all in its defence of a continued aid effort. Instead it held that the popular call

---

[52] *III Commissione*, 7 December 1989: 79, 102, 94. In fact, virtually every participant in this debate referred to the fact that Italy had lost face, both in general and with respect to particular recipient states (see e.g. pp. 85–6 in the same debate).

[53] Italy, *Raccolta di atti della Commissione Parlamentare d'Inchiesta sull'attuazione della politica di cooperazione con i paesi in via di sviluppo*, 1184–5.

Changes over time in aid frames 93

to cancel aid altogether 'is unfounded, dangerous, and also damaging to our dignity and our international interests'.[54] More notably, growing streams of refugees, as well as renewed concerns about international instability (associated with the Balkan crises), increased the salience of enlightened self-interest once more.

In the Netherlands, the 1980s saw the appointment of the first Development Minister from the main conservative party (the Liberal Party, VVD), Eegje Schoo. Interestingly, although her own rhetoric consistently emphasized economic self-interest as a valid frame for approaching aid policy, the overall Dutch aid discourse changed very little. Indeed, throughout the 1980s, the two most salient aid frames, in relative terms, continued to be power and humanitarianism. Rather than agreeing with the minister in her emphasis on economic interests, many legislators were instead concerned with the potential impact of her proposals on the international image and power of the Netherlands.[55]

As in Belgium and Italy, the end of the Cold War and a growing awareness of international interdependence increased the salience of the enlightened self-interest frame. For example, the government White Paper *A world of difference* emphasized the global repercussions of inaction, especially regarding human rights and the environment.[56] The report received a lot of media attention and was translated into several languages. However, the enlightened self-interest frame hardly replaced the power and humanitarian frames, which remained dominant throughout. As post-Cold War changes in the international system spurred a review of aid policy in many donor states, chances for the Netherlands to pursue a leadership position grew. The power frame accordingly increased in salience, while enlightened self-interest became somewhat less important after a peak in the mid 1990s. Legislators insisted that 'the Netherlands assumes responsibility as the largest of the smaller member states', and that the goal was to

---

[54] *Ibid.*, 1191.
[55] See, for example, contributions by representative (and future Development Minister) Herfkens as well as a representative from Schoo's coalition partners, the Christian Democrats, in the 1985 budget debate (*Handelingen*, 7 November 1984: 1257, and 8 November 1984: 1386, respectively).
[56] Netherlands, *Een wereld van verschil. Nieuwe kaders voor ontwikkelingssamenwerking in de jaren negentig (Tweede Kamer document 21 813).*

'maintain maximum influence over the issues that are meaningful to us'.[57] Indeed, Figure 3.4 showed an increase in importance for the power frame by the end of the century.

In Norway, finally, the obligation frame rapidly lost in salience after 1980. By almost any measure, the country was more than fulfilling its international obligations. The emphasis, therefore, turned once again to reputation, along with a consistent role for the humanitarian frame. In 1981, although one legislator still emphasized 'first and foremost the political and moral obligations that we as a nation have taken upon ourselves', a more common sentiment was that failure to continue to live up to these obligations 'would be a disaster for Norway's reputation in important circles in the poor world'.[58]

With humanitarianism and reputation in place as the dominant themes in Norway's aid discourse, the main change during this period was the emergence of enlightened self-interest as an important additional frame. In the late 1980s, this trend was driven by international environmental concerns associated with aid policy. The international visibility of the report produced by the UN-sponsored Commission on the Environment (WCED), chaired by former prime minister Brundtland, helped inspire Norway to pursue 'a – if not *the* – leading role in the international debate on the environment'.[59] Once again, the personal involvement of a leading citizen in an international initiative had a clear impact. Indeed, the aid policies of other donor states at this time displayed much less of an environmental focus.

The emphasis on reputation did not derive solely from Brundtland's international activities, however. It also flowed almost naturally from the realization that Norway had attained a certain status as a major international donor. As the chair of the parliament's Foreign Aid Committee noted in 1988: '[N]one of the parties in the committee want[s] Norway to relinquish its position among the world leaders where development aid is concerned.'[60] After a short-term decline, the enlightened self-interest frame rose in salience again during the second

---

[57] Quotations from Van Middelkoop, and Van Traa, respectively. *Handelingen*, 24 November 1994: 27–1707, and 23 November 1994: 26–1670.
[58] Representatives Rossbach and Brundtland, respectively. *Stortingstidende*, 23 November 1981: 677, 687.
[59] H. H. Lembke, *Norway's development cooperation*, 28.
[60] *Stortingstidende*, 30 November 1987: 1118. Norway's status in particular aspects of aid policy was praised as well: 'Emergency aid and refugees is one

half of the 1990s. This new trend appears to have been driven by the salience of refugee issues, a policy area added to the Development Minister's competences in 1997. However, it is worth noting that concerns with migration and overpopulation were already evident in Norway's very first aid debate: in many ways this focus was a return to the original framing of Norwegian aid.

Discussion

The patterns of change in the aid discourse point to domestic factors as the driving forces in changing the framing of aid. The basic themes of the four aid discourses proved remarkably durable and were relatively unaffected by pressures towards international convergence. The most dramatic changes in the discourse, in Belgium and Italy during the 1990s, were caused not by a rejection of the main frames in principle, but rather by accumulating evidence indicating that the actual implementation of aid policy was frustrating the goals envisioned in those frames.

Nevertheless, during the 1970s and the 1990s, international influences did have measurable effects on the aid discourses in the different countries. In the 1970s, a combination of domestic economic crises and fear of international economic instability changed the relative appeal of various frames, including wealth and enlightened self-interest. However, the degree to which these changes durably reshaped the aid discourses depended heavily on the frames that were salient in particular countries, as well as on the compatibility between different frames and perceptions of national identity and purpose. In Italy, the reaction was defensive, and enlightened self-interest as well as the wealth frame both grew in salience. In the Netherlands and Norway, on the other hand, the situation was largely seen in terms of international and distributive justice, strengthening the obligation and humanitarian frames.

---

issue area where Norway can justly be called a superpower' (Representative Lahnstein, *Stortingstidende*, 25 November 1991: 1115. See also *ibid*., 21 February 1995: 2280). Janne Haaland Matlary, state secretary for foreign affairs from 1997 to 2000, similarly emphasized Norway's 'international reputation as humanitarian superpower' (quoted in F. Liland and K. A. Kjerland, *Norsk utviklingshjelps historie, bind 3: 1989–2002. På bred front*, 86).

In the 1990s, the end of the Cold War and the growing international preoccupation with conflicts in developing countries increased the potential appeal of enlightened self-interest. The Netherlands reacted first, but the long-standing dominance of the power and humanitarianism frames won out, and the salience of enlightened self-interest declined during the second half of the decade. In Norway, on the other hand, refugee and population issues had been a concern in the aid discourse from the very beginning, and thus the enlightened self-interest frame proved more durably appealing. In Belgium and Italy, more immediate concerns with conflicts in and refugees from areas of direct national interest – the former colonies and the former Yugoslavia, respectively – helped promote the strength of particularistic takes on enlightened self-interest. In sum, national experiences and enduring themes in the national aid discourses shaped the impact of even such a dramatic international change as the end of the Cold War.

Governments as frame entrepreneurs

Although the previous section concentrated on the effect of national experiences and international influences on composite aid frames in different states, we also encountered several instances of frame entrepreneurship on the part of political actors, from the Dutch queen to the Italian Radical Party. This section of the chapter looks more closely at such efforts by government actors to affect the aid discourse. The most important reason for such initiatives is to address a divergence between the composite frame for aid and empirical evidence about aid policy. After all, policy-making elites have only limited slack: when the discordance between policy and the public's beliefs becomes too great, public pressures may well force a change in policy. In order to reduce this discordance, governments can change the policy, but often they would prefer not to do so.

This leaves two alternatives: change the balance of frames used to evaluate a policy, or limit and distort the information the public receives about the policy. As we shall see, each tactic has its own advantages and disadvantages. This section of the chapter focuses on the first approach; limiting and distorting policy visibility is the subject of the next section. Changing the balance of frames relevant to an issue area is a costly and involved process that will likely take some time. Moreover, it does not guarantee results, as conservative Dutch

Development Minister Schoo discovered in the 1980s. On the other hand, success is likely to have long-term effects. This option is most attractive, therefore, when elites become committed to an enduring change in policy orientation, as was the case in the Netherlands during the 1950s.

A concerted effort to increase the salience of a particular frame is most likely for the humanitarianism and enlightened self-interest frames. Humanitarianism is a comparatively new frame, historically. Hence it is not likely to be prominent initially in the public discourse on new foreign policy issues. Elites for whom humanitarianism is an important frame may, therefore, need to make a particular effort to promote this frame. Similar efforts are less likely to be necessary for frames such as power or wealth, which have a long tradition as foreign policy goals. Some aspects of the enlightened self-interest frame are similar to humanitarianism in this respect. While international instability is often a concern of long standing, interest in the environment, distributive justice and democratic governance are more recent, and hence more likely to require an extra push to be accepted into the general policy discourse.

To test this prediction, I examine efforts at 'aid education' on the part of the four governments. All governments publish materials explaining and promoting their policies. If our expectations about particular government efforts are correct, we should see a greater effort in this field in the two countries where humanitarianism has been a major frame for aid, starting some time *after* it has become an important frame in elite discourse (on the assumption that elites lead the public on these issues). This would be around 1980 for the Netherlands, and around 1975 for Norway. In Belgium and Italy, government efforts should be much less distinctive, but the salience of enlightened self-interest might suggest some extra effort in Belgium starting around the mid 1970s and peaking around the late 1980s and again in the late 1990s. In Italy, the same argument suggests some effort starting in the late 1970s, with peaks soon after and during the late 1990s.

In fact, almost every aid debate in the Netherlands has included comments regarding the importance of public support and the need to make an official effort to stimulate this support. As the humanitarian frame came to the fore in the 1970s, such comments became more prevalent. In 1972, the government announced that 'The costs associated with the domestic activation of shaping public opinion will increase quite rapidly'. In response, legislators emphasized the need not only to inform but also to explain: 'The official information service should not tell us that our policy is praiseworthy, but rather must increase the public's awareness of development issues.'[61]

By the late 1970s, Development Ministers routinely emphasized the importance of public awareness-raising,[62] and legislators have always been supportive.[63] The allocation of resources for this purpose had remained rather small until then. From this point forward, however, spending on aid education as a share of the total aid budget rapidly grew to over 0.5 per cent. At the start of the 1990s it increased further, to over 0.6 per cent.[64] Up to one-third of aid education funds were spent on distributing a free monthly magazine to the higher elementary school grades, with a total circulation of about 500,000. The magazine focused on the humanitarian aspects of aid, as well as its contribution to international peace and justice.[65] The government also produced a magazine for the general public, as well as a broad range of information brochures, folders and annual reports.

In Norway, too, legislators and the government emphasized a need to galvanize public support for development cooperation from the beginning: '[I]t is necessary for the Storting, and the authorities, to promote a certain conception in this area which simply is not [yet] unanimously shared by the broader public today.'[66] Indeed, many legislators viewed Norway's first aid initiative (a fishery project in

[61] *Handelingen*, 25 November 1971: 1357, 1370. The second statement is by representative De Gaay Fortman.
[62] See, for example, statements by Ministers De Koning, *Handelingen*, 22 February 1978: 1005, and Schoo, *Handelingen*, 8 November 1984: 1379.
[63] Moreover, during the 1990s a number of legislators became increasingly concerned with the apparent spread of aid fatigue among the public, further strengthening their resolve regarding the need for public education. See e.g. contribution by De Haan, *Handelingen*, 5 December 1997, meeting 34.
[64] Aid education data in this section are drawn from the annual reports on Dutch development cooperation, various years.
[65] *Handelingen* 1984–5:Documents 18600, chapter V, §76. See also *Handelingen* 1987, nr 26: 1268–9.
[66] Representative Wormdahl, *Stortingstidende*, 21 May 1968: 3805. Similarly, in the mid 1970s, representative Haugstvedt emphasized his desire 'to contribute to raising awareness among the people of our responsibility to address the poverty and deprivation from which great parts of the world's population suffer, even though such viewpoints at times can be unpopular among the voters' (*Stortingstidende*, 14 November 1974: 934).

Kerala, India) at least in part as a means to impart to the Norwegian people a greater understanding of the problems of developing countries.[67] As in the Netherlands, the government generally agreed with such assessments: in September 1974 the Minister of Foreign Affairs stated that 'the attitude of public opinion towards development aid is a question of the way in which we implement our public education efforts'.[68]

When Norway's Directorate for Development Aid was created in 1962, a separate information office was set up to handle the public education aspects of the aid programme. Expressed as a share of the total aid budget, spending on aid education was stable. It reached between 0.5 and 0.6 per cent of the total aid budget by 1964 and remained around that level throughout the mid 1970s. At that point, Norway's total aid budget started to grow rapidly, and total aid education funds likewise ballooned.[69] In addition to a detailed annual report, Norway's development administration (NORAD) published a number of different information magazines, several of which were aimed at the general public. Morever, several periodicals published by development-oriented non-governmental organizations (NGOs), using funding from NORAD, enjoyed a wide circulation. In the late 1990s, for example, Save the Children distributed 90,000 copies of its magazine, or about one for every fifty Norwegians.[70]

In contrast to its Dutch and Norwegian counterparts, the Belgian government was not very interested initially in expending resources on promoting public awareness of aid issues. In fact, in the 1968 budget debates, Minister Scheyven noted that

I was ... asked what was required to sensitize public opinion and parliament. I replied ... that I do not believe that it is necessary to sensitize either public opinion or the parliament other than by [demonstrating] the will to make a start. If that will manifests itself clearly, one can at that moment

---

[67] Balsvik, 'U-landsdebatt', 192.
[68] Cited by representative Longva, *Stortingstidende*, 14 November 1974: 950.
[69] Information from annual reports of the Directorate for Development Aid and NORAD, various years.
[70] Norway, *FN-sambandet i Norge (Evalueringsrapport nr 2.95)*, appendix 7; cf. also A. E. Ruud and K. A. Kjerland, *Norsk utviklingshjelps historie, bind 2: 1975–1989. Vekst, velvilje og utfordringer*, 59–61.

obtain both the approval of the parliament and the approval of public opinion.[71]

However, by the mid 1970s this attitude began to change. In his commentary on the 1974 budget, Minister Cudell argued that it was 'a primary task to inform public opinion sufficiently'.[72] As a result, during a 1976 reorganization, the development administration officially became charged with 'sensitizing the Belgian population to the problems of development, in order to promote the required adjustments to the Belgian economic and social structures'.[73] The second part of the quotation highlights the centrality of enlightened self-interest in fostering the adoption of this new policy.

Throughout the 1980s, aid education expenditures remained at the low level they had reached by the late 1970s, about 0.3 per cent of the total aid budget. The situation changed only in the late 1980s, as our model predicted. In his 1989 budget presentation, Development Minister Geens announced his determination to increase credits for public awareness-raising.[74] Overall aid education efforts grew to occupy 0.45 per cent of the total aid budget by 1992.[75] Soon after, however, government interest in mobilizing the public waned once more, and there was little evidence of the predicted second peak by the late 1990s.

In Italy, interest in aid education has been less even than in Belgium, as we would expect. Law 1222 of 1971 provided for a consultative committee on aid that could 'perform those initiatives it deems useful to publicize and illustrate ... Italy's actions in this field'.[76] As a result, the government in 1973 began publishing a periodical, *Cooperazione*, with information about Italy's aid policy. However, the publication

---

[71] *Parlementaire Handelingen*, 9 July 1968: 55.
[72] *Kamer Documents* Special Session 1974, 4-VIII, nr 6:17.
[73] Cited in R. Vaes, 'Het officiële Belgische beleid inzake ontwikkelingssamenwerking: Een beleidsanalyse', 100.
[74] See *Senaat Documents*, 1 February 1989, 352–5 and *Kamer Documents*, 15 June 1989, 4/8–794/4–88/89.
[75] Data on aid education expenditures are derived from the ABOS annual report, various years. See also J. Randel and T. German, *The reality of aid 1998/99*, who note that spending on domestic awareness-raising had risen to 1.07 per cent of the aid budget by 1996. However, this jump is due to a reduction in the aid budget, not to an increase in government education activities.
[76] Representative Salvi, presenting the government's proposal. *III Commissione*, 11 November 1971.

Governments as frame entrepreneurs 101

was almost entirely concerned with describing the legal framework associated with Italy's aid efforts. It had essentially no awareness-raising or educational function, and circulation was very limited. In fact, it appears to have been aimed more at Italian firms that might have wished to compete for foreign aid contracts than at the broader public.

From the late 1970s, as enlightened self-interest became a more prominent frame for aid, *Cooperazione* became glossier and the intended audience broader, with wider distribution to the media, as well as to schools and universities.[77] However, the new law nr 73 of 1985 did not earmark any funds for public information purposes,[78] and by the early 1990s, publication was halted. By that time, total spending for information purposes, including some other activities besides *Cooperazione*, was less than $0.01 per capita, compared to about $1 in the Netherlands.[79] After the mid 1990s, when enlightened self-interest had increased in salience again, the Ministry of Education began to get involved, along with regional and local governments.[80] As a result, education spending rose again. Still, the overall scope of government activity remained minimal.

Overall patterns of spending on aid education closely match our predictions. Where the humanitarian frame is salient among the policy-making elites, they are most likely to emphasize aid education; where the enlightened self-interest frame is important, the same tendency exists, albeit more weakly. In both cases, we observe a bit of a lag between a frame becoming salient and increased spending, also as predicted. Where neither of the two frames is salient, there is little or no spending on aid education.

It is worth asking whether these activities have any impact. The evidence seems to suggest that they do, as long as they are maintained for a number of years.[81] In Norway, regular public opinion polls on development assistance indicate that the government's initiatives have been

---

[77] At its peak, the magazine had a circulation of about 30,000. C. Foy and H. Helmich, *Public support for international development*, 151.
[78] L. Ardesi, 'L'impatto della cooperazione allo sviluppo sulla società italiana', 35.
[79] J. Randel and T. German, *The reality of aid 1996*, 115; J. Randel and T. German, *The reality of aid 1997/1998*, 239.
[80] G. Busini and E. Taviani, 'Italy', 91.
[81] Cf. J.-P. Thérien and A. Noël, 'Political parties and foreign aid'.

quite successful. In 1983, for example, 76 per cent of those polled said their opinions about aid policy had changed as a result of their exposure to aid information on television.[82] Similarly, representative Tøsdal felt as early as 1980 that 'we have really succeeded in steadily increasing the [public's] understanding of the goals behind our development aid principles'.[83] Finally, the 1999 DAC review of Norway's aid policy attributes its success to 'a broad national consensus, underpinned by the churches, a strong NGO community and an ongoing development education effort'.[84]

Though less information is available about the impact of the Dutch government's initiatives, these, too, appear to have been effective. Reviewing evidence from a range of surveys, a 1992 study found that, over time, opinions about the Third World among the Dutch public had become more informed and more nuanced.[85] In contrast to these findings for the Netherlands and Norway, the effect of aid education spending by the Belgian and Italian governments appears to have been negligible, both in terms of public support and as regards promoting an understanding of aid policy.[86]

Governments and policy visibility

Governments attempting to limit or distort public knowledge about a policy are engaging in a rather different kind of entrepreneurship from that discussed in the preceding section. This second type of initiative may be much cheaper, especially in the short run and in foreign policy, where policy specifics may be difficult to verify without travelling abroad. On the other hand, limiting policy visibility may require subverting well-established reporting procedures within the administration, which introduces additional costs. Moreover, it carries a considerable risk, as a public outcry may result if the discordance between frames and policy eventually comes to light. At that point, a serious revision of the policy may become inevitable, as Belgian and Italian policy-makers both discovered during the 1990s.

[82] Norway, *Holdninger til Norsk utviklingshjelp 1983*.
[83] *Stortingstidende*, 15 November 1979: 814.
[84] OECD, *Development co-operation review series: Norway*, 1.
[85] Netherlands, *Beweging gewogen. Impactsstudie NCO*, 84.
[86] E.g. Foy and Helmich, *Public support*.

A first general prediction concerns the monitoring and evaluation of aid policy. Different frames for aid not only suggest different goals; they also require different types of data to demonstrate policy 'success'. For example, if the goal of aid policy is to express a certain identity, putting the policy in place and publicizing it may suffice. However, if the goal is humanitarian, information about policy outcomes is necessary to determine whether or not the goals are being met. In other words, we expect governments to expend an effort on ongoing policy evaluations only to the extent necessary to establish that the goals associated with the dominant frames for the policy are being met. The two frames that are most closely associated with measurable goals are wealth and humanitarianism. When the former is strong, the emphasis in policy evaluation should be on the economic benefits to the home economy; for humanitarianism, it should be on the success of projects in the field.

A second prediction addresses overall policy visibility. The greater the divergence between the dominant frames and policy reality, the more we expect governments to minimize the amount of information available to the public about the policy. In particular, aid readily lends itself to rent-seeking on the part of private economic actors. Therefore, the more willing an administration is to allow its aid policy to be captured by private economic interests – at the expense of national economic welfare – the more it is likely to keep policy visibility low.

On average, the visibility of development assistance has been relatively high in the Netherlands and Norway, lower in Belgium, and lowest in Italy. The visibility of aid has never been as high in Belgium as in its neighbour to the north, due in part to structural and administrative realities. As we shall see in the next chapter, aid budget items are spread across several ministries, making it difficult for legislators and the public alike to develop an integrated understanding of Belgium's aid policy. The government also has a history of not consulting parliament before it introduces new initiatives. It consciously decided against introducing the first major legislation on development cooperation into parliament – passing it by decree instead – in order to avoid a public debate on the issue.[87] Similarly, legislators were

---

[87] A. A. J. Van Bilsen, *Structurele aspecten van de ontwikkelingssamenwerking. Deel I: Donorbeleid*, 222.

denied the opportunity to discuss the 1971 reorganization of the aid programme, much to their dismay.[88]

During the 1980s, Belgian budget debates ran further and further behind schedule, to the point that the 1986 and 1987 development budgets were discussed, together, in June 1988! Most of the arrears were eliminated when the budgets for 1988, 1989 and 1990 were all debated and approved in 1990, at two to three month intervals. In should come as no surprise, then, that legislative deliberation became increasingly superficial. In addition, the government made access to information difficult even for legislators. For example, Senator Maes found in 1982 that 'upon requesting the relevant documents, it even turned out that the [1981] budget document itself was no longer available'.[89] As representative Van der Maelen later argued, 'certain abuses could come into being because decision-making regarding development cooperation often took place in the shadows, in specific working groups or committees, without any reporting to the outside world'.[90]

In sum, aid policy's lack of salience in Belgium appears to have resulted from a combination of inefficient administrative structures and a deliberate policy on the part of the executive. The latter almost certainly was inspired by a realization that the aid programme had gradually become captured and distorted by private economic interests, and was no longer in line with ideas about the goals of aid policy shared by the broader elites and the public alike. Aid policy was dramatically brought out of the shadows only by corruption scandals in the mid 1990s. These scandals erupted when the strategy of minimizing policy visibility could no longer hide the divergence between the dominant frames regarding aid policy and the policy's empirical reality.[91] As predicted earlier for such a situation, the scandals inspired a wholesale reorganization of Belgium's aid programme. Both enlightened self-interest and a concern with Belgium's reputation grew in salience relative to the traditional wealth and obligation frames.

---

[88] For criticism of the government's behaviour by a legislator from one of the government's own coalition partners, see Senator Bogaert, *Parlementaire Handelingen Senaat*, 24 March 1971: 1184.

[89] 1981 Budget debate, *Parlementaire Handelingen Senaat* 1982, nr 27: 799. Contrast this state of affairs with the complaint by representative Terlouw in the Netherlands, that the government provided the legislature with perhaps too much information (*Handelingen*, 15 February 1978: 866).

[90] *Kamer Documents*, Committee Meetings 414 and 415, 5 November 1997.

[91] De Coninck, *Witte olifanten*.

Governments and policy visibility 105

Turning next to Belgium's policies regarding aid evaluation, it comes as no surprise that the emphasis has traditionally been on 'flow-back': the fraction of aid funds that returns to the Belgian economy in the form of goods and services. Even one of Belgium's most ambitious international aid proposals, the Pact for Solidary Growth, was explicitly promoted for its ability to guarantee 'an optimal use of the financial resources and an increase in the "flow-back" to Belgian industry'.[92] A NGO representative summed up the requirements for large aid projects in 1983 as follows: 'For bilateral projects, Belgium demands a flow-back of 75%; for projects in cooperation with other rich countries (e.g. via the UN), a flow-back of 100% is demanded; where the African Development Bank is concerned, the figure rises to 800%!'[93]

While flow-back was monitored quite closely, the Belgian government paid far less attention to the success of projects in the field. A study of the role of project evaluation in the Dutch and Belgian aid programmes noted that it was far less important in the latter, as evident 'both from the resources that are made available and from the special procedures and institutions that are created for this purpose'. The study estimated that the Netherlands spent 0.18 per cent of its bilateral aid on assessments, whereas the figure for Belgium was only one-third as high.[94]

Patterns in Italy resemble those in Belgium, albeit with an even more deliberate government strategy aimed at minimizing the visibility of aid policy than was the case in Belgium. Low levels of public awareness caused, as in Belgium, by various structural and administrative factors, meant that the Italian government 'has felt itself less constrained than other governments as far as [the DAC's] controls and efforts are concerned'.[95] The government made a concerted effort to ensure the continuation of this situation throughout the 1970s and

[92] Minister Eyskens, explaining the proposal to the Senate. *Senaat Documents* 1980–81, nr 5-VIII #4: 9. For a statement by his successor similarly emphasizing flow-back, see H. Achten, *Ontstaansgeschiedenis van de wet van 10 augustus 1981 tot oprichting van een fonds voor ontwikkelingssamenwerking. Overzicht van de parlementaire standpunten en verklaringen*, 17.
[93] B. Cleymans, 'Ronde tafel gesprek', 23.
[94] L. Berlage and R. Renard, *Evaluatie van ontwikkelingshulp in België en Nederland*, 6, 11, 25.
[95] R. Aliboni, 'Italian aid policy in the 60's', 63.

1980s. Although the Ministry of Foreign Affairs was supposed to provide an annual overview of its aid activities to the legislature, this document was rarely produced. Whenever it was produced, it was both too sketchy to permit an independent assessment, and usually designated for internal use within the Ministry only, making it difficult for legislators to obtain.[96] Legislators repeatedly complained about this state of affairs: 'the government has ignored requests for explanation that have been put forward by multiple political parties, including those forming part of the majority ... we are often denied the right to be informed'.[97]

By the late 1980s, growing suspicions about the actual implementation of the aid programme led the government increasingly to emphasize the reputational benefits of aid, which were of course harder to verify than economic ones. Foreign Minister De Michelis took the unusual step of convening a general legislative debate on aid policy in 1989, in order to emphasize the reputational payoffs of Italy's aid. This initiative was repeated several years in a row, finally providing legislators with a semblance of a general debate on aid policy after thirty years of requests. Not surprisingly, the practice was suspended once corruption scandals began to break in the early 1990s, just as they had in Belgium, although corruption ran both deeper and wider in Italy.[98] Since the authorities were cognizant of the degree to which aid policy was corrupted, Italy only very sporadically performed any evaluation of its aid projects at all.[99]

The situation has been rather different in both the Netherlands and Norway. Starting in the mid 1960s, Dutch aid policy was debated as a separate issue, no longer included in general foreign affairs debates as in Belgium or Italy. By 1975, opinion leaders felt that development cooperation was the issue area that had in recent years seen the

---

[96] Similarly, the Ministry was required to construct a database with information about the approval, funding and progress of different projects, to provide the legislature with accurate and up-to-date statistics on Italy's aid, but this database was never created. Rhi-Sausi et al., 'Italian bilateral aid policy', 20–24.
[97] Representative Crippa, *III Commissione*, N. 2043–4, 16 December 1987: 36. See also a similar comment nearly two decades earlier by Bartesaghi, *III Commissione*, N.1987-A, 19 November 1969: 20.
[98] Italy, *Raccolta di atti*.
[99] P. Hoebink, *The comparative effectiveness and the evaluation efforts of EU donors*.

greatest increase in both public interest and political salience.[100] As a result of the increased salience of aid issues, political parties began to feature aid more prominently in their election platforms, and growing numbers of voters indicated that this was a question they considered in determining their vote.[101] In Norway, too, the visibility of aid issues in the media, in political party platforms, and in legislative debates has been consistently very high.

Finally, these two countries also have active aid project evaluation programmes, as predicted. The Norwegian government has produced numerous reports both on individual projects and on the overall lessons that could be drawn from these evaluations.[102] As representative Steensnæs said in 2000, 'We have to see how the funds are being used, and follow the money even further to the final recipients in order to assure ourselves that they reach the right destination.'[103] Similarly, in the Netherlands a first major evaluation of the aid programme took place as early as 1968,[104] and an independent organization was created in 1977 to evaluate both individual projects and overall aid policy. Its reports have often been quite critical, and resulted in widespread discussions regarding the best way to improve the effectiveness of the Dutch aid programme in reaching those whose standard of living it aims to improve.[105]

Overall, the patterns described here match the predictions that follow from our model. In both Belgium and Italy, aid visibility has been low at least in part as a result of structural and administrative peculiarities. However, in both cases governments actively worked to make it difficult for legislators and other interested observers to obtain accurate information about aid policy. As aid policy was increasingly

[100] P. R. Baehr et al., *Elite & buitenlandse politiek in Nederland*, 250.
[101] J. Stapel, 'Onderzoek 26 mei 1981', 121.
[102] For example, O. D. K. Norbye and A. Ofstand, *Norwegian development aid experiences: A review of evaluation studies 1986–92*; K. Samset, K. Forss and O. Hauglin, *Learning from experience: A study of the feedback from evaluations and reviews in Norwegian bilateral aid*; see also O. Stokke, 'The evaluation policy and performance of Norway'.
[103] *Stortingstidende*, 16 May 2000.
[104] E. W. Hommes, 'Evaluaties van een evaluatie: I. Commentaar van een socioloog'; H. Van der Heijden, 'Evaluaties van een evaluatie: II. Commentaar van een economist'.
[105] Hoebink, 'Geven is nemen'; P. Hoebink, *De effectiviteit van de hulp: Een literatuuroverzicht van macro- naar micro-niveaus*.

captured by rent-seeking private interests, such efforts increased. Of the two countries, only Belgium performed any form of systematic monitoring of aid policy. As expected, however, the government did not monitor the success of aid projects in the field, but rather the flow-back of funds from those projects into the hands of Belgian companies. In contrast, the visibility of aid was higher from the start in the Netherlands and Norway, but both governments actively worked to ensure that it remained so, and even grew. Moreover, as the humanitarian frame became increasingly dominant, systematic efforts at evaluating the success of aid projects became ever more thorough, and were publicly debated.

Conclusion

Patterns in the relative strength of different frames for aid are driven by a number of factors. First, and perhaps most importantly, national traditions and core beliefs about national identity were fundamental at the inception of foreign aid in the 1950s, setting the stage for all later developments. The initial shape of the aid discourse established during those years has proven remarkably durable over the subsequent decades, with dramatic shifts occurring only in Belgium and Italy. These shifts took place not because of international trends or pressures for convergence, but rather because accumulating evidence showed that the central goals of aid policy were being undermined rather than helped by the actual implementation of that policy.

In fact, international organizations, and the norms and ideas they promulgate, played a minor role at best in the evolution of frames over time. They had some influence in the Dutch and Norwegian cases, but primarily as a result of feelings of obligation towards the United Nations that derived from the involvement of prominent national leaders of both countries in that organization's activities. The evidence clearly contradicts the common claim that international organizations have had a strong normative influence on national aid policies.[106] International economic and political trends have been more important, most notably the widespread economic crises of the 1970s and the growing salience of conflicts in (and refugee flows from) developing countries in the 1990s. Here too, however, the impact of

---

[106] E.g. Lumsdaine, *Moral vision*.

these trends on aid frames depended on the pre-existing balance of different frames in the discourse of each country.

Finally, governments are far from passive participants in the aid discourse. Where humanitarianism was a dominant frame for elites, governments expended considerable resources trying to bring the public discourse in line with this pattern. Similar, but weaker, efforts characterized situations where enlightened self-interest was a salient frame. Other frames inspired little effort to raise public awareness. To the contrary, where the economic frame was dominant we more often found active government policies aimed at minimizing the salience and visibility of aid policy. In an interactive process, low visibility led to greater distortion of the broad policy goals envisioned in the aid discourse, which in turn inspired government efforts to lower visibility further. Both Belgium and Italy had a tradition of insufficient consultation with the legislature, but in Italy the government's deliberate efforts to restrict access to information about aid policy began earlier and went further. As a result, the shift in the overall aid discourse generated when scandals erupted in the early 1990s was also more profound in that country.

The main goal of this chapter, as noted in the introduction, was to shed some light on the changing salience of different frames about aid policy over time in each country. The evidence presented here undermines the sceptical claim that the causal arrow runs in the opposite direction from that proposed in my model – in other words, that aid policy is prior to the ideas about aid we find expressed in legislative debates. The central goal of this study, however, is to demonstrate conclusively that these ideas drive the policy choices of decision-makers. The next three chapters take up this challenge.

5 | *The administration of aid policy*

> The full programme of our aid is placed at a very honourable level ... we are among the countries where the development policy is least bad.
> – Belgian Development Minister Outers, 1978[1]

What might Belgium's Development Minister have meant when he argued that his country's aid programme was 'least bad'? Regular reviews of aid programmes produced by the Development Assistance Committee suggest that an important part of the answer lies in the overall administration of aid policy. When the DAC reviewed Belgium's aid programme in 2001, it emphasized the implementation of 'major legislative changes and sweeping administrative reforms'.[2] Similarly, the central finding in its 2000 review of Italy's policies was that 'Considerable progress has been made in the management of Italian aid'.[3]

Another important factor in evaluating an aid programme is the quality of the aid it disburses: the fewer strings are attached to particular aid flows, the higher the quality is generally deemed to be. This chapter analyses both the overall administration of the aid programmes in Belgium, Italy, the Netherlands and Norway, as well as their performance on two key indicators of aid quality: tied aid and multilateral aid. Among others, this will help us decide the accuracy of Minister Outers' assessment of his country's programme.

In the first part of the chapter, I show that differences in composite national frames for aid explain a lot about the initial administration of aid policy. Moreover, subsequent reorganizations have tended to be cosmetic, unless preceded by a shift in the overall aid discourse. The

---
[1] *Parlementaire Handelingen*, 17 May 1978: 2080.
[2] OECD, *Development co-operation review of Belgium*, 1.
[3] OECD, *Development co-operation review of Italy: Main findings and recommendations*, 1.

second part of the chapter focuses on aid quality. The evidence shows that high levels of tied aid tend to be correlated with a strong economic self-interest frame. The story is somewhat more complicated for multilateral aid commitments: the allocation of aid to multilateral organizations is not just shaped by dominant policy frames but also by beliefs about the nature of those organizations and the quality of their initiatives.

The administration of aid policy

Administrative organization is of considerable importance to the quality of an aid programme, though it is rarely studied.[4] In this section, I show that the relative strength of different frames for aid has a noticeable impact on the evolution of aid administrations. Several different frames have implications for the size and organization of the aid administration. In addition, they affect the nature and success of reorganizations over time. To begin with, the distribution of frames helps explain peculiarities in the creation and consolidation of aid administrations. For example, although Belgium, Italy and the Netherlands all had colonies, each handled the transition from colonial administration to development cooperation in a different fashion, because aid was framed differently from the start.

Creating and consolidating aid administrations

Throughout the 1950s, Belgium provided bilateral aid only to its colonies Congo, Rwanda and Burundi. The country was ill-prepared for the end of the colonial era, in part because its national identity was closely tied to its status as a colonial power. Belgium's bilateral aid programme officially began in 1962, and was staffed mostly by former colonial civil servants. Many of these were traumatized by their sudden relocation from Congo back to Brussels. Not surprisingly, they focused most of their attention on continuing relations with the former colony.[5]

---

[4] See W. Easterly and T. Pfutze, 'Where does the money go? Best and worst practices in foreign aid', for a valuable recent contribution. For a more detailed account of the aid administrations of the four case study countries, see Chapters 6–9 in Van der Veen, 'Ideas and interests in foreign policy'.
[5] M. Vandommele, 'Twintig jaar Belgisch ontwikkelingsbeleid. Op zoek naar een visie en naar een houding'.

This was in line with the overwhelming importance of the obligation frame in the overall discourse. Initial aid projects were administered through the Commerce Ministry, with obvious implications for the importance of economic interests. This, too, reflected the contents of the national aid discourse, where wealth was the second dominant frame. In fact, apart from prioritizing commercial considerations and relations with Congo,[6] the development programme had no real purpose: its first Minister admitted in 1965 that it had 'neither a doctrine, nor a policy, nor an administration'.[7]

In Italy, the wealth frame was even more salient, whereas the obligation frame was much weaker. There were, however, a number of inescapable expenditures. For much of the 1950s, for example, Italian 'aid' funded Second World War reparation payments to Yugoslavia, Ethiopia and a few other countries. The administration of Italy's UN protectorate, Somalia, accounted for the bulk of the remainder. As in Belgium, a clear vision for development cooperation was absent.[8] Instead, particularistic economic interests rapidly came to dominate.[9] In 1962, the passage of law 1594 marked Italy's first official bilateral aid initiative. As we saw earlier, the importance of the reputation frame was obvious in government claims that 'there is reason to believe that most of the underdeveloped countries await our initiative with interest', a claim that even some legislators found rather comical.[10]

Italian aid legislation continued to be closely connected to the promotion of foreign investment, in line with the dominance of the wealth frame. The task of administering aid was often assumed by the large firms that absorbed most of Italy's aid-related export credits.[11] In 1972, the administration of aid was put on a more formal

---

[6] The public debt of Congo's colonial administration at independence, as well as the pensions of former colonial civil servants, continued to absorb a large share of the 'aid' budget. In 1968, eight years after Zaire's independence, these budget posts still accounted for close to 50 per cent of total bilateral aid. Vaes, 'Het officiële Belgische beleid', 136.
[7] Minister Brasseur, *Parlementaire Handelingen Senaat*, 3 March 1965.
[8] A. Monti, *Economia e politica dell'aiuto pubblico allo sviluppo. Il sistema italiano di cooperazione con i paesi in via di sviluppo: Un'analisi critica*, 44.
[9] E.g. F. Forte, 'Il programma di aiuti economici ai paesi arretrati', 628–9.
[10] *III Commissione*, 12 July 1962: 199. For a critical reaction, see the contribution by Bartesaghi, *ibid.*, 200.
[11] R. Aliboni, 'Italy and Africa: The aid policy'.

The administration of aid policy 113

footing within the Foreign Affairs department, with the creation of a directorate-general for development cooperation (DGCS). However, its administrative mandate was inadequate to keep Italy's aid programme well organized, and resources allocated to aid administration remained negligible throughout the remainder of the 1970s.[12]

In the Netherlands, official aid activities began a decade earlier than in Belgium or Italy, as the government reacted quickly to the first international initiatives promulgated by the United Nations. In October 1949, just nine months after President Truman introduced his 'Point Four' programme for international assistance, the government produced a report discussing a Dutch contribution to his plans.[13] At the same time, the Dutch government allocated an initial sum of 1.5 million guilders to UN aid initiatives. This rapid reaction showed the Dutch interest in being an influential actor from the start. Among others, the government hoped to generate jobs for Dutch technical specialists and academics, 'now that Indonesia will become less important as an export market for Dutch brainpower'.[14] The aid programme was rapidly consolidated and expanded: an official Committee on Technical Assistance was set up by 1950, in 1963 the government appointed a State Secretary whose sole mandate was aid policy, and in 1965 that position was upgraded to the cabinet level.

Whereas Belgium looked to the Ministry of Commerce as a place to park many of its former colonial employees, and Italy had too few such employees even to manage successfully its meagre aid efforts, the Netherlands tried as much as possible to farm them out internationally, through the United Nations. As Foreign Minister Luns argued in 1954, with the international influence and reputation of the Netherlands in mind: 'The Netherlands prefers the multilateral approach ... because it has too much to offer to be content with providing Dutch services to only one country.'[15]

---

[12] Actually, the problem was not inadequate legislation per se, since decrees in 1960 and 1966 had already provided for centres of policy coordination. However, both of these were buried by the Department of Foreign Affairs bureaucracy, or simply never came into being. Aliboni, 'Italian aid policy', 65.
[13] J. J. P. de Jong, 'Onder ethisch insigne: De origine van de Nederlandse ontwikkelingssamenwerking'.
[14] Netherlands, *Nota betreffende de bijdrage aan het programma der Verenigde Naties voor technische hulp aan economisch laag ontwikkelde landen*, 8.
[15] *Handelingen*, 18 June 1954: 1077–9.

The situation in Norway was different from that in the other three countries, because there were no former colonial employees to deal with. Norway's first aid initiative was a result at least in part of its choice to give up neutrality and join NATO. This decision had not been an easy one, and many groups on the political left had been strongly opposed. Afterwards, 'the governing Labour Party ... left the aid arena to those in the party who had lost the fight on the NATO issue, in a deliberate effort to keep them busy with what might be perceived as a positive way of building peace'.[16] On 21 March 1952, the full legislature submitted a letter to the government requesting proposals for an aid policy, and an extensive legislative debate followed on 5 May. The debate resulted in a decision to fund a fisheries development project in Kerala, India, which was to remain Norway's sole bilateral aid initiative for the next five years.

Norway's initial aid activities were heavily influenced – both inside and outside the legislature – by those who had been active in missionary work, and who accordingly combined a more humanitarian vision with a sense of obligation. When aid initiatives spread out beyond the India Project in the early 1960s, an official aid administration was put in place. Enlightened self-interest emerged as a prominent motivation, together with a sense that Norway was obliged to do at least as much as its Scandinavian neighbours. The creation of the Swedish International Development Agency (SIDA) in 1965 thus spurred the Norwegian government to appoint a committee to review and expand its own aid programme even further. The committee's report inspired the creation of a new Norwegian Development Agency (NORAD), with the responsibility of planning and implementing bilateral aid.[17]

Adaptation and reorganization in the 1970s and 1980s

By the mid 1960s, all four countries had more or less well-established aid administrations, each coloured both by the particular national context and by the composite frame that characterized the aid discourse. At this point, international organizations increasingly began evaluating and comparing the aid programmes of different donor

---

[16] O. Stokke, 'The determinants of Norwegian foreign aid policies', 163.
[17] Norway, *I. Om den videre utbygging av Norges bistand til utviklingslandene. II. Om opprettelse av 'Direktoratet for utviklingshjelp'*.

states. Given the strength of the obligation frame in Belgium, this development was of particular concern, and the country's reaction was quite interesting. Belgium showed itself to be less interested in meeting international standards than in not looking bad relative to other donor states. In 1972, for example, representative Colla complained: 'we have to admit that Belgium for far too long … has done no more than dabble in the area of development cooperation'.[18] Belgium's interest in its relative performance remained strong for many years, as we saw in the quotation opening the chapter.

Belgium's bare-bones, commercially oriented aid programme increasingly threatened to place Belgium in a bad light, especially relative to the Netherlands, a logical comparison country. One major problem was that aid budget items were spread across the departments of Development Cooperation, Finance, Foreign Affairs, Education, and even Defence.[19] However, although the government had announced plans for the reorganization of the aid programme as early as 1965, and taken some action in this direction in 1971, the basic set-up appeared adequate to handle the twin goals of pursuing Belgium's economic self-interest and meeting perceived international obligations. Repeated attempts at reorganization during the next two decades always followed the same pattern: a concern that Belgium was falling short of its international obligations inspired action, but the feeling among those involved that the current model was largely satisfactory meant that changes were largely cosmetic.

In Italy, a similar concern with international obligations was largely absent. New laws governing the aid administration were passed when the old ones expired, not because of any sense of unease regarding the current organization of aid policy. After two minor renewals in

---

[18] *Parlementaire Handelingen*, 31 May 1972: 1347.
[19] The Department of Defence allocated funds for the military training of officers of Mobutu's repressive government, and the Belgian government was clearly embarrassed about the reputational implications of this programme. The Minister of Defence refused to discuss these funds since, he claimed, they were subject to the authority of the Minister in charge of development cooperation; the latter, conversely, abjured responsibility because the funds were listed in the Defence Department's budget. As representative De Facq noted in the 1972 budget debates: 'In a sense it is understandable that nobody likes to defend this [policy] since our military technical assistance in fact is a policy that damages our prestige both domestically and abroad' (*Parlementaire Handelingen*, 21 June 1972: 1694).

1967–8 and 1971, the first 'real' development assistance law was approved in 1979 (law 38). Unfortunately, 'the law almost completely lack[ed] references to the substance of development cooperation'.[20] Instead, as had been the case with previous legislation, more attention was paid to legislative constructs related to administrative personnel, rules for tenders, etc.[21] In the meantime, Italy's aid policy continued to be seriously hampered by administrative disarray. For example, of the 2,500 billion lire allocated to development cooperation in the government's 1984 budget, only about 10 billion appeared on the Foreign Affairs budget. Fully 700 billion went to a special Development Cooperation Fund, 1,500 billion appeared on the Treasury budget under various headings (multilateral aid, export credits, etc.), 230 billion was without a budget allocation at all, and the rest was distributed over a variety of other ministries.[22] This made it almost impossible for legislators and observers – as well as the government itself – to keep track of spending.

The dispersion of aid funds across different departments also facilitated the 'pollution' of the aid budget with non-aid items. In 1982, for example, the budget included allocations to the Treasury Ministry for its contribution to the international theoretical physics institute in Trieste (2.4 billion lire), to the Ministry of Defence for the maintenance and repair of civilian aircraft, as well as for cleaning buildings (6.7 billion), and to the Ministry of Industry for Italy's participation in multilateral meetings regarding international property rights (215 million). All in all, at least 143 billion lire had not the faintest relevance to development.[23]

The next legal reorganization, law 73 of 1985, has been described as 'an attempt to overcome the "improvisation" characterizing Italian development cooperation'.[24] Its main result was to set up a large

---

[20] Rhi-Sausi *et al.*, 'Italian bilateral aid policy', 7.
[21] D. Menichini, *Cooperazione Italiana allo sviluppo: Analisi e proposte*, 5.
[22] R. Maurizio, 'I prossimi tre anni di cooperazione'.
[23] Monti, *Economia e politica*, 131–2. Nor was this an unusual year. The comparable figures for 1983 were considerably higher. The data are from a report by the national accounting office (Corte dei Conti). Other departments cited by the office for using aid funds for completely non-aid-related purposes included the Ministry of Transport, the Postal Service, the Health Ministry, and the Ministry of Foreign Affairs itself.
[24] Rhi-Sausi *et al.*, 'Italian bilateral aid policy', 6.

The administration of aid policy 117

emergency fund to fight world famine, a late response to an international surge of public interest in the issue of deprivation and famine prevention in sub-Saharan Africa in the early 1980s.[25] Despite the good intentions of its original sponsors, law 73 is commonly judged to represent one of the worst failures of Italian development cooperation.[26] Only a small fraction of the allocated resources was used for the original purpose of the law: the alleviation of suffering in Africa. Instead, spending was almost entirely concentrated on industrial and infrastructure investments, with no thought for appropriateness or long-term sustainability.[27] In addition, projects were exempt from the overly bureaucratic tendering system governing most Italian public spending. Although the intention was for aid to be granted more efficiently, this implied that spending was scrutinized even less than was normally the case. Pressures to spend money rapidly only aggravated the endemic corruption. In the end, the operation absorbed 2.5 times the originally allotted budget. Moreover, numerous lawsuits by Italian companies against the Italian state for non-disbursement of funds were still pending a decade later.[28]

As early as 1987, a new law (nr 49) was passed to supplement the ill-fated law 73. However, a parliamentary commission of inquiry later argued that 'it strikes one that this law has omitted almost entirely to provide for an administrative apparatus for the management of cooperation'.[29] Indeed, the law did little to change the long-term patterns in Italy's aid programme. It appears clear that legislative initiatives in Italy were doomed to have little impact so long as the main frames for aid remained wealth and reputation. As long as the government could claim to be improving Italy's status while simultaneously benefiting the Italian economy, few cared how aid funds were used in practice. In fact, for many years it was relatively easy to convince the public as well as the legislature that Italy looked good: reference

---

[25] After government foot-dragging for several years, legislative action was finally spurred in part by the highly visible antics of representative Pannella of the Radical Party (PRI), who went so far as to conduct a hunger strike to force the government to allocate more development aid. P. Giordano, 'Intervista a Pannella: "Quale crisi? La gente ci segue"'; 'Per la fame 350 miliardi. Pannella ne chiede 3 mila'.
[26] See Italy, *Raccolta di atti*.
[27] Rhi-Sausi *et al.*, 'Italian bilateral aid policy', 46.
[28] *Ibid*.
[29] Italy, *Raccolta di atti*, 1187.

to a few high-profile projects and to the florid preambles of various laws sufficed. Even academic coverage of Italy's aid programme often concentrated on legal texts rather than on experiences with the implementation of aid in practice.[30]

In the Netherlands, the government faced administrative challenges that were rather different from those in Belgium and Italy. In accordance with the targets set for the second UN Development Decade, the Dutch aid budget nearly tripled during the first half of the 1970s. At the same time, the number of officials in charge of managing these funds increased by less than 25 per cent. As a result, Dutch aid administrators were each in charge of a far greater sum than were their counterparts in other states.[31] This resulted in a ballooning reservoir of allocated but unspent funds, and reduced spending oversight. Nevertheless, the Dutch programme never fell victim to the type of malversations that came to light in Belgium and Italy in the 1990s. The difference in outcome must be attributed at least in part to the different frames that shaped the Dutch aid programme.

The early 1980s provide another good example of the ability of aid frames to constrain government policy. As noted in Chapter 4, the conservative party (VVD) increased its apparent control over the aid programme in 1982, with the appointment of the first conservative Development Minister. The new government's stated policy was that 'Dutch development cooperation will have to react to the possibilities and capabilities of the Dutch economy and society'.[32] A White Paper published in 1984 even indicated that 'the main goal of Dutch development policy will be supplemented by a sub-goal: increasing the importance of development cooperation to the economy and to employment in the Netherlands'.[33] However, Minister Schoo's ideas were at odds with the main aid discourse, and her tenure in office was characterized by near-constant disagreements with interest groups, the media and the legislature. As we saw in Chapter 4, her influence on the relative

---

[30] For example, Istituto Ricerche Studi Economici e Sociali, *Emergenza, fame e cooperazione allo sviluppo: Analisi, documentazione, proposte*; C. Vangi, *Cooperazione con i paesi in via di sviluppo: criteri pratici orientativi per l'applicazione delle norme della legge n.38 del 9 febbraio 1979*.

[31] J. Verloren van Themaat, 'Loopt Nederland achter met de organisatie van zijn ontwikkelingshulp?'.

[32] Cited in Maas, *Kabinetsformaties en ontwikkelingssamenwerking*, 80–89.

[33] Netherlands, *Ontwikkelingssamenwerking en werkgelegenheid: Nota*, 42.

strength of different frames for aid was negligible. More importantly for our present purposes, aid policy itself changed remarkably little, much to the disappointment of certain actors in private industry.[34] Indeed, throughout Schoo's tenure, policy choices continued to reflect the importance of the power and humanitarianism frames.

In Norway, finally, the early 1980s brought a noticeable reorganization of the administration of development assistance, but only on the surface. In 1983, the government established a separate Ministry of Development Cooperation, which was to house both NORAD and the multilateral aid division of the Foreign Affairs department. However, the Ministry was created largely for political reasons, in order to allow the Conservative Party (Høyre) to give its coalition partner, the Christian Democrats (KrF), some influence in foreign policy, without having to cede the entire Ministry of Foreign Affairs.[35] As a result, the reorganization was primarily symbolic, and the overall impact of this reorganization on the actual administration of aid policy was minor.

Crises and new mandates in the 1990s

In the 1990s, administrative problems came to a head in Belgium and Italy. From the mid 1980s, Belgium's aid administration had been increasingly affected by a variety of problems, most notably a Flemish–francophone imbalance in both employees and attitudes towards aid. Regarding the latter, Flemish representative Demeester-De Meyer noted in a 1985 interpellation that 'Over the years it has become clear … that Flemish and francophones have visions of development cooperation that differ on essential points'. Challenging the government's handling of the differences between the linguistic groups, her colleague Caudron complained in the same debate that 'When the government … tries to appease the Flemish with projects in Indonesia and Suriname, former Dutch colonies, this is less relevant to including the Belgian or Flemish people in the issue of development than to underscoring the neocolonial policy vision of the government'.[36]

---

[34] See, for example, the interview with a high-ranking aid official published in *De Volkskrant*, 20 June 1986.
[35] Tamnes, *Norsk utenrikspolitikks historie*, 390.
[36] *Parlementaire Handelingen*, 8 May 1985: 2588, 2590.

The need to ensure a balance between Dutch and French speakers within the aid administration increasingly hampered effectiveness, as the administration became more and more top-heavy and often had two separate officials in charge of the same task. Dissatisfaction with the administration of aid grew, both within and outside the government. The main administrative agency, ABOS, was reorganized again in 1992, but its reputation was fatally undermined when serious corruption scandals came to light in the mid 1990s, implicating several top administrative officials.[37]

In debates over a new, post-scandal, aid policy, an emphasis on enlightened self-interest grew simultaneously with the decline in salience of the twin frames of wealth and obligation, neither of which the existing aid programme was perceived to have met successfully. A new Minister for Development Cooperation, Réginald Moreels, was appointed, in line with this changing vision of aid. His background in Médecins sans Frontières (Doctors without Borders) set him apart from his predecessors, most of whom had ties to private industry and evinced no prior personal interest in aid or development.[38] Moreels produced a major policy paper in October 1996, proposing a renewed focus on poverty and civil society. Spurred by disillusionment with aid politics as usual, as well as by a concern for Belgium's reputation if serious reforms were not implemented, the legislature accepted his proposals a year later.[39]

Still, the administration of Belgium's aid policy remained problematic. A considerable share of the aid budget continued to be allocated without any oversight.[40] Moreover, the Flemish and francophone communities continued to disagree, with the former vastly more committed to improving and reforming the aid programme. Perhaps as a result, the government decided in October 2000 to devolve aid policy to the two linguistic communities. The Flemish and Walloon

---

[37] De Coninck, *Witte olifanten*.
[38] B. Speelman, 'Tussen droom en daad …? Ontwikkelingssamenwerking als politiek instrument in België'; Vaes, 'Het officiële Belgische beleid'.
[39] J. Oppewal and D. Seroo, 'De moraal van Réginald Moreels: "Als ethiek ten koste gaat van effectiviteit, dan moet dat maar"'.
[40] For example, representative Versnick complained in a 1997 debate on the reorganization: 'We know that your administration at the end of the year randomly spends the remaining millions on allegedly "sympathetic" countries without being concerned with objective criteria.' *Kamer Documents* Committee Meeting 415, 5 November 1997.

communities were to be given almost full responsibility over the entire ODA budget by 2004. Although the DAC opposed the move for fear that it would hamper the effectiveness of Belgium's aid policy, differences between the communities appeared to have become irreconcilable.[41]

In Italy, too, the disconnect between the frames for aid and the empirical reality of aid policy became increasingly visible by the late 1980s. It was obvious that neither Italy's reputation nor its economy were benefiting from its aid policy. At the same time, cost overruns and project commitments several years into the future came into conflict with increasing budget pressures. In December 1989, Foreign Minister De Michelis informed parliament that, whereas official commitments already amounted to over 20,000 billion lire, available funds totalled less than half that sum.[42] These problems led to a number of lawsuits between the Directorate General (DGCS) and firms in charge of implementing aid projects. At the end of 1993, the DGCS estimated that litigation was pending against it for up to 500 billion lire.[43]

A fact-finding commission of the Italian Senate was called into being during the late 1980s to help assess the extent and nature of the divergence between government claims and the actual results of Italy's aid efforts. It published its findings in 1991, criticizing both 'the lack of correspondence between many projects and the spirit of the law' and 'the preoccupation with a policy that appeared to support domestic commercial interests more than it did the interests of the recipient states themselves'.[44] In its conclusion, the Commission adopted an attitude to Italy's aid policy similar to one that was beginning to characterize the public debate: aid was still seen in terms of image and reputation, but now Italy's policy was felt to have deleterious effects. In this light, the Commission re-emphasized 'the inalienable necessity of safeguarding the image and the credibility of our

---

[41] OECD, *Development co-operation review of Belgium*, 1.
[42] The issue of overcommitment was to paralyse Italy's aid efforts well into the 1990s. In 1994, for example, commitments of 7,200 billion vastly outstripped the 3,500 billion in available resources. Rhi-Sausi *et al.*, 'Italian bilateral aid policy', 23.
[43] *Ibid.*
[44] Italy, *La politica di cooperazione dell'Italia con i paesi in via di sviluppo: Indagine conoscitiva della 3a Commissione Permanente (Affari Esteri, Emigrazione): Raccolta di atti e documenti*, 558.

foreign and development cooperation policy relative to developing countries'.[45]

The publication of the 1991 report increased the government's concern with salvaging Italy's image. As a first step, law 412 of 1991 attempted to correct some of the problems associated with project approval, calling for contracts to be tendered and spending to be monitored. Prior to this time, almost all projects had been characterized as urgent or extraordinary, allowing the administration to bypass tendering and to negotiate directly with interested Italian firms. In fact, between 1987 and 1991 no projects had been offered for tender at all, except, ironically, in the field of emergency aid, where the tendering process caused delays of up to three-and-a-half years in the disbursement of aid funds.[46]

Along with these changes, government and legislature took steps to redress some of the damage already done to Italy's reputation, both internationally and in the eyes of the public. In the 1991 budget debate, representative Crippa argued that 'we have the responsibility to respond ... in proportion to the greater or lesser contribution of these resources to increasing the prestige of our country'.[47] This marked the beginning of a complete overhaul of Italy's policies, along with a drastic reduction in Italy's aid volume. Averaging 5,000 billion lire in the early 1990s, it fell to 3,000 billion in 1993 and 2,300 in 1994, to the dismay of legislators and external observers alike: 'Belonging to the club of nations that really count is a long-standing goal of Italy's foreign policy', but 'There is little doubt that ... the present cuts will entail a sharp reduction in Italy's influence and prestige'.[48]

---

[45] *Ibid.*, 560. In order to limit further damage, the Commission proposed that the government release enough funds at least to cover just one-third (!) of the projects already approved by the planning department. In doing so, it also referred to the continuing economic interests associated with development cooperation, noting the importance of aid 'for the positive developments that it can provide to important sectors of the Italian productive system'. Italy, *La politica di cooperazione*, 562. However, the wealth frame had become decidedly less salient than self-affirmation in light of the accumulating evidence.

[46] Cf. representative Crippa in the 1991 budget debate, *III Commissione*, 12 June 1991: 27.

[47] *III Commissione*, 12 June 1991: 30 (cf. also p. 25).

[48] M. Dassù and M. De Andreis, 'Italian foreign and development cooperation policy', 35–8.

Interestingly, there was remarkably little public resistance to the budget cuts, largely because of escalating disillusionment with Italy's aid programme. Added to the media coverage of the government's failure to live up to its financial commitments was a growing stream of newspaper articles about malfeasance in the administration of Italy's development programme.[49] Wide-ranging judicial inquiries into *Tangentopoli* ('bribe city') implicated many of those involved in aid policy. In response, a new bicameral commission of inquiry was launched in 1995. At its opening meeting, representative Falqui argued that the decline in Italy's aid had caused, 'by a kind of transitive property, the reduction in the role of Italy on the international political scene … There is no doubt, therefore, that it is important to know the causes that have led to a political decision of such great importance to our country'.[50]

The Commission's findings were damning:

Among donor countries, Italy … distinguishes itself by the particular seriousness of malversations in the use of cooperation funds … Moreover, the corruption in the sphere of cooperation appears to have been widely diffused and to have enjoyed widespread complicity.[51]

Corruption and malfeasance were identified in aid relations with nearly every single recipient state: not only top targets such as Somalia and Ethiopia, but also recipients of smaller allocations such as Vietnam and Peru.[52] Public outrage was greatest in the case of Somalia, both due to a lingering sense of a special relationship with the former protectorate, and because for so many years Italy's aid efforts in that country had been held up by the government as examples of the exceptional, reputation-building work performed under the auspices of the aid programme.

---

[49] An early example was 'Tangenti sugli aiuti? Per i Somali, "un'offesa"'. By 1991, the sums implicated were staggering: for relations with Somalia alone, alleged corruption accounted for a total of 1,500 billion lire, representing a considerable share of Italy's annual aid budget. ('Nei rapporti Italia-Somalia uno scandalo da 1.500 miliardi'). In the early 1990s, newspapers published hundreds of articles detailing corruption in Italy's aid programme.
[50] Italy, *Raccolta di atti*, 70.
[51] Ibid., 1184–5.
[52] Ibid., 1186.

The report also acknowledged that many among the public were so upset that they wanted do away with Italy's aid policy altogether. Strikingly, the Commission's argument against such a drastic step highlighted the familiar reputation frame, while giving no evidence of thinking about aid in humanitarian terms:

> only a little additional thought suggests that this argument [about canceling the aid programme] is unfounded, dangerous, and also damaging to our dignity and our international interests ... if Italy wants to play a role of its own in important organizations such as the G-7 or the Security Council of the UN, it cannot exempt itself from the tasks that face it in the sector of cooperation.[53]

For the Netherlands and Norway, the situation in the 1990s was rather different. Their main concern was with the degree to which their aid programmes had become 'polluted' by non-aid expenditures. The DAC sets and monitors standards regarding the types of spending that can be labelled official development assistance. In both countries, an increasing share of the aid budget fell outside these definitions. In each case, this situation was a result of increasing budget pressures during the 1990s pushing up against official commitments to keep the aid budget fixed at a high level relative to GNP. Other departments faced with painful cuts increasingly attempted to place some of their programmes into the aid budget, where they would be safer.

By 1993, for example, sums allocated for the domestic support of foreign workers, refugees and asylum-seekers in the Netherlands exceeded 550 million guilders, or about 10 per cent of the total aid budget. At this point, rather than allow the 'real' aid budget to become ever more affected, Minister Pronk chose to accept budget cuts and relinquish the heretofore sacred indexation of the aid budget to 1.5 per cent of national income.[54] A new target of 0.8 per cent of GNP in 'pure' ODA was adopted, and this helped stem the slide.

---

[53] *Ibid.*, 1191.
[54] The calculation of net national income (NNI) differs from that of GNP: 1.5 per cent of NNI was usually about equivalent to 1 per cent of GNP. In the 1993 budget debates, Pronk noted that, in dealing with budget cuts and the use of aid funds for other purposes, he felt like 'Hansje Brinker [of finger-in-the-dike fame] who at a certain point saw the flood threatening to wash over him'. *Handelingen*, 19 November 1992: 25–1841.

The departure from the long-standing 1.5 per cent norm engendered considerable debate regarding its potential symbolic costs to the international stature of the Dutch aid programme.[55] However, in the interest of influence and status, many preferred to focus on aid initiatives that would show up in DAC statistics, even at the symbolic cost of relinquishing the automatic indexation of aid to national income.

The importance of the influence and humanitarian frames also inspired a wide-ranging re-evaluation of the entire Dutch foreign policy administration in the mid 1990s. Minister Pronk argued in the White Paper *A world in conflict* that development cooperation could never achieve much if conflicts continued to rage.[56] As a result, the Department of Foreign Affairs was 'decompartmentalized' so that foreign policy and foreign aid were no longer handled by separate desks. In return for giving up some control over the management of aid policy, the Minister of Development Cooperation was to have more input on foreign policy initiatives affecting development issues, such as sanctions, peacekeeping efforts, and North–South relations in general.[57] This would not only leverage the humanitarian impact of the Dutch aid programme, but it would also increase the influence of the Dutch within these broader issue areas. The goal was to 'maintain maximum influence over the issues that are meaningful to us' and to make it easier for 'the Netherlands [to assume] responsibility as the largest of the smaller ... states'.[58]

A similar process took place in Norway, where the long-standing prominence of the reputation and humanitarian frames was supplemented by a comparatively salient influence frame during the 1990s. Development cooperation began to be seen not only as a goal in itself, but also as an instrument to pursue other foreign policy goals. In 1997, the Development Minister's portfolio was expanded and renamed to become International Development and Human Rights. This brought additional competencies for refugee issues and humanitarian relief,

---

[55] E.g. R. J. Van den Dool, *Normverva(n)ging: Een bijdrage aan de discussie over de budgetaire norm voor internationale samenwerking.*
[56] Netherlands, *Een wereld in geschil.*
[57] Netherlands, *Hulp in uitvoering: Ontwikkelingssamenwerking en de herijking van het buitenlandse beleid.*
[58] Quotations from representatives Van Traa and Van Middelkoop, respectively, in the 1995 budget debate. *Handelingen*, 23 November 1994: 26–1670 and 24 November 1994: 27–1707.

areas that consumed an increasing share of the aid budget. By the end of the decade, the Minister's mandate was to use aid not only to further development, but also to promote human rights, democracy and peaceful conflict resolution, as well as sustainable environmental development.[59]

Aid quality

We now move from a broad-brush overview of aid administration to two measures of aid quality that are much more specific: levels of tied aid and multilateral aid, respectively. Tying aid to purchases in the donor country is costly to the recipient because it both reduces choice and increases costs. Donor country producers or contractors will not always be able to supply the products that recipient countries are most interested in. Moreover, even when they are, these products often cost considerably more than they would on the world market. The latter factor can be exacerbated if the donor country firm is aware that the recipient has no alternatives and raises prices even further.[60]

Another common measure of the quality of an aid programme is the share of aid that is channelled through multilateral organizations. States have less control over the use of these funds, so multilateral aid is usually considered to be less likely to be distorted by ulterior motives, and more likely to aim directly at the well-being of the recipients. Of course, governments can attach conditions to the way their contributions are used, and have done so from time to time. Moreover, they can selectively support multilateral initiatives in line with their own goals for their aid policy. On the other hand, multilateral organizations might themselves be inefficient in the management of their funds, and may have their own ulterior motives. These may not only be equally damaging to the quality and nature of aid, but also more difficult to control than are those of individual states.

Much depends, therefore, on the causal beliefs associated with multilateral aid in each nation's aid discourse. Are its goals and contents thought to be more or less in line with the nation's own goals? Is the lack of national control a cost or a benefit, and for what reason?

---

[59] Tamnes, *Norsk utenrikspolitikks historie*, 408.
[60] C. Jepma, *The tying of aid*; C. Terlinden and L. Hilditch, *Untie aid: Towards effective partnership*.

Aid quality 127

Since we cannot answer those questions using information about the strength of different frames alone, it becomes difficult to make straightforward predictions about the relative importance of multilateral aid within the aid budgets of different donor states. On the other hand, we shall see that this makes for an interesting illustration of the interaction between frames and causal beliefs, as the latter affect the implications of different salient frames in the aid discourse.

Tied aid

Table 5.1 reviews the general hypotheses regarding tied aid presented in Chapter 2, together with information about the salience of the different frames in each of the four countries. Putting the two together suggests that in Belgium as well as Italy, we can expect high levels of tied aid, at least until 1990, when the wealth frame lost some of its salience. In the Netherlands, the situation is rather different. The importance of humanitarianism from the mid 1970s suggests low levels of tied aid from that point. In Norway's case, humanitarianism became a dominant frame even sooner, and thus we expect tied aid levels to be low already from the early 1970s. The table also indicates that the introduction of international standards may affect these predictions somewhat.

As predicted, the tied aid share in Belgium averaged well over 70 per cent during the 1970s and 1980s, according to DAC statistics.[61] During the 1980s, industry groups fought for, and to some extent obtained, an ever tighter link between the Ministry of Foreign Trade and the aid administration. Some ABOS projects were taken over by private firms, and conversely some private initiatives were converted into government-funded development projects. This process was part of a conscious policy of greater integration between official aid and the activities of private industry. Indeed, an unofficial memo from a top ABOS official in early 1983 suggested that only NGO projects that guaranteed orders for Belgian suppliers were likely to be approved.[62]

---

[61] All data on tied aid and multilateral aid in this chapter is derived from annual reports of the Development Assistance Committee, as well as its online database, available at www.oecd.org.
[62] Vaes, 'Het officiële Belgische beleid', 489.

Table 5.1 *Hypotheses about the relationship between frames and tied aid*

Category	Salient when?	Tied aid
Power	**Italy** late 1970s to early 1980s **Netherlands** throughout **Norway** mid 1990s	Possibly meet standards (depends on nature of influence pursued)
Wealth	**Belgium** throughout early 1970s, 1980s **Italy** throughout 1990	High
Reputation	**Belgium** second half of 1990s **Italy** throughout 1960, 1990s **Norway** 1960s, mid 1980s to mid 1990s	Possibly meet standards (depends on nature of reputation pursued)
Obligation	**Belgium** throughout, with occasional minor dips **Italy** early 1970s **Netherlands** 1970s (but emerging by mid 1960s) **Norway** mid 1960s throughout 1980	High
Humanitarianism	**Belgium** early 1990s **Netherlands** from mid 1970s **Norway** from early 1970s	Low

The emphasis in Belgium is more on 'flow-back' than on tied aid per se, as we saw in the preceding chapter. The government actively collects information regarding the fraction of aid funds that returns to the Belgian economy for each aid initiative. For many years the government expected flow-back figures of over 100 per cent on average. Although some flow-back is indirect, and not directly tied to aid disbursements, such high levels could never be attained unless most aid was either explicitly or implicitly tied. With the decline in the salience of the wealth frame after the early 1990s, however, tied aid levels fell off considerably, from well over 50 per cent at the beginning of the decade to about 30 per cent by 1998.

In Italy, with private industry setting the agenda in terms of development assistance, the situation has been even starker. For many years, virtually all aid flows were tied to domestic purchases. While the government bore most of the costs of repeated refinancing and 'soft' loans, private firms sold their products at prices up to 60 per cent above those prevailing internationally.[63] As might be expected given the salience of the reputation frame, a central concern among observers regarding this state of affairs was not its impact on the effectiveness of aid, but rather the fact that 'for all these reasons ... Italy never excels in the various classifications of the member nations that the secretariat of DAC draws up'.[64]

During the 1980s, with a succession of new legislative initiatives, the wealth frame continued to dominate and the share of aid tied to purchases in Italy grew further still. Levels were over 80 per cent for much of the decade, higher even than in Belgium. Moreover, nearly 50 per cent of all aid credits were coupled with standard export credits (creating so-called mixed credits), making the implicit level of tying even higher. Both of these patterns contrasted sharply with Italy's formal commitment to the DAC goal of dissociating aid disbursements from export credits and from the purchases of goods in the donor state.[65] Although the preamble to law 49 of 1987 struck some humanitarian notes, the tying of aid remained a prominent goal, as evident from the actual text of the law, which allowed exceptions to the requirement that aid money be spent in Italy only with great reluctance:

> [Only] where required by the nature of the development projects and programs, may aid credits be used, in particular in the least developed countries, for the partial financing of local costs and of possible purchases in third countries of goods needed for the approved projects. (Article 6.4)

In his presentation to the 1996 Commission of Inquiry, Director General of Development Cooperation Aloisi de Larderel conceded that 'the extremely high level of tying in our aid' had been a major problem: 'In these years, 96% of our aid, in fact, has been tied to the acquisition of Italian goods and services, a figure much higher than the international average.'[66] It is difficult to get good statistics on

---

[63] Aliboni, 'Italian aid policy', 55.
[64] *Ibid.*
[65] Monti, *Economia e politica*, 165.
[66] Italy, *Raccolta di atti*, 66.

levels of tied aid in Italy after the Commission's report was published, since the aid programme was in such turmoil. However, there are indications that levels did decline somewhat.

In the Netherlands, the level of tied aid dropped over the course of the 1970s, as humanitarianism became a dominant frame. For most of the decade the comparative salience of the obligation frame slowed down the rate of the decline. Nevertheless, tied aid levels were – at 40–50 per cent – already well below the levels in Belgium and Italy. After 1979, when the humanitarianism frame assumed prominence for good, the level dropped further, below 20 per cent; by the mid 1980s it had fallen below 10 per cent. The decline in tied aid occurred in parallel with the increasing influence of the conservative party as a government coalition partner during the late 1970s and early 1980s, indicating once more that frames predict aid policy better than do government composition or the strength of particular political parties.

In Norway, finally, humanitarianism became a dominant frame even earlier than in the Netherlands. Inspired by a desire to pursue an identity as a generous donor, the government adopted an informal guideline against tying most aid already in the early 1960s. In 1967, this rule was made more formal, although exceptions were introduced for situations where tying was likely to be particularly helpful to domestic industries.[67] In 1972, with humanitarianism becoming dominant, the government reaffirmed its principled objection to tied aid and extended the range of aid programmes in which the rule against tied aid was applicable.

A number of outstanding loans were retroactively converted to grants over the course of the 1970s. The government also emphasized its desire to keep prices of tied goods and services more or less in line with world price levels.[68] In 1981, further legislation introduced a limit of 10 per cent for the maximum surcharge over international prices.[69] Overall, Norwegian practices in this respect compare favourably to those of other donor states. The level of tied aid has been below the

---

[67] Norway, *Om den videre utbygging*.
[68] Norway, *Stortingsmelding nr 29*, 31–2.
[69] Norway, *Innstilling S. nr 255*, 6. It should be noted that these rules were often violated in practice, and actual surcharges reached as high as 40 per cent. See O. Stokke, 'Spenningen mellom egeninteresse og altruisme i Norsk bistandspolitikk'; Stokke, 'The determinants of Norwegian', 206–7.

Aid quality 131

DAC average in most years. During the late 1970s, it hovered around 30%, compared to a DAC level around 50%. In the 1980s, it dropped to around 20%, and further declines in the 1990s brought the level down to just over 10%.

It has long been a DAC principle that untied aid is the preferred form of aid, with partial tying – allowing purchases in other developing countries but not in other donor states – as a second-best alternative. By the end of the 1990s, the Netherlands had gone furthest in following DAC recommendations, outperforming even Norway much of the time from the late 1970s onward. This record can be attributed to the Dutch interest in pursuing international influence through aid policy, which would be more difficult if international recommendations were not met. It thus appears the power frame was a stronger motivating factor than Norway's interest in developing a reputation as a generous and humanitarian state.

Finally, both Norway and the Netherlands consistently supported international initiatives to abolish tied aid, though they refused take such a step unilaterally. Of course, talk is cheap, and many donor states officially adopted the same position. Nevertheless, there is evidence that Norway and the Netherlands were more willing to push the issue and to bear some costs for doing so than were other donors such as Belgium and Italy.[70] Even though the wealth frame lost influence in the latter countries during the second half of the 1990s, Italy, in particular, was rarely supportive of proposals to end tied aid altogether. In fact, the position of each country within these international policy discussions continued to be in line with the enduring themes in its aid discourse.

Multilateral aid organizations

Making predictions regarding the prominence of multilateral aid is more difficult than is the case for tied aid, since much depends on how the former is viewed in a particular context. However, Chapter 2 did provide some general suggestions, which are summarized in Table 5.2. Given the salience of the wealth frame in Belgium, we expect little aid through multilateral organizations before 1990. After that, as

---

[70] For example, see Minister Herfkens in the Dutch 2000 aid budget debates, *Handelingen*, 8 December 1999: 32–2460; also United Kingdom, *Ministerial round table on trade and poverty in least developed countries*.

Table 5.2 *Hypotheses about the relationship between frames and multilateral aid*

Category	Salient when?	Multilateral aid
Security	**Belgium** around 1960, around 1990 **Italy** 1960s **Netherlands** mid 1950s to 1960s **Norway** around 1960s	Low unless see UN as a security instrument
Power	**Italy** late 1970s to early 1980s **Netherlands** throughout **Norway** mid 1990s	Low unless pursue influence in international fora
Wealth	**Belgium** during early 1970s, 1980s **Italy** in 1990	Low
Enlightened self-interest	**Belgium** mid 1980s, mid 1990s **Italy** late 1970s to 1980s, late 1990s **Netherlands** late 1980s to 1990s **Norway** around 1970, late 1980s, late 1990s	High
Reputation	**Belgium** second half of 1990s **Italy** 1960, 1990s **Norway** 1960s, mid 1980s to mid 1990s	Low unless pursue visibility in international fora
Obligation	**Belgium** throughout, with occasional minor dips **Italy** early 1970s **Netherlands** 1970s (but emerging by mid 1960s) **Norway** mid 1960s to 1980	Low unless inescapable
Humanitarianism	**Belgium** early 1990s **Netherlands** from mid 1970s **Norway** from early 1970s	High unless lack faith in quality of multilateral aid

Aid quality 133

humanitarianism and enlightened self-interest come to the fore, we expect to see higher levels. The predictions for Italy are similar, but the salience of the enlightened self-interest frame from the mid 1970s to the mid 1980s may bring multilateral aid more prominence during that period. In the Netherlands, the salience of humanitarianism is likely to result in higher multilateral aid at least throughout the early 1980s, while increasing concerns with the effective administration of many multilateral aid agencies might reduce such levels after that time. Predictions for Norway are similar. Here, however, the renewed importance of self-affirmation from the mid 1980s may provide an extra incentive to emphasize bilateral over multilateral aid, unless generous participation in multilateral organizations is perceived to improve Norway's international image.

As the salience of the wealth and obligation frames leads us to predict, the share of multilateral aid in Belgium's total aid budget has been well below the overall DAC average. The difficulty of obtaining flow-back information for multilateral aid has been one the factors reducing its appeal. Moreover, the fact that recipients might not know Belgium was the donor also hurt the multilateral aid agencies: 'Our contributions to multilateral programs cannot, after all, be identified by the recipient states as an explicit effort for them on the part of Belgium.'[71] Throughout 1970, the multilateral aid share rarely exceeded 20%, compared to DAC levels well over 25%. As with many of its aid efforts, the main impression is that Belgium made as much of an effort as it felt obliged to, but not more.

The multilateral aid share grew slowly during the 1980s, repeatedly reaching 40 per cent of the aid budget, in line with the prediction following from the temporary salience of the enlightened self-interest frame. In fact, however, this trend was more obligation-related, as the government itself pointed out:

this evolution is primarily due to the very steady increase of Belgian contributions to the European Development Fund [EDF] ... The contribution to the Fund represents 54.5% of the multilateral contributions by ABOS. It needs to be said that this contribution is a legal commitment and that the sum was imposed on Belgium.[72]

---

[71] State Secretary De Donnea, speaking in 1984. Speelman, 'Tussen droom en daad', 59.
[72] Belgium, *ABOS jaarverslag 1983*, 27.

It is also worth noting that most EDF contracts represent tied aid, and that Belgian firms have traditionally done quite well in winning such contracts, recouping more than their country's share of the fund in the form of orders. This 'flow-back' of greater than 100 per cent made the EDF contribution quite attractive viewed through the wealth frame.[73] The share of multilateral aid rose further during the 1990s. Once again, this was in line with the rising salience of enlightened self-interest. In addition, it was partially a result of prior multilateral commitments consuming a growing share of a shrinking total aid budget.

In Italy, the relative importance of multilateral aid fluctuated considerably from year to year, affected both by the size of the total aid budget and by the practice of making contributions to multilateral organizations at irregular, multi-year intervals. An interest in showing Italy's generosity as visibly as possible – the reputation frame in action – ensured that Italy would always make a contribution when a new multilateral aid initiative was undertaken. Nevertheless, multilateral aid levels rarely exceeded 20 per cent during the 1960s.[74]

The average level during the 1970s rose to nearly 70 per cent, far above the level prevailing in most other DAC countries. However, as was the case in Belgium, this jump was due largely to the growing importance of the EDF; it was not, in other words, a matter of choice. As Italy's aid budget began to grow rapidly during the 1980s, the relative share of multilateral aid declined, since Italians saw little tangible benefit deriving from such aid. Nevertheless, the decline was moderated both by the fixed commitment to the EDF, and by the 'driving factor' of Italy's continuing interest in international prestige.[75]

The Netherlands adopted a clear policy in favour of multilateral aid from the very beginning, in line with its interest in establishing Dutch

---

[73] Along similar lines, the government also increasingly favoured so-called multi-bi aid in the 1980s. This was a relatively new type of aid, in which a multilateral organization helped identify and administer a project, but Belgian firms and goods were used in its implementation. Such aid allowed the government to obtain the benefits of tied bilateral aid through disbursements that appeared in official statistics as multilateral aid.

[74] The figure jumped briefly in 1965–6 (52% and 39%, respectively) as a result of Italy's first contribution to the newly created International Development Association of the World Bank.

[75] Rhi-Sausi *et al.*, 'Italian bilateral aid policy', 5.

Aid quality 135

leadership and influence as broadly as possible. As the government's 1956 White Paper proclaimed:

Direct, bilateral Dutch aid will be little more than a drop in the ocean and will thus put us at a disadvantage, because we are operating in an area where far stronger partners are already active. A multilateral approach better ensures our participation and influence.[76]

By the beginning of the 1960s, however, pressures for more bilateral aid initiatives coincided with growing legislative demands for increased overall transfers. Over the course of that decade, multilateral aid's share of total ODA fell from 70% to about 30% – a level at which it has since remained – as the aid budget rose without a corresponding growth in multilateral contributions.[77]

Interestingly, as humanitarian views of aid increasingly came to the fore, the Dutch often worried that multilateral aid would not be as 'pure' in humanitarian terms as their own bilateral aid, and could be distorted by the aid goals of other contributors to the same multilateral fund. From the 1980s onward, concerns about the efficacy and equity of multilateral aid administration were added to the mix.[78] A practical expression of such concerns was the Dutch use of bilateral aid during the 1980s to counterbalance the effect of structural adjustment policies pushed by the World Bank, which were felt to hurt disproportionately the main targets of humanitarian aid: the poorest groups in developing countries.[79] Such considerations also underscore the difficulty of deriving predictions about multilateral aid from aid frames without knowing more about beliefs regarding multilateral organizations and aid.

The case of Norway is similarly complex. Norway's contribution to the UN Special Fund for Technical Assistance remained low relative

---

[76] Netherlands, *Nota inzake de hulpverlening aan minder ontwikkelde gebieden*, 9. See also the statement by Foreign Minister Luns cited earlier in the chapter.

[77] Of course, the total Dutch aid budget has grown dramatically since those early days, so even a declining share of multilateral aid represents a sizable commitment. Expressed as a share of GNP, the Dutch contribution to multilateral aid agencies continues to be well above average.

[78] See e.g. the discussion of multilateral aid by Minister Herfkens in the 2000 budget debate, *Handelingen*, 8 December 1999: 32–2458.

[79] E.g. Netherlands, *Een wereld van verschil*.

to the contributions of its peer states, as the government argued that Norway already contributed sufficient funds to its India project in Kerala.[80] Multilateral assistance did not enjoy the same initial priority as in the Netherlands, because the Norwegians were less interested in using aid as an instrument for obtaining international influence. Nevertheless, policy-makers argued for the importance of contributing to multilateral aid initiatives, emphasizing the need to '[make] our peace with the fact that we are a small country which cannot do great things by itself'.[81] Starting in the 1960s, the stated aim was to maintain a 50–50 split between bilateral and multilateral aid.[82] In fact, however, Norway's performance on this score resembled that of the Netherlands, albeit with a lag of a few years: the multilateral aid share declined gradually from about 70% to about 40% from 1965 to 1980, as Norway increasingly expanded its bilateral aid programme.

In 1986, the government reaffirmed the 50–50 principle. However, driven in part by the renewed importance of the reputation frame – and the corresponding value placed on the visibility of Norway's own efforts – policy-makers implicitly accepted the reality of a 60–40 split.[83] Starting in the early 1990s, a further decline took place, and the level dipped below 30 per cent by 1995, close to that of the Netherlands, and slightly below the DAC average. As in the Netherlands, moreover, the further decline in the multilateral aid share during the 1990s was associated with growing suspicion of the administration of multilateral aid funds by organizations such as the UN. An increasing awareness of administrative inefficiencies in those institutions reduced their perceived utility as aid channels, whether seen through a humanitarian frame or through a prestige- or influence-oriented frame.

Conclusion

This chapter highlighted the influence of aid frames over the administration and implementation of development assistance programmes.

---

[80] See Balsvik, 'U-landsdebatt', 45. However, all political parties had agreed in the 1952 aid debate that the India Fund ought to be considered a separate, *additional* activity.
[81] Representative Aasen. *Stortingstidende*, 2 June 1970: 3066; cf. also Simensen, *Norsk utviklingshjelps historie*, 110–111.
[82] E.g. Norway, *Stortingsmelding nr. 29*.
[83] Norway, *Innstilling S. nr. 186 (1986–1987)*.

Conclusion

The frames that dominated the aid discourse in the early years clearly shaped the conversion of colonial administrations into aid administrations in the Netherlands, Italy and Belgium. Whereas the latter used its aid programme as a place to park former colonial employees, the Netherlands instead tried to increase its international influence by seconding those same employees to international aid initiatives as much as possible. In Italy, the aid programme was so small and the government's efforts so minimal that there simply were insufficient resources to pay a lot of attention to colonial administrators – or, for that matter, to the former colony itself – leaving the door wide open for corruption and rent-seeking by private actors.

Patterns in the subsequent evolution of these aid programmes also illustrate the influence of different frames. Reorganizations only had a real impact on aid policy if preceded by either a shift in the aid discourse or widespread agreement that the existing policy was not adequately meeting the main purposes of aid suggested by the composite aid frame. Otherwise such reorganizations remained largely cosmetic. Similarly, attempts by governments to reorient aid policy in new directions often encountered resistance from administrators and the broader elite, whose aid frames – and thus policy preferences – were not so readily shifted. As a result, governments usually gave in or were replaced before any real policy changes had been implemented.

The case of Belgium illustrates how different communities may have different composite frames for aid, even within a single country. Flemish views of aid inevitably drew from the Dutch discourse almost as much as they did from the bilingual debate within Belgium. Differences in emphasis between the linguistic communities contributed to the problems in organizing and administering Belgium's aid programme. By the end of the century, goals for and ideas about the aid programme had diverged so far that the central government felt forced to devolve aid administration to the two linguistic communities.

Our predictions regarding two common measures of the quality of an aid programme were also largely on the mark. The observed patterns in multilateral aid can be explained in large part by the salient frames in each case. Nevertheless, both the range of potential opinions about the quality of multilateral aid and structural issues related to mandatory contributions to certain multilateral initiatives make this a difficult variable to explain neatly. Tied aid is much less open to multiple interpretations or external constraints, and our predictions for this variable proved to be both straightforward and accurate.

The features of national aid programmes discussed in this chapter are significant aspects of a country's overall aid policy; however, they are not very visible to the average observer and are not often studied. In the next chapter, the focus shifts to the single measure most often used to evaluate a country's aid programme: the overall aid volume, expressed as a share of GNP.

6 | *The generosity contest: determinants of aid volume*

Norway loses lead to Denmark as accounts reveal foreign aid as percentage of GNP dropped drastically.

Norway again largest OECD donor, as emergency relief aid funds ... grow rapidly.

– Headlines in *Development Today*, 1994 and 1995[1]

Aid levels of the OECD donor states have varied considerably over time, ranging from virtually nothing to well over 1 per cent of GNP. Interestingly, despite four decades of activity in standard-setting and monitoring of donor state performances, the OECD's Development Assistance Committee shows no signs of producing convergence among individual donor states on the international norm of 0.7 per cent of GNP. Instead, aid levels in many donor states dropped throughout the 1990s, moving further away from the norm, before increasing again during the first decade of the twenty-first century, albeit without reaching the levels of the 1980s.

Explaining patterns in overall aid levels has proven difficult: neither changes in government composition nor the economic fortunes of the donor states correlate highly. The end of the Cold War may have had an impact, but if so, it was in the opposite direction of that expected: many observers initially predicted aid levels would rise as military expenditures declined. Some explained the declining levels by pointing to public disillusionment or to a waning political commitment, but arguments along those lines date back at least to the mid 1960s,[2] making them poor explanations for trends several decades later. In this chapter, I

---

[1] *Development Today* is a Nordic journal focusing on development assistance. The headlines are from the front pages of issues 1994/9 and 1995/10, respectively.
[2] For an early example, see representative Mommersteeg's contribution, *Handelingen, Comité Buitenlandse Zaken*, 16 November 1967: B5.

argue that the impact of various explanatory factors depends crucially on the relative strength of different frames for aid. The data about the salience of these frames presented in Chapter 3 help us explain patterns in aid volume from the 1950s throughout the end of the twentieth century.

In Belgium, for example, the dominance of the wealth frame has made trade with developing countries – and in particular with its former colony of Congo/Zaire – an important determinant of aid volume. In addition, the performance of Belgium's peer states has been of considerable interest to Belgian decision-makers, given the salience of the obligation frame. In Italy, on the other hand, the salience of the reputation frame helps explain the dramatic decline in aid levels during the 1990s. In the Netherlands, the power and obligation frames spurred the country to meet international standards and stake out a leadership position on this measure. Moreover, the combination of a strong domestic welfare state and a dominant humanitarian frame helped push aid levels up further. In Norway, finally, humanitarianism played a similar role, but even more striking is the impact of the reputation frame in the early 1990s on Norway's efforts to hold on to first place in the 'generosity contest' – an interest reflected in the quotations opening the chapter.

The chapter proceeds in three stages. In the first section, I discuss patterns of variation over time and across donor states in the total size of the aid budget, and briefly review the literature on the determinants of aid volume. Next I analyse the evolution over time of aid levels in Belgium, Italy, the Netherlands and Norway, in light of the frames prominent in their respective aid discourses at different times. The third section, finally, illustrates the value of frames in quantitative analyses of aid volume. I show that we can increase the leverage of standard dependent variables by interacting them with measures of frame strength. Moreover, doing so also uncovers patterns that would otherwise remain hidden.

The dependent variable - trends and characteristics

The total amount of money spent on development assistance is the most concise measure available of a state's aid efforts. Moreover, since domestic and international audiences alike widely use it as an indicator of the performance of donor states, it is also an important decision variable in itself. Indeed, donor states consistently evince an

The dependent variable - trends and characteristics 141

interest in international comparisons concerning this measure and some states actively pursue prominent positions in such comparisons, as the headlines opening this chapter indicate. In other words, aid volume is more than just the incidental result of adding up the costs of the individual aid projects sponsored by a donor state.[3]

Discussions of development assistance were couched in terms of internationally comparable data regarding aid volume as early as the 1960s. For example, in 1969 Belgian Minister Scheyven noted that 'We have not yet reached this one percent of GNP', the accepted international standard at the time.[4] The media, too, was quick to focus on such international yardsticks: *The Economist* of 4 November 1967 noted that aid as a percentage of national income had recently fallen in almost all of the rich countries.[5] Expressing aid volume as a share of the national product permits cross-national comparisons of relative aid effort between small and large states. Most comparative analyses of aid budgets accordingly focus on volume as a fraction of gross national product (GNP) or income (GNI).

Standards regarding what constitutes development assistance slowly evolved during the 1950s and 1960s, and often differed from one country to the next. However, by 1969 the DAC promulgated the formal definition of official development assistance quoted in Chapter 1. Prior to that time, reporting of aid data was not uniform, and some states included non-concessional loans and export credits in their statistics. Nevertheless, differences were sufficiently minor to obviate the need to consider pre-1969 and post-1969 data separately.[6] Measured as a share of the combined GNPs of DAC members, ODA

---

[3] Actually, this has been the case only since the mid 1960s, when aid volume first began being tracked as a variable by international organizations and the media. Until that time, aid volumes often do appear to have been determined largely by the projects states chose to sponsor.
[4] *Parlementaire Handelingen*, 6 March 1969: 41.
[5] Cited by representative Mommersteeg. *Handelingen, Foreign Affairs Committee*, 16 November 1967: B5.
[6] One might fear that combining data will distort analyses (cf. M. McGillivray and H. White, *Explanatory studies of aid allocations among developing countries: A critical survey*, 31). However, the data do not show any shock to aid figures around 1969, nor do statistical analyses on post-1969 data produce substantively different results from analyses starting in 1960. Moreover, insofar as aid volume is a variable of widespread interest, we would expect donor states to adjust outlays so as to avoid unwanted shifts in the published data from year to year.

reached a peak of 0.54% in 1961, the very year the DAC was created. It fell off rather dramatically for the next ten years, fluctuated around one-third of a percent during the 1970s, and began another gradual decline in the 1980s, falling to 0.22% by 2000, before picking up again in the new century.[7]

Measured in terms of average aid volume across donor states, the pattern is similar, albeit with a much later peak. Expanded programmes in smaller states resulted in a steep increase starting in the mid 1960s, with average volume rising from 0.3% of GNP to a high of nearly 0.5% about twenty-five years later. After the early 1990s, this measure, too, declined steadily, dropping just below 0.4% by the turn of the millennium, before inching up again by the middle of the next decade.

There is considerable cross-national variation in the evolution of aid budgets. Figure 6.1 illustrates some of this variation, showing aid levels as a share of GNP, in 1960, 1980 and 2000 for all DAC donor states. The horizontal lines show the average level across all DAC donors in each year: 0.35, 0.47 and 0.39% of GNP, respectively. The figure also illustrates the degree to which relative rankings have changed over time. For example, we see the United States moving from left to right over time, while the Scandinavian countries follow the opposite trajectory. Indeed, whereas the United States allocated 0.6% of its GNP during the early 1960s, by 2000 it had become the least generous aid donor among all DAC states, allocating just 0.1% of GNP. Conversely, aid budgets in the Netherlands and in most Nordic countries grew rapidly starting in the mid 1960s. They continued to do so until a period of stagnation and decline began during the late 1980s. By the late 1990s, Dutch, Norwegian and Swedish aid volumes had declined as much as 20% below their peak levels.[8] Only Denmark still allocated a sum approximating 1% of its GNP at the turn of the millennium, making it the undisputed leader in the generosity contest, as Figure 6.1 shows.[9]

---

[7] Data in this section is drawn from OECD, *ODA steady in 2000*.
[8] Several states, including Norway, introduced significant changes in national accounting procedures during the 1990s. This has resulted in much higher estimates for GNP, and retroactively reduced aid volume expressed as a share of GNP.
[9] Five years later, however, Norway and Sweden were the leaders once again, with 0.94% of GNI going to ODA in 2005, while Denmark's aid volume fell to 0.81% of GNI. OECD, *Development co-operation report 2006*.

The dependent variable - trends and characteristics 143

ODA levels in 1960 (%GNP)

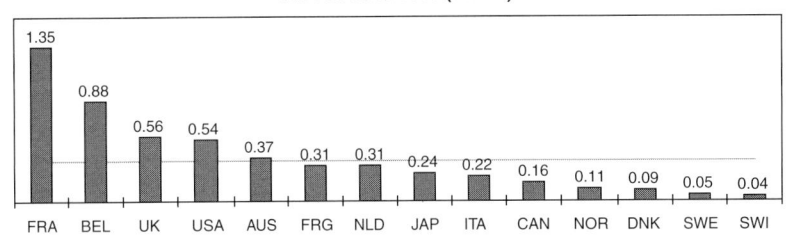

FRA	BEL	UK	USA	AUS	FRG	NLD	JAP	ITA	CAN	NOR	DNK	SWE	SWI
1.35	0.88	0.56	0.54	0.37	0.31	0.31	0.24	0.22	0.16	0.11	0.09	0.05	0.04

ODA levels in 1980 (%GNP)

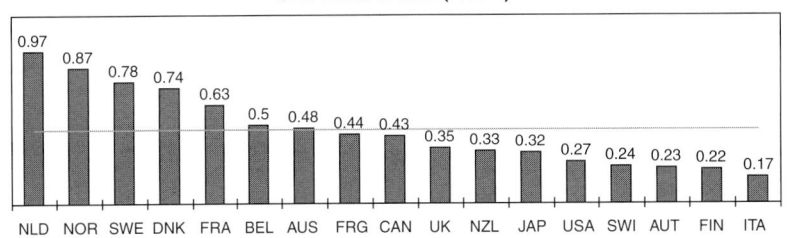

NLD	NOR	SWE	DNK	FRA	BEL	AUS	FRG	CAN	UK	NZL	JAP	USA	SWI	AUT	FIN	ITA
0.97	0.87	0.78	0.74	0.63	0.5	0.48	0.44	0.43	0.35	0.33	0.32	0.27	0.24	0.23	0.22	0.17

ODA levels in 2000 (%GNP)

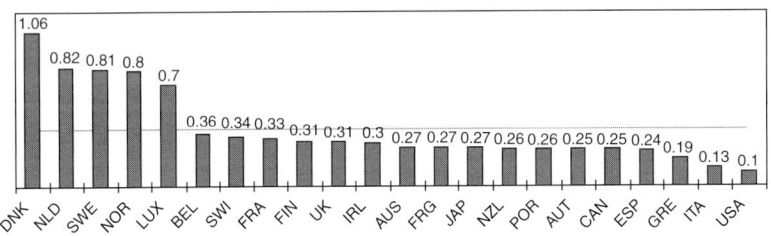

DNK	NLD	SWE	NOR	LUX	BEL	SWI	FRA	FIN	UK	IRL	AUS	FRG	JAP	NZL	POR	AUT	CAN	ESP	GRE	ITA	USA
1.06	0.82	0.81	0.8	0.7	0.36	0.34	0.33	0.31	0.31	0.3	0.27	0.27	0.27	0.26	0.26	0.25	0.25	0.24	0.19	0.13	0.1

Figure 6.1 Aggregate ODA performance of DAC member states
Source: Calculated from OECD national accounts and aid data.

The performance of most other donor states falls somewhere closer to the DAC average. Belgian aid peaked around 1960, coinciding with the independence of Congo. For many years afterwards it fluctuated around 0.5% of GNP, reaching a second, smaller peak of 0.6% in the early 1980s. After that point, aid levels gradually declined to half that level. Italy, on the other hand, remained near the bottom for many years. It initiated a dramatic increase in aid activity in the 1980s, reaching a volume of about 0.4% of GNP by the end of the decade. Mounting corruption scandals in the 1990s resulted first in a freezing of aid budgets and later in a precipitous decline back to the levels of the 1970s. Nevertheless, it still outperformed the United States in

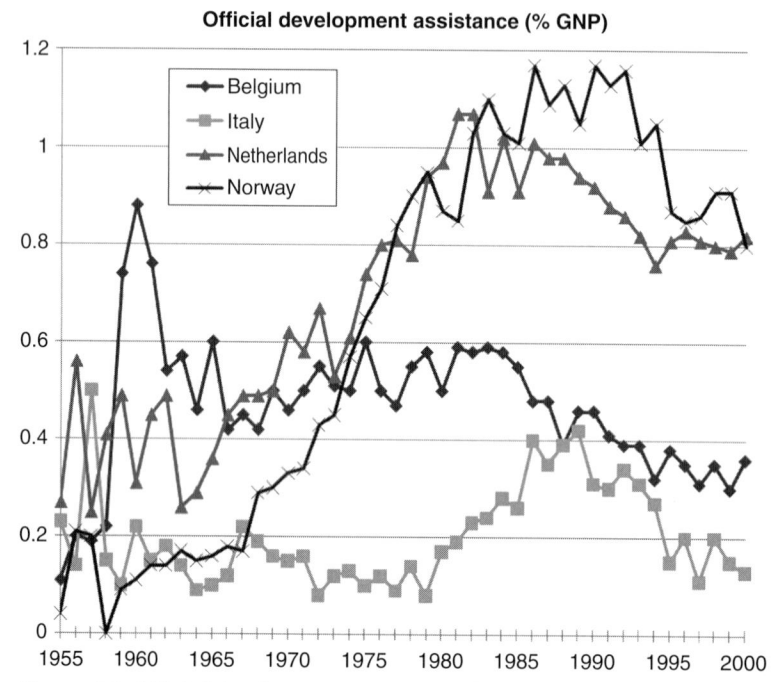

Figure 6.2 Official development assistance of Belgium, Italy, the Netherlands and Norway, expressed as a percentage of each country's gross national product
Source: Calculated from OECD national accounts and aid data.

2000. Figure 6.2 gives a more detailed overview of the evolution of aid volumes in our four countries.

The impact of international norms: the 0.7 per cent of GNP target

All of this variation in aid levels occurs in the context of an internationally accepted norm that the advanced, industrialized states ought to allocate 0.7 per cent of their GNP to development assistance. Some institutionalists have argued that this target, combined with the DAC's function as an institution monitoring compliance in the aid 'regime', serves to increase aid levels.[10] However, Figure 6.1

---

[10] Holdar, 'The study of foreign aid'; Lumsdaine, *Moral vision*; but see L. Botcheva and L. L. Martin, 'Institutional effects on state behavior: Convergence and divergence'.

The dependent variable - trends and characteristics 145

shows that average aid levels have never even approached the target level, and they show no signs of doing so in the near future. Nevertheless, given the importance of this norm at least in the official rhetoric of many donor states, it is worth briefly reviewing its history.

A concern with the size of the overall aid budget arose almost simultaneously with the creation of a bilateral aid programme in many donor states. In 1958, the World Council of Churches recommended a target of 1 per cent of the national income of the rich states, in public and private investment combined. This general target found its way into the programme for the UN Development Decade in 1960,[11] and was explicitly translated into a donor-specific target for the first time in 1964, at the UN Conference on Trade and Development (UNCTAD). Around the same time, the issue also gained prominence in national debates. For example, in the Dutch parliament, representative Patijn noted that 1 per cent of the national income was hardly too much for a country in which the national income itself was increasing by 3 per cent annually. In Belgium, similarly, representative Saintraint criticized the Belgian effort at that point as 'far from the norms to which we should adhere, quite far from the 1 per cent of national income that is being discussed in international assemblies'.[12]

The DAC adopted the 1 per cent target as a recommendation in 1965, and it was officially endorsed by all DAC members by 1968. In 1966, the Netherlands became the first state to commit publicly to raising its official aid budget to 1 per cent of net national income (NNI), by 1971.[13] At UNCTAD II in 1968, the Netherlands was joined by several other donor states in expressing a willingness to provide a target level of 0.75 per cent of GNP in net official flows, i.e. excluding private investment. The 1969 Pearson Report, commissioned by the World Bank, crystallized ongoing debates by proposing two related aid targets:

---

[11] The programme called for an increase in the flows of international assistance and capital 'so as to reach as soon as possible approximately 1 per cent of the combined national incomes of the economically advanced countries'. General Assembly resolution 1522 (XV), 1960.

[12] *Handelingen*, 2 February 1960: 614, and *Parlementaire Handelingen*, 14 January 1964: 33, respectively.

[13] See articles about aid volume in *De Volkskrant*, 28 September, 10 November and 9 December 1967. Future Minister Jan Pronk was among the NGO activists pushing for higher aid levels.

1. Each developed country should increase its resource transfers to developing countries to a minimum of 1 per cent of its gross national product.
2. Each developed country should increase its commitments of official development assistance to the level necessary for net disbursements to reach 0.70 per cent of its gross national product by 1975.[14]

These recommendations found their way into the declaration of the second UN Development Decade, as goals to be reached by 1975. Some observers were concerned about the feasibility of these goals, but they did not seem out of reach to most states.[15]

Due to its extensive aid disbursements to former colonies and current territories, France was already in compliance with the 0.7% target at the time of its official adoption. However, it began to fall below the target level just as other states began to reach it. In 1973, Sweden became the second state to allocate 0.7% of its GNP in ODA. It was followed by the Netherlands in 1975, Norway in 1976, and Denmark in 1978. France's aid programme was in compliance with the 0.7% norm on and off during 1980s. After that time, aid levels dropped down closer to the DAC average. Although twelve donor states expressed reservations about the 0.7% target at the beginning of the 1970s, a decade later only Switzerland and the United States remained as DAC members without a stated goal of attaining the target. Only one new country has achieved the target since 1980: Luxembourg, which did so first in 2000, and became one of the most generous aid donors in the ensuing decade. Throughout the 1990s, most donor states kept the 0.7% target level as an official, rhetorical goal, while shying away from setting an explicit date for attaining it. As we saw in Chapter 1, the introduction of the Millennium Development Goals brought new visibility to the target, without, however, appearing to have much of an impact on policy outcomes.

Explaining aid volume: the literature

The aid literature has not been very successful in isolating the main determinants of aid volume. As noted in the introduction, some

---

[14] Pearson and the Commission on International Development, *Partners in development*, 152.
[15] OECD, *Development co-operation: Efforts and policies of the members of the Development Assistance Committee: 1971 report*, 14.

observers have suggested that the end of the Cold War explained declining aid levels throughout the 1990s.[16] However, in many countries aid levels already declined during the 1980s. Moreover, some other countries actually increased their aid effort during the 1990s, using part of the 'peace dividend' for development cooperation. In fact, military expenditures during the Cold War do not seem to have been systematically correlated with aid levels, as one would expect if aid were a security instrument.[17] For example, military expenditures as a share of GNP in Belgium and Norway were very similar for many years, but their aid contributions diverged considerably.

The size of states has also been proposed as a causal factor affecting aid levels. Smaller states might give more aid because they have fewer alternative instruments for the pursuit of power.[18] However, the United States *was* at one point one of the most generous donors, and France was in compliance with the 0.7 per cent norm for a while during the 1980s. Conversely, New Zealand and Australia, much smaller states, are not particularly generous donors. The per capita GNP of a state also has surprisingly little explanatory power, though it is sometimes suggested as a causal factor.[19] Although the most generous donors are all quite wealthy, greater wealth seems to have little influence on generosity. The United States and Switzerland – for years two of the richest countries in the world – are usually found far down in the rankings, for example. Moreover, per capita GNP levels are far too steady to explain the dramatic fluctuations over time in aid levels and in the relative rankings of donor states.

Even if overall or per capita wealth cannot explain aid levels, one might think that changes in economic fortunes can.[20] However, during the economic crisis of the 1970s the Netherlands and Sweden both raised their aid volumes considerably, despite high levels of inflation and unemployment.[21] Nor do budget deficits provide much explanatory power, since aid budgets have been considered nearly inviolable

---

[16] Griffin, 'Foreign aid'; H. White, 'Trends in the volume and allocation of official flows from donor countries'.
[17] See McKinlay and Mughan, *Aid and arms*.
[18] Hoadley, 'Small states'; J. I. Round and M. Odedokun, 'Aid effort and its determinants'.
[19] E.g. Round and Odedokun, 'Aid effort'.   [20] Mureddu, 'Obiettivi espliciti'.
[21] Similarly, the global economic crisis that began in 2007 had far less of an impact than many observers initially feared.

in some countries (e.g. Norway), whereas in others they have been the first target of budget cuts (e.g. the United States). Thus budget pressures alone cannot explain the patterns we observe. Nor can exposure to international trade, another popular candidate. The more a country trades with developing countries, the larger we might expect its aid budget to be.[22] However, although the extent of trade with LDCs in Italy has been up to two times as great as in Norway, relative to GNP, Italy gives far less aid than does the latter. Similarly, the importance of LDCs in the overall trade of the Netherlands and Belgium is comparable, yet their aid levels show very different trends.[23] In fact, Belgium is one of the most trade-dependent countries in Europe, yet it has never been a particularly generous donor.

The most intriguing finding in the literature is associated with arguments about humanitarian motivations for aid. A fairly consistent correlation exists between domestic welfare expenditures and the foreign aid budget.[24] Moreover, policy-makers themselves have often depicted aid programmes as international reflections of the values shaping the domestic welfare state. Indeed, a strong, positive correlation (of 0.85 or higher) exists between social security expenditures and aid levels over the period 1960–95 in a range of countries including Ireland, the Netherlands and Norway. However, a strong correlation in the opposite direction is present for the United States and the United Kingdom, and to some degree in other states such as Belgium or France. This casts some doubt on the nature (and universality) of the causal link between welfare and aid. Moreover, Noël and Thérien find an equally strong correlation with the overall government budget, suggesting that perhaps the connection to welfare considerations is spurious.[25] It is possible that the size of the government budget is a general proxy for faith in the state as an actor. In countries where citizens look to the state to solve a lot of problems, we might therefore also see high levels of aid.[26] For now, the precise causal factor behind these suggestive correlations remains unclear.

---

[22] Maizels and Nissanke, 'Motivations for aid'.
[23] Comparisons based on data from the IMF's *Direction of Trade Statistics*, various years.
[24] Lumsdaine, *Moral vision*; D. Tingley, 'Donors and domestic politics: Political influences on foreign aid effort'.
[25] Noël and Thérien, 'From domestic to international'.
[26] A. Chong and M. Gradstein, 'What determines foreign aid? The donors' perspective'; OECD, *Development co-operation: Efforts and policies of*

Case studies - from aid discourse to aid volume 149

Finally, we turn to political pressures as explanatory factors of aid volume. Public support for aid as expressed in opinion surveys is almost entirely uncorrelated with aid levels.[27] Italians, for example, have often been among the more enthusiastic supporters of foreign aid, at least in opinion polls, yet aid levels have remained very low. Political party strength is a more promising candidate factor. Supporters of left-wing and Christian Democratic parties usually favour aid more than do voters for right-wing parties, and party platforms reflect this fact.[28] However, this association between political orientation and rhetorical support for aid is not systematically reflected in aid budgets.[29] In fact, some evidence indicates that right-wing party strength has at times been associated with *larger*, not smaller, foreign aid programmes.[30] As is the case with the other candidate factors, then, the status of this explanation remains inconclusive.[31]

Case studies - from aid discourse to aid volume

One conclusion to be drawn from the literature on aid volume is that different causal factors have been relevant to different donor states at different times. In this section, I discuss the evolution of aid levels in Belgium, Italy, the Netherlands and Norway, showing that their composite aid frames explain why certain factors had an impact only in particular situations. In turn, this explains why it has been so difficult to find systematic overall patterns in the determinants of aid

 the members of the Development Assistance Committee: 1977 report, 135; Round and Odedokun, 'Aid effort'.
[27] M. Otter, 'Domestic support for foreign aid: Does it matter?'; A. M. Van der Veen, 'Not whether but why: Using public opinion to explain foreign policy'.
[28] E.g. 'Politieke partijen en de Derde Wereld'.
[29] L.-M. Imbeau, *Donor aid – The determinants of development allocations to Third World Countries: A comparative analysis*.
[30] W. Hout, 'European development aid: A cross-national analysis of competing explanations', 480.
[31] It is possible that right-wing parties 'purchase' coalition support from Christian Democrats by giving them larger aid budgets. Here too, however, the evidence is at best anecdotal. Stokke, 'The determinants of Norwegian'. In response to these ambiguous results, Thérien and Noël ('Political parties') argue that social democratic parties *are* in fact associated with higher aid spending, but that the causal link is indirect. They suggest that such parties produce changes in public beliefs about aid, and that these beliefs in turn promote higher aid levels. Their model thus resembles my discussion of frame entrepreneurship on the part of governments in Chapter 4.

volume. Table 6.1 combines the hypotheses derived in Chapter 2 with the empirical patterns in frame salience presented in Chapter 3.

Belgium: about average, but not much more

Over the years, the Belgian authorities often used their aid programme as a locus for correcting administrative and budget imbalances in other departments: 'Development cooperation is political small change, used during cabinet formations and budget planning to re-balance at the last minute the complex relations between the linguistic communities and among the political orientations.'[32] In fact, one observer claimed that 'great changes in aid volume are largely due to coincidental factors or to factors that are not directly related to the issue of development', such as internal political conflict or trends in relations with Zaire.[33] However, patterns have not been as arbitrary as these assessments might suggest.

The salience of the wealth frame in Belgium's aid discourse suggests we look at the importance of trade with developing countries. LDC trade (especially trade with the former colonies) has long been relatively important to Belgium, so if the wealth frame were the only important consideration, we would expect above-average aid levels. However, we need to take into account the importance of the obligation frame as well. The sum a state feels obliged to give will depend in part on which states it considers its peers. Evidence from public discourse suggests that, for obvious linguistic reasons, Belgians pay particular attention to France and the Netherlands. Beyond that, they are concerned mostly with averages across all DAC donors. Since obligation predicts an aid volume that matches the peer group, we would expect an aid volume somewhere between the DAC average and the Netherlands and France: above average but not too much so.

Belgium's aid volume fluctuated quite strongly during the early 1960s. Figure 6.2 showed that it shot up at the end of empire, after hovering at a low level during the 1950s. Once Belgium had acquitted itself of the duties immediately associated with granting its colonies independence, the sense of obligation attenuated somewhat. As a result, aid volume fell below 0.6% of GNP by 1962 (after a peak of 0.88% in 1960), never

---

[32] Vandommele, 'Twintig jaar Belgisch ontwikkelingsbeleid', 500.
[33] Vaes, 'Het officiële Belgische beleid', 289.

Table 6.1 *Hypotheses about the relationship between frames and aid volume*

Category	Salient when?	Aid volume
Security	**Belgium** around 1960, around 1990 **Italy** 1960s **Netherlands** mid 1950s to 1960s **Norway** around 1960s	Correlated with military expenditures
Power	**Italy** late 1970s to early 1980s **Netherlands** throughout **Norway** mid 1990s	Inversely correlated with relative GDP
Wealth	**Belgium** through early 1970s, 1980s **Italy** throughout 1990	Correlated with LDC trade (and investment)
Enlightened self-interest	**Belgium** mid 1980s, mid 1990s **Italy** late 1970s to 1980s, late 1990s **Netherlands** late 1980s to 1990s **Norway** around 1970, late 1980s, late 1990s	Correlated with LDC trade
Reputation	**Belgium** second half of 1990s **Italy** throughout 1960, 1990s **Norway** 1960s, mid 1980s to mid 1990s	Correlated with peer aid volume
Obligation	**Belgium** throughout, with occasional minor dips **Italy** early 1970s **Netherlands** 1970s (but emerging by mid 1960s) **Norway** mid 1960s to 1980	Correlated with peer aid volume, government expenditures
Humanitarianism	**Belgium** early 1990s **Netherlands** from mid 1970s **Norway** from early 1970s	Correlated with wealth, welfare spending

again to exceed that level. During the second half of the 1960s, aid levels remained below 0.5% of GNP. Five different ministers were in charge of aid during the decade, serving five different governments, but these government changes had little impact on aid volume.

By the end of the 1960s, the obligation frame grew once again in salience, stemming any further decline. Over time, the balance of individual arguments within this frame had shifted, from specific post-colonial concerns to a view of aid as an obligation imposed on Belgium by virtue of its status as an industrialized country. Aid levels accordingly began to inch up, following the lead of the Netherlands and France. The Chamber of Representatives passed a motion in support of this trend on 30 April 1970, charging the government with the task of reaching a minimum percentage of 0.75 per cent of GNP in official government contributions to development aid. The government accepted the motion on 25 September, but failed to allocate the required resources.[34] Although aid volume grew somewhat, it remained well below the motion's target level.

In 1975, aid volume rose to a level it had last attained in 1965, fell for a couple of years, and then held close to 0.6 per cent for the first half of the 1980s. The trend here cannot be explained by pointing to the colour of the government, as the drop-off from 1975 to 1977 occurred on the watch of Minister Van Elslande, one of the most development-oriented ministers in Belgium's history. Instead, the answer lies in the declining salience of the obligation frame, as well as in changes in the economic factors associated with the wealth frame. Trade with Zaire had long been quite important to Belgium's economy. However, a notable reduction in the volume of trade with that country occurred from the mid 1970s forward, caused by the deterioration of its economy under Mobutu. As a result, the predicted aid volume associated with the wealth frame also declined. Interestingly, the drop in aid levels appears to have been stemmed by the temporary prominence of the self-affirmation frame.

Starting in the mid 1980s, and lasting about a decade, Belgium's aid effort began a sustained decline. Although the obligation frame

---

[34] Actually, the government passed the buck to the legislature, charging it with finding the additional resources needed. A proposed 'solidarity tax' was rejected, as the humanitarian frame to which this tax appealed was insufficiently strong in Belgium.

Case studies - from aid discourse to aid volume 153

had become salient again by this time, both the Dutch and French aid levels had begun to fall – Dutch aid had peaked in 1982, French aid in 1985 – and their upward pull diminished accordingly.[35] We might have expected the salience of the wealth frame, coupled with the importance of trade with Zaire, to keep aid levels up a while longer. However, this same period also saw a further decline in the volume of that trade.[36] By the early 1990s, the 0.7 per cent international aid target was officially abandoned.[37]

From the mid 1990s, enlightened self-interest became more prominent. The relevant variables here are international tension and vulnerability. Belgium's vulnerability was rather high, since it was both highly trade dependent and a likely target for refugee flows from Congo, Rwanda and Burundi. On the other hand, global tension levels were low in the 1990s, and although all three countries were in nearly continuous crisis, few refugees made it to Europe. Hence there was little or no incentive for Belgium to increase its overall aid levels during the second half of the decade. Indeed, as Figure 6.2 shows, they remained more or less steady. At the end of the century, the aid level of 0.36 per cent of GNP corresponded to just over half of the international target so ardently espoused during the 1970s and 1980s, and remained just below the overall DAC average of 0.39 per cent.

Italy: enough not to be embarrassed

The dominance of the wealth frame in Italy's aid discourse, combined with the fact that Italy's trade with developing countries has

---

[35] Nevertheless, throughout the 1980s, the government continued to cling to its official commitment to the 0.7 per cent standard. For example, Foreign Minister Tindemans claimed in a 1986 interview, without a trace of irony, that 'the target has been established and is known. The rest is a question of budgeting'. M. Vandommele and D. Barrez, 'Interview met L. Tindemans: "Stapsgewijs naar 0,70% van het BNP tegen 1989"', 22.

[36] Interestingly, the salience of the humanitarian frame in the early 1990s appears to have had no impact on aid volume. Given the emerging information about malversations in the aid programme at the time, doubts about the ability of Belgium's aid programme to pursue humanitarian goals likely prevented that frame from exerting the upward pressure on aid levels we would otherwise have expected to see.

[37] Nevertheless, State Secretary Derycke continued to insist in 1992 that the international norm ought to be a medium-term goal. *Senaat Documents* Special Session 1991–2, nr 351–8, 20 May 1992: 5–7.

long been comparatively insignificant, would lead us to expect low aid levels. The frequent prominence of the reputation frame, however, suggests a potential adjustment to this prediction: as Table 6.1 suggests, we would expect Italy to take into account the aid levels of its peer group. Italy has long aspired to be a major power; its logical peers in the European context are Great Britain and France. Given the relatively high aid levels of these countries, we might expect the reputation frame to exert an upward pull on Italy's aid levels. Finally, the security frame was more salient in Italy than in the other countries during the 1960s. The relevant variable for this frame, Italy's military spending, was comparatively low during that period. As a result, we would expect this frame simply to reinforce the prediction derived from the dominance of the wealth frame.

During the 1950s, when Somalia was still a colony, Italy's aid volume fluctuated considerably, suggesting that it was largely determined by the costs of different aid initiatives, rather than coordinated to add up to an overall target. In this respect, Italy did not distinguish itself much from the other former colonial powers studied here. However, whereas the Netherlands and Belgium spent an average of about 0.4 per cent of GNP on aid during the 1950s, aimed mostly at current and past colonies, Italy spent only half as much in relative terms. Hence, when it made the same transition from minor colonial power to aid donor in the early 1960s, its initial aid level was also considerably lower, as Figure 6.2 showed.

Why, then, did Italy's aid level not rise to converge with that of Belgium and the Netherlands during the 1960s? Why did it not even keep up with the efforts of Norway, which was setting up an aid programme from scratch, but whose efforts exceeded those of Italy by 1968? As predicted, the answer lies in the dominance of the wealth frame within Italy's overall aid discourse. Since aid was seen primarily as an instrument for economic progress, the limited significance of trade with LDCs not surprisingly caused policy-makers to view Italy's *domestic* economic goals as more pressing. Why spend a lot on export promotion when there is enough work internally for firms producing goods in and for the Mezzogiorno, Italy's internal 'less developed country'?

The reputational interests that were also evident from the start did not change this basic attitude, for two reasons. First and foremost, Italy's aid discourse has not been much about quantity or quality, but rather about Italy's performance in specific cases. Hence, as long as the government could point to some highly visible projects as activities that were contributing to Italy's international reputation, Italy's overall volume performance compared to its peers was of little concern. Second, and relatedly, the low public visibility of aid restricted the ability of the interested public to compare Italy's performance to those of its peer states. This also made it more difficult to assess the validity of the government's claims regarding Italy's international status.

In the late 1970s, the power and enlightened self-interest frames temporarily replaced reputation as complements to the wealth frame in Italy's aid discourse, with effects that quickly became visible. Given Italy's enduring aspirations to great power status, it seized upon any issue area that offered the potential for some international influence, including development cooperation. Moreover, the variables associated with the enlightened self-interest frame also suggested increasing aid levels. Although international tension levels were moderate around 1980, Italy's perceived vulnerability was above average, in light of its exposed location on the Southern flank of Europe. Finally, the experience of the oil crisis led to a greater appreciation of the potential value of aid for ensuring access to reasonably priced raw materials as well as promoting international stability and growth.

Given these factors, the pronounced rise in aid levels from the late 1970s to the late 1980s comes as no surprise. Aid levels reached a peak of just over 0.4 per cent of GNP by 1989.[38] As policy-makers hoped, Italy's growing aid volume did win it some additional influence within the DAC and related institutions, especially concerning Mediterranean issues. However, rising aid levels exacerbated the effects of the capture of the Italian aid budget by rent-seekers, producing rampant corruption. Commenting on increasingly brazen demands by political leaders for spoils to be divided among them and their cronies – in a distorted version of the wealth frame – some observers drily concluded that 'corruption played a role in increasing development assistance at the time'.[39]

---

[38] Looking back, State Secretary Raffaelli in 1986 judged Italy's aid volume in 1979 to have been 'ridiculous'; implying that an aid programme worthy of the name had not yet been started (*III Commissione*, 9 December 1986: 23). Ironically, Italy would find itself back at those same 'ridiculous' aid levels ten years later.

[39] Rhi-Sausi *et al.*, 'Italian bilateral aid policy', 19.

The growth in Italy's aid levels came to an abrupt halt in 1989. During the subsequent decade aid volume plummeted, relegating Italy once again to a status as one of the least generous DAC donors. Why did aid disbursements fall so rapidly after 1989? Budget pressures and corruption scandals were certainly important factors; however, Belgium experienced similar problems, with rather less drastic results. The difference, in Italy's case, was the salient presence of the reputation frame, which magnified the impact of those corruption scandals. In fact, judging that Italy's international image and status were being seriously harmed rather than helped by its aid programme, many Italians were supportive of simply eliminating the aid programme altogether, as we saw in Chapter 5. However, concerns about Italy's reputation, as well as its international exposure and vulnerability, ensured a continued aid effort, albeit at a mostly symbolic level.

The Netherlands: influence by setting an example and exceeding standards

In the Netherlands, the salience of the power frame, combined with the country's status as a small power, ought to translate into relatively high aid levels. Indeed, as early as 1962 a motion demanding a 'significant expansion' in Dutch aid disbursements received support from legislators across the political spectrum, many of whom expressed an interest in seeing their country extend its international influence in this issue area: 'We, as the Netherlands, can not permit ourselves to fall short.'[40] Soon after, aid levels began a sustained climb that was to continue for nearly two decades.

The growing salience of obligation from the mid 1960s added an extra impetus to the drive to meet international standards. We saw in Chapter 4 that Dutch economist Tinbergen was actively involved in drawing up the UN's programme for the second Development Decade. Not surprisingly, we see a spike in aid levels right around 1970, when this decade began. Perhaps even more interestingly, a temporary plateau lasting from 1975 to 1978 is evident in Figure 6.2. The former was the first year in which the Netherlands met the international norm of 0.7 per cent of GNP, as we saw earlier. It appears that meeting this

---

[40] Representative Stoffels-van Haaften, *Handelingen*, 9 January 1962: 631; see also 4 January 1962: 589.

Case studies - from aid discourse to aid volume 157

standard fulfilled the main goal associated with the obligation frame at the time, and further upward pressures were low.[41]

Renewed upward pressure came from a different frame. From the late 1970s, humanitarianism became ever more salient in the Dutch aid discourse, and it contributed to pushing the aid volume over 1 per cent of GNP by the early 1980s, a process almost certainly strengthened by the generosity of domestic welfare policies in the Netherlands.[42] The Dutch aid performance during the late 1970s and early 1980s is particularly noteworthy because it goes against expectations based either on economic or political factors. Aid volume grew or remained steady notwithstanding the economic crises associated with the second oil shock. Nor did a political shift to the right from the mid 1970s to the early 1980s bring the reduction in aid levels one might expect. Instead, it saw Dutch aid volume reach its peak.

From 1982 to 1986, under the most conservative Development Minister the Netherlands had yet seen, Schoo, aid levels remained more or less constant, fluctuating between 0.9 and 1.0 per cent of GNP. Ironically, it was Pronk, the country's most progressive and pro-aid Minister, who was forced to preside over the decline in aid levels from the late 1980s to the mid 1990s. This decline negated nearly all the gains that had been made since Pronk first left office in 1977. Once again, therefore, changes in the political composition of government are of no help in explaining this trend.

Instead, two factors related to the composition of the aid discourse appear to have been decisive. First, the association between domestic welfare spending and foreign aid came into play again. From the late 1980s, the welfare state increasingly came under pressure and budget cuts could not be avoided. It thus made sense to cut back the aid programme – as a form of international welfare – too. Second, a decline in the international political visibility of aid made this a less valuable issue area for the pursuit of international influence and status. Whereas debates over North–South relations and NIEO (during the 1970s) as well as structural adjustment (during the 1980s) had kept development cooperation quite visible for several decades, the emphasis during the 1990s increasingly turned to peacekeeping and

---

[41] From 1976, the aid budget was pegged explicitly at 1.5 per cent of Net National Income. (Van den Dool, *Normverva(n)ging*).
[42] Cf. Lumsdaine, *Moral vision*.

conflict prevention. At the same time, international scepticism grew regarding the importance and effectiveness of aid.[43] As a result, the perceived value of aid as a tool for the pursuit of Dutch international influence declined, and the sustaining effect on aid levels exerted by the influence frame declined.

As we saw in the previous chapter, Pronk reacted to these changes by shifting the aid programme's emphasis in the direction of conflict prevention and governance. At the same time, the increasing 'pollution' of the budget by items that did not meet the DAC definition of ODA began to affect the international leverage the Netherlands derived from its aid programme. Pronk accepted an end to the indexation of the overall aid budget to national income in 1992; instead, a target of 0.8 per cent of GNP for 'pure' ODA was adopted.[44] After the reorientation of the programme and the elimination of non-ODA items from the budget, the renewed utility of development cooperation as an issue area for pursuing international influence prevented further declines in aid levels.

Different authors have proposed alternative explanations for Dutch aid generosity. Hoebink, for example, argues that the volume is determined by 'export interests, and the "internationalized" character of the Dutch economy'.[45] However, developing countries have become less important economically to the Netherlands over time, without an analogous reduction in aid levels.[46] The strength of humanitarian norms is another common explanation, but the present discussion illustrates that humanitarianism by itself is not enough, as the humanitarian frame became steadily more salient throughout the period of declining aid levels from the late 1980s to the early 1990s. Others, still, make a more institutional argument, emphasizing faith in the state as an agent for international redistribution.[47] Yet changes

---

[43] Cf. H. Doucouliagos and M. Paldam, 'The aid effectiveness literature: The sad results of 40 years of research'.
[44] Van den Dool, *Normverva(n)ging*, 364.
[45] Hoebink, 'Geven is nemen', 232.
[46] Nor does Hoebink's hypothesis travel well: few of the most generous aid donors conduct a lot of trade with (or investment in) LDCs compared to the other advanced industrialized states.
[47] C. Cooper and J. Verloren van Themaat, 'Dutch aid determinants, 1973–85: Continuity and change', 154. Interestingly, the same article also emphasizes a key factor highlighted in the present analysis: the Dutch interest in international power (*ibid.*, 127–8).

Case studies - from aid discourse to aid volume 159

in aid levels over the past four decades bear no systematic relationship to changes in public support of the state as an international actor, as expressed, for example, in Eurobarometer surveys. Overall, the evidence presented here supports my claim that Dutch generosity can only be explained by looking at shifts in the aid discourse *together* with changes in the explanatory variables associated with different frames for aid.

Norway: matching and outperforming peers

Throughout the 1950s, the volume of Norwegian aid was determined mainly by the costs of the India Project, together with contributions to different multilateral aid initiatives. This produced sharp fluctuations, including one year – 1958 – in which the government budget contained no new aid allocations at all, as funds from previous years had not yet been exhausted. Reputation became a prominent frame from the late 1950s, generating a prediction that Norway would make an effort to match its closest peers, Sweden and Denmark. In fact, Sweden was an early leader in aid policy, and its initiatives were closely followed – and imitated – in Norway.[48]

In 1962, legislative deliberation over a major report on aid by the Engen Commission resulted in the establishment of a first target for aid volume: 0.25% of national income, with a long-term goal of 1%.[49] Nevertheless, aid volume remained quite modest until 1967, never exceeding 0.2% of GNP. Although Norway was largely keeping up with Sweden and Denmark, a number of other countries were well ahead, thanks to the head start provided by colonial programmes. The 1967 DAC aid review criticized Norway as one of the least generous OECD donors. Political leaders were embarrassed at being singled out internationally, and legislators demanded that the government produce a plan to raise the volume.[50] The concern for reputation was joined – and even partially displaced – by the obligation frame, as aid became accepted as a policy area in which Norway had an international obligation to become more active.[51]

[48] See e.g. Norway, *Budsjett Innstilling S. nr. 4*.
[49] Norway, *Engen-utvalget*.
[50] Tamnes, *Norsk utenrikspolitikks historie*, 391.
[51] E.g. Norway, *Om den videre utbygging*.

In fact, following the 1967 DAC report Norway dramatically increased its overall aid volume, pushing the country over its own target of 0.25 per cent of national income for the first time in 1968. This marked the beginning of a sustained and steep rise in aid levels that more than quadrupled aid flows as a share of GNP over the next decade. In 1969, the government adopted a four-year plan to bring total aid levels (including private flows) to 1 per cent of national income, inspired again by the UN's standard and the obligation frame: 'Norway has morally and politically committed itself to reach the 1% target in 1974.'[52] A sense of obligation, combined with a traditionally strong allegiance to the UN, also caused Norway to attach extra significance to that organization's introduction of the 0.7 per cent norm for total public assistance: 'both government and Parliament are sensitive to recommendations by the UN system, in particular if commitments have been given'.[53]

In 1972, Norway exceeded the DAC average for the first time. That same year, the government proposed a target of 1 per cent of GNP for ODA, to be reached by 1978. The legislature approved the plan one year later, proud that Norway had now become a front-runner in aid generosity.[54] By this time, humanitarianism had become prominent in Norway's composite frame for aid. As in the Netherlands, we expect humanitarian motivations to be associated with high aid levels, in part because Norway has a generous domestic welfare state as well. Indeed, aid levels continued to rise rapidly, and when the final budget allocations necessary to reach 1 per cent of GNP were tabled in 1977, the Storting voted unanimously in favour.

A temporary decline in the relative salience of humanitarianism around 1980 resulted in a halting of the upward trend in Norway's aid volume. The obligation frame, which was still prominent at the time, was insufficient to sustain aid levels, since Norway was already exceeding its international obligations by any measure. Despite proposals for continued growth in the share of aid in GNP, the

---

[52] State Secretary Stoltenberg, cited in Tamnes, *Norsk utenrikspolitikks historie*, 391.
[53] Stokke, 'The determinants of Norwegian', 210.
[54] Consider, for example, representative Karstensen's contribution to the 1978 budget debate: 'We justifiably place a great emphasis on the fact that Norway is one of the very first countries in the world that has passed the goal the UN has set for the second Development Decade' (*Stortingstidende*, 21 November 1977: 582). See also Stokke, 'The determinants of Norwegian', 210.

Case studies - from aid discourse to aid volume 161

government froze the aid volume. In fact, Finance Minister Kleppe actually wanted to reduce aid levels, but both Prime Minister Nordli and Foreign Minister Frydenlund blocked this proposal, on the grounds that 'such a step would generate domestic and international reactions'.[55] The ever-present reputation frame thus helped prevent a further decline in aid levels in 1980 and 1981.

An increase in the importance of the humanitarian frame translated quite quickly into a renewed rise in Norway's aid volume the next year. Interestingly, this occurred despite the fact that the main conservative party (Høyre) won the 1981 elections. Indeed, although the government proposed a continued freeze in aid levels, it was overruled by the legislature, which voted increases in aid allocations to 1.05% and 1.1% of GNP in 1982 and 1983, respectively.[56] From the mid 1980s, the reputation frame became even more prominent in the overall aid discourse. As predicted, this fired Norway's interest in matching, and if possible outdoing, Norway's peers. In 1983, Norway took over from the Netherlands as the most generous DAC donor, and, except in 1993, it held this rank throughout 1994, matching almost exactly the period during which the reputation frame was particularly salient. Even when Norway lost the lead in the generosity contest to Denmark – as reported in the quotations opening the chapter – the DAC's review emphasized the fact that 'Norway can be proud of the consistently high level of its aid volume', quite a contrast to the negative comments three decades earlier.[57] Norway continued to be the second most generous aid donor until 2000, when it dropped to third place just below the Netherlands.

As in Netherlands, some concern arose in the early 1990s regarding the value of development cooperation as an issue area in which to pursue international influence and reputation. The reaction, too, was similar: Norway's aid programme was reoriented to place greater emphasis on international environmental issues in the wake of the well-publicized report by the UN's World Commission on Environment and Development, chaired by former Prime Minister Brundtland.[58]

---

[55] Tamnes, *Norsk utenrikspolitikks historie*, 392.
[56] The Storting's role in pushing for a high aid volume during this period is also noted in Ruud and Kjerland, *Norsk utviklingshjelps historie*, 2022.
[57] OECD, *Development co-operation review series: Norway*, 13.
[58] G. H. Brundtland and the World Commission on Environment and Development, *Our common future*.

However, a different reaction could be observed as well, at the expense of the aid programme. Brokering the Oslo Accords between Israel and the PLO in 1993 proved to be a far more visible international endeavour, and was thus preferable from the point of view of the reputation and power frames alike. It is not surprising, therefore, that the drop in aid volume during the second half of the 1990s coincided closely with the emergence of the new opportunities presented by these peace brokerage activities.

Statistical analysis - uncovering patterns and establishing causes

In each of the four case study countries, the evolution of aid volume over time closely matches our predictions based on the relative salience of different aid frames at different times. Moreover, in each country we encountered situations where the trend in aid volume was directly opposite to what might be expected if aid volume were determined either by the shifting political composition of the government or by economic variables related to trade, growth or employment. The fact that such variables provide no systematic explanatory leverage explains why observers have sometimes concluded that patterns in aid volume are largely arbitrary.

This final section of the chapter presents a quantitative test of my argument about the importance of aid frames. The preceding qualitative analysis demonstrated how to combine our measures of frame salience with the variables expected to be associated with each frame. Doing so systematically – by creating interaction variables – will adjust the size of those causal factors in accordance with their expected contribution to aid policy. Ideally, this should allow us to accomplish two things: first, to explain variation in aid volume better than we would without the frame data; and second, to uncover patterns that might otherwise not be obvious.

Data for the statistical analysis were derived from a variety of sources. Figures for aid volume were drawn from the database of the OECD's Development Assistance Committee (DAC), both the CD-ROM and the online versions (see www.oecd.org/dac). This same dataset was also used for the measures of relative aid performance. Three additional datasets provided the data necessary to construct the explanatory variables: the Comparative Political Dataset for OECD

Uncovering patterns and establishing causes 163

countries, the Comparative Welfare States dataset, and Gleditsch's trade and GDP dataset.[59] The data were used to generate the following variables:

aid	aid volume as a percentage of GNI *(dependent variable)*
generosity	relative aid volume calculated as a percentage of the highest aid volume among DAC donors (expressed as a percentage of GNI) in a given year
outperform	aid volume minus the average DAC aid volume in a given year
military	military expenditure as a percentage of GDP
size	natural log of the percentage share of the total DAC GDP (a measure of total economic wealth)
rich	GDP per capita as a percentage of the DAC average (a measure of relative economic wealth)
openLDCs	total trade with developing countries accepted by the DAC as ODA recipients as a percentage of GDP
government	total general government disbursements as a percentage of GDP[60]
welfare	social security transfers as a percentage of GDP

The size of the dataset is limited, since we can go back only as far as 1960, the first year for which many comparative international statistics on OECD countries are available. With four observations per decade during the year 2000, this gives a total of seventeen observations over time, for four countries each, or a total of sixty-eight observations in the dataset. Given the limited number of observations, we cannot include many explanatory variables in our statistical analysis.[61] Moreover, the two aid performance variables (generosity

---

[59] K. Armingeon *et al.*, 'Comparative political data set 1960–2006'; E. Huber *et al.*, 'Comparative welfare states data set'; K. S. Gleditsch, 'Expanded trade and GDP data'. Each of these datasets draws on other data sources in turn. For example, the military expenditure data in the Comparative Welfare States dataset come from the Stockholm International Peace Research Institute, while the trade data originate from the International Monetary Fund's *Direction of Trade Statistics*.

[60] In the case of the Netherlands, the data for 1999 and 2000 were missing, and were supplied by extrapolation from the preceding years.

[61] In particular, earlier research has shown that control variables representing the political composition of the government add no significant explanatory

Table 6.2 *Summary statistics for dependent and explanatory variables*

Variable	Lag	Mean	Std. dev.	Min	Max
aid	0	0.535	0.313	0.08	1.17
generosity	2	54.263	31.283	6	100
outperform	2	0.114	0.294	−0.4	0.650
military	1	2.851	0.687	1.4	4.5
size	1	0.587	0.880	−0.616	2.017
rich	1	96.535	9.026	75.347	122.049
openLDCs	1	7.703	4.173	2.066	19.029
government	1	44.134	8.175	30.1	62.5
welfare	1	15.287	4.751	7.6	28.743

Variable	Mean	Std. dev.	Min	Max
security * military	0.172	0.172	0.013	0.774
power * size	0.046	0.068	−0.055	0.227
wealth * openLDCs	0.902	0.721	0.721	3.067
ESI * openLDCs	1.084	0.798	0.025	3.428
reputation * generosity	10.075	7.194	0.628	28.620
obligation * outperform	0.020	0.053	−0.097	0.201
humanitarianism * government	3.956	2.470	0.148	12.886
humanitarianism * rich	24.432	11.070	1.138	56.826

Sources: see text. Std. dev. = standard deviation.

and outperform) are highly correlated, as are the two government expenditure variables (government and welfare), so one of each pair is dropped in the analyses reported below, except when interacted with different measures of frame strength.

Since we are trying to *predict* aid volume, all independent variables are lagged by one year. Moreover, since relative aid performance only becomes clear at the end of a year, the aid performance variables are lagged by an additional year. Both of these steps protect against the possibility of inadvertently misinterpreting the direction of the

leverage. Van der Veen, 'Ideas and interests in foreign policy', Chapter 4. Since they are not directly associated with any frame, I have omitted them here.

Uncovering patterns and establishing causes 165

Table 6.3 *Determinants of aid volume,* uninteracted, *panel-specific autocorrelation*

Variable	Coefficient	Standard error	P>|z|
Military	0.0186	0.0270	0.492
Size	−0.0128	0.0287	0.655
OpenLDCs	0.00672	0.00475	0.157
Generosity	0.00788***	0.000814	0.000
Welfare	0.0000354	0.00476	0.994
Rich	0.00415	0.00276	0.133
Constant	*−0.383*	*0.311*	*0.217*

N = 68. Wald chi-squared(6) = 334.87.
Statistical significance: *** < 0.01.

causal arrow.[62] Finally, each of these variables can be interacted with a particular measure of frame strength, as suggested in Table 6.1. Table 6.2 gives summary statistics for both the plain and the interacted variables.[63]

To test the explanatory power of these variables, I performed a cross-sectional time-series feasible generalized least squares regression, with panel-corrected standard errors.[64] The first regression uses the uninteracted variables, the second replaces these by interacted variables, thus introducing the frame information.[65] The results are shown in Tables 6.3 and 6.4. Though each of the basic variables in

---

[62] To increase our confidence in the posited causal direction, I ran the same regression model but with all independent variables advanced, rather than lagged. This model performs worse, as we would expect if aid volume is indeed caused by these variables, instead of being prior to them (or, more specifically, causally prior to the measures of aid frames).
[63] Two variables listed in Table 6.1 are not represented. It is difficult to find good measures for international tension and investment in LDCs. The few promising candidates were not available for the entire period. Moreover, exploratory analysis showed they were of little or no explanatory value in the years where data was available (Van der Veen, 'Ideas and interests in foreign policy', Chapter 4).
[64] N. Beck and J. N. Katz, 'What to do (and not to do) with time series-cross section data'.
[65] The statistical package used was Stata (xtgls). Although the error structures for the different countries do not have identical variances, the variation is

Table 6.4 *Determinants of aid volume*, interacted, *panel-specific autocorrelation*

Variable	Coefficient	Standard error	P>|z|
Security * military	0.0999	0.114	0.382
Power * size	0.0584	0.273	0.830
Wealth * openLDCs	0.0487*	0.0262	0.063
ESI * openLDCs	0.0263	0.0232	0.257
Reputation * generosity	0.0125***	0.00296	0.000
Obligation * outperform	2.545***	0.3569	0.000
Humanitarian * rich	0.0130 ***	0.00177	0.000
Constant	−0.0543	0.0823	0.509

N = 68. Wald chi-squared(7) = 300.87.
Statistical significance: * < 0.1, *** < 0.01.

Table 6.3 has been found to have some explanatory influence on aid volume in other subsets of donor states and years, all but one perform rather poorly in this smaller subset. Moreover, the sole significant variable, not surprisingly, was the measure of the donor's relative aid performance in the previous year. In contrast, when we interact these variables with our measures of frame strength, we get four statistically significant estimates. Two of these are still related to aid performance, but two others capture the importance of per capita income and trade with developing countries.

The overall explanatory power of the two regressions is roughly equal, with the uninteracted regression performing slightly better (Wald statistics 334.87 vs 300.87). This pair of regressions thus meets just one of our expectations: interacting measures of frame strength with standard explanatory variables *does* uncover additional patterns in the data, but it does not increase the overall explanatory power. The problem lies at least in part in the fact that panel-corrected standard errors require the estimation of four autocorrelations (one for each country). Especially given our small sample size, this places steep demands on the data. In fact, each regression

small. I imposed homoscedasticity; allowing for heteroscedasticity across states does not significantly improve the estimation.

Uncovering patterns and establishing causes 167

Table 6.5 *Determinants of aid volume,* uninteracted, no autocorrelation

Variable	Coefficient	Standard error	P>|z|
Military	0.00770	0.0224	0.731
Size	−0.00792	0.0245	0.747
OpenLDCs	0.00397	0.00429	0.355
Generosity	0.00830***	0.000720	0.000
Welfare	0.000780	0.00428	0.856
Rich	0.00373	0.00239	0.119
Constant	*−0.335*	*0.263*	*0.203*

N = 68. Wald chi-squared(6) = 490.53.

Statistical significance: *** < 0.01.

already includes a proxy for a lagged dependent variable, in the form of a measure of aid performance in the previous period. As a result, it is not unreasonable to eliminate the estimated autocorrelations and rerun the analysis.[66]

As Tables 6.5 and 6.6 show, both of our expectations are now met: the interacted regression performs considerably better (Wald statistic 608.34 vs 490.53). Reassuringly, the coefficient estimates of the statistically significant variables change little, if at all. Though a statistical analysis on such a small dataset has its limits, the results affirm the impact of frames on this key dimension of development assistance programmes. Richer countries, as measured by per capita GDP, do tend to give more development assistance, but only if humanitarianism is a strong frame for aid. On the other hand, countries where economic interest is a strong aid frame give more development assistance as they trade more with developing countries. Each of these patterns matches our predictions, but neither could be identified without the frame data.

The results also underscore the importance of non-material considerations. In addition to the humanitarian frame, the reputation and obligation frames are each associated with statistically significant coefficient estimates. A concern with reputation induces countries

[66] Indeed, tests show relatively little evidence of autocorrelation.

Table 6.6 *Determinants of aid volume*, interacted, *no autocorrelation*

Variable	Coefficient	Standard error	P>|z|
Security * military	0.126	0.0975	0.195
Power * size	0.183	0.217	0.398
Wealth * openLDCs	0.0502**	0.0235	0.032
ESI * openLDCs	0.0298	0.0206	0.149
Reputation * generosity	0.0124***	0.00267	0.000
Obligation * outperform	2.718***	0.327	0.000
Humanitarian * rich	0.0140***	0.00165	0.000
Constant	*−0.0941*	*0.0729*	*0.197*

N = 68. Wald chi-squared(7) = 608.34.
Statistical significance: ** < 0.05, *** < 0.01.

that already give a lot of aid to give still more, whereas the influence on aid volume is less for countries that already do comparatively poorly. A concern with obligation has a comparable impact. Though this same basic pattern is also evident in the uninteracted regression, the results here show that the reputation and obligation frames, in particular, help drive the pattern.

Conclusion

Although it is one of the most visible measures of a donor state's aid programme, aid volume has proven difficult to explain. Indeed, some observers have concluded that much of the observed variation in aid volume is arbitrary or random. Although unforeseen and idiosyncratic factors undoubtedly come into play, this chapter demonstrated that much of the variation *can* be explained successfully, once one has a measure of the frames that dominate the aid discourse.

The association between aid volume and welfare state expenditures provides a prime example. As noted earlier in the chapter, a strong positive correlation between these two variables can be found in some countries, such as the Netherlands or Norway, whereas in other countries, such as Belgium, this correlation is absent or even negative. We have now seen that this difference can be explained by the strength of the humanitarian frame in the aid discourse of the former two countries, and its relative weakness in the latter. Our measures of frame strength not only allow us to explain the pattern, but also save us from having to impute motivations or generate ad hoc explanations for the presence of a particular pattern in one case but not in another.

The case studies in the second part of the chapter showed that the relative strength of different frames, combined with the empirical variation in the associated explanatory variables, explain a large part of the observed variation in aid levels. The discussion also illustrated how different nuances in frames may imply that different explanatory variables are relevant. Thus, the obligation frame in the Netherlands and Norway implied a heavy emphasis on meeting international norms and standards promoted by the United Nations, in part because a prominent citizen of each country was strongly associated with the organization in the public's mind. In Belgium, however, the perceived obligation was much more a combination of duties towards the former colonies and the responsibilities of an advanced industrial state. Both of these aspects of the obligation frame were much weaker in Italy, even though the latter, too, had a background as a minor colonial power.

Similarly, donor-specific nuances in the self-affirmation frame inspired dramatically different patterns in Norway and Italy. In the former, the salience of reputational considerations had a direct and measurable impact on aid volume from the mid 1980s, as Norway strove to attain the top ranking in the generosity contest. In the latter, aid volume never featured prominently in the overall aid discourse, and reputational considerations mainly served to make sure that Italy provided enough aid not to be embarrassed internationally. Moreover, when corruption scandals broke, the realization that the aid programme was actually damaging Italy's international image resulted in a sharp decline in aid volume, the opposite of our prediction in Chapter 2.

The third section of the chapter illustrated that aid frames can help explain patterns in aid volume not only using a case study approach, but also in a statistical analysis. The regression analyses showed that interacting measures of frame strength with the associated explanatory variables can uncover single-variable patterns that would otherwise not emerge, as well as explain the total variation better. Even though the overall explanatory strength of the regressions was not overwhelming and several interacted variables were not statistically significant, the fact that introducing frame strength into the analysis can improve our predictive ability, even using such a limited dataset, must qualify as strong evidence in favour of the overall theoretical model.

7 | *The popularity contest: selecting the recipients of aid*

Criteria for the choice of main recipient countries must be taken seriously!

– Headline, *Norkontakt*, 1983[1]

No aspect of aid policy attracts more attention, in political debates and in academic circles, than does the distribution of aid funds across recipient countries. Studies of the determinants of aid allocation date back to the early 1960s and continue to account for the bulk of the literature today.[2] Such studies have posited causal effects for a wide range of explanatory variables, but definitive conclusions have been elusive. On the one hand, theoretical as well as methodological problems frustrate the quantitative analysis of aid allocation. On the other hand, virtually all qualitative analyses, whose findings might offer a richer understanding of the factors driving the geographical distribution of aid, are single-country studies. This chapter addresses each of these problems.

An analysis of aid distribution decisions in Belgium, Italy, the Netherlands and Norway demonstrates that this aspect of official aid programmes is shaped by aid frames just as much as are the other aspects we considered in the preceding chapters. In Belgium, economic self-interest has been pre-eminent in the selection of new countries, whereas the obligation frame has kept the share of aid allocated to the former colonies high. In Italy, the wealth frame has been so dominant

---

[1] *Norkontakt* was a public information magazine published by Norway's aid administration. The headline is from 1983, issue 2, page 10.
[2] Examples of early studies are Kirschen, 'Objectifs et determination' and M. S. Levitt, 'The allocation of economic aid in practice'. Some recent studies include Alesina and Dollar, 'Who gives foreign aid'; J.-C. Berthélemy and A. Tichit, 'Bilateral donors' aid allocation decisions – A three-dimensional panel analysis'; Bueno de Mesquita and Smith, 'A political economy'; Schraeder *et al.*, 'Clarifying the foreign aid puzzle'.

that the country long avoided even setting criteria for the selection of aid recipients, preferring to let private industry find projects wherever it might. In the Netherlands, the power frame increased the emphasis on taking the lead in initiatives suggested by the humanitarian frame, with the result that aid became increasingly dispersed in response to a succession of different priorities. In Norway, finally, the reputation and enlightened self-interest frames generated a preference for larger LDCs, whereas the humanitarian frame inspired an emphasis on the poorest recipient states from the beginning.

In the first part of the chapter, I define and introduce the dependent variable and describe its empirical variation. The second part provides an analysis of the recipient selection process in the four case study countries. The final part presents quantitative analyses offering a comparative overview of the statistical patterns in recipient selection in each country. As was the case in the previous chapter, combining measures of frame prominence with the appropriate independent variables helps uncover and illustrate several important patterns and trends that would otherwise remain obscure.

Geographical patterns in aid flows

The Development Assistance Committee tracks several measures of aid allocation: aid commitments (the sums that donors promise to make available), disbursements (actual transfers from donor to recipient), net disbursements (gross disbursements minus repayments of principal from earlier loans), and net ODA (net disbursements minus interest payments). There are plausible reasons for focusing either on commitments or on disbursements as the decision variable. On the one hand, disbursements are affected by the actions of the recipient states. Some recipients may not succeed in proposing enough projects to consume the funds committed to them by a donor. Conversely, sudden emergencies such as famines or political upheaval may result in supplies of aid over and above committed levels. In view of these factors, one could argue that disbursements are 'likely to represent the results of a compromise between the aid demand of recipient countries and the aid supply of donor countries'.[3] Hence, if we are interested in aid selection choices by donors, commitments might be preferable.

---

[3] L. Dudley and C. Montmarquette, 'A model of the supply of bilateral foreign aid', 138.

On the other hand, there is evidence that donors systematically commit more funds than they intend to spend.[4] In some cases, excess commitments are saved in a reservoir for future use,[5] but often they revert to the general state budget. In either situation, decision-makers are likely to be cognizant of these possibilities and, at least roughly, of the sums involved. Taking these considerations into account, I follow the standard practice in the literature, which is to use net ODA figures.

We also need to decide in what form to use these data. Some studies use per capita aid as the dependent variable, in part to facilitate assessment of the ability of aid to address the humanitarian needs of target populations.[6] However, it seems implausible that aid allocation decisions are made on this basis. In pragmatic terms, it is quite difficult to calculate allocations per capita for different recipients in such a way as to satisfy an overall budget target or constraint. Nor do the data suggest per capita aid is the decision variable. In particular, the smallest states are systematically over-represented by this metric. For example, in 1997 the Netherlands gave Dominica, with its 73,800 citizens, $2 per capita, compared to a mere $0.03 per capita for the 960 million citizens of India, whose per capita income was rather lower than that in Dominica. It is implausible that the Netherlands really values Dominicans sixty-six times higher than it does Indians.[7] The data make rather more sense if we look at total aid receipts, by which measure India received about 200 times as much aid as did Dominica.

Table 7.1 shows the evolution over time in the set of most favoured aid recipients, and the percentage of total bilateral ODA each receives,

---

[4] Total commitments were as high as 2.8 times actual net ODA in Italy in 1978 and 1979. On the other hand, there are also cases where disbursements were twice as high as commitments, for example in Belgium in 1985 and Norway in 1988.

[5] This has been the case most notably in the Netherlands. The presence of a reservoir, in turn, will bias commitments downwards since expected disbursements from the reservoir will be taken into account in the decision-making process.

[6] E.g. P. Bowles, 'Recipient needs and donor interests in the allocation of EEC aid to developing countries'; F. Tarp et al., 'Danish aid policy: Theory and empirical evidence'; W. N. Trumbull and H. J. Wall, 'Estimating aid-allocation criteria with panel data'.

[7] OECD, *Geographical distribution. 1998 report*.

Table 7.1 Top aid recipients over time, all DAC donors. Figures are percentages of total bilateral ODA.

DAC	1960		1970		1980		1990		2000
India	20.86	India	15.53	Egypt	8.22	Egypt	9.93	Indonesia	6.39
Algeria	10.06	Indonesia	9.27	Israel	6.18	Indonesia	4.83	China	4.97
Pakistan	7.21	Vietnam	8.96	Bangladesh	5.89	China	4.73	Vietnam	4.93
Korea	7.09	Pakistan	7.94	Indonesia	5.85	Israel	4.29	Egypt	4.50
Vietnam	5.43	Korea	5.53	Turkey	4.94	Philippines	3.46	Tanzania	3.08
Egypt	4.84	Turkey	3.15	India	4.39	Bangladesh	3.45	India	2.57
Turkey	3.89	Papua NG	3.02	Tanzania	3.63	Tanzania	2.64	Thailand	2.47
Taiwan	3.12	Brazil	2.70	Pakistan	2.35	India	2.36	Mozambique	2.46
Israel	2.98	Colombia	2.53	Zaire	2.19	Mozambique	2.35	Bangladesh	2.44
Indonesia	2.30	Algeria	2.25	Thailand	2.11	Kenya	2.30	Yugoslavia	2.34
Total	67.77	Total	60.88	Total	45.75	Total	40.35	Total	36.17

Note: This table and those that follow, as well as figures given throughout the chapter, are derived from the OECD's annual publication and CD-ROM *Geographical Distribution of Financial Flows*. The percentages listed are shares of total net bilateral ODA disbursed to specified LDCs. Some donor states regularly allot aid funds at a regional level, leaving it to the recipient states within regions to compete for the available funds. Hence, DAC statistics list categories such as 'Latin America, unallocated', and some of these regional entries account for considerable sums. I follow standard practice and assume that the empirical distribution of aid listed as 'unallocated' and 'undecided' in the official statistics does not differ systematically from the distribution of those funds for which the national destination is specified. However, this is a largely untested assumption. In addition, the DAC lists 'negative' aid flows, which represent loan repayments. These explain why the aid shares listed below occasionally add up to more than 100 per cent.

Geographical patterns in aid flows 175

for all DAC donors combined. Table 7.2 shows the same data for Belgium, Italy, the Netherlands and Norway. In the early years of development assistance, present or former colonies received the bulk of aid, but the concentration of aid has fallen considerably since then. Nonetheless, Belgium in particular continued to prioritize its former colonies throughout the 1990s.[8] Indonesia remained a prominent recipient of Dutch aid until it decided in 1992 not to accept such aid any longer, because the Netherlands too openly criticized president Suharto's policies. After Suharto's fall in 1998, Indonesia reassumed its place at the top of the rankings. The episode illustrates both the continuing importance of former colonies and the potential influence of recipients on aid flows.

A few states appear to be favourites of all donors. Tanzania is an oft-cited example, but Indonesia, Mozambique and Bangladesh are prominent too. A comparison of Tables 7.1 and 7.2 shows that European donor states tend to concentrate on Africa more than do non-European DAC donors. Some observers have suggested that this pattern results from a division of labour within the DAC, with Japan concentrating on Asia, the United States on Latin America, and Europe on Africa. It is equally plausible, however, that the bias is generated by a combination of historical ties and the disproportionate poverty of African LDCs. The tables also document the rise to prominence during the 1990s of some states that were not previously candidates for aid, such as Bosnia-Herzegovina and the Palestinian Administrative Areas. Conversely, some recipients, such as the Netherlands Antilles and Israel, disappear from the rankings because they are now deemed too rich to be eligible for ODA. Specific changes aside, the distribution of aid flows has been relatively stable over time. Indeed, potentially attractive new aid targets, such as some of the poorer former Soviet republics, rarely found their way into donors' top-ten lists during the 1990s.

Over time, the share of aid flows allotted to the top recipients has declined significantly. All donor states give aid to far more countries than are on their official lists of target recipients. For example, in 1997 Norway allocated over 1% of its aid budget to each of twenty recipients. Another fifty recipients received between 0.1% and 1% of

---

[8] Note that Zaire's name changed to the Democratic Republic of Congo during the late 1990s.

Table 7.2a Top aid recipients over time: Belgium

Belgium	1960		1970		1980		1990		2000	
Zaire	82.56	Zaire	55.20	Zaire	39.82	Zaire	25.16	Vietnam	12.02
Burundi	8.72	Rwanda	12.22	Rwanda	8.50	Rwanda	11.45	DR Congo	8.43
Rwanda	8.72	Burundi	10.67	Burundi	6.50	Burundi	10.43	Rwanda	5.03
		Indonesia	4.05	Indonesia	4.82	Tanzania	3.76	Côte d'Ivoire	4.39
		Tunisia	3.47	Philippines	4.03	Uganda	2.78	Niger	3.10
		Pakistan	2.30	Tunisia	3.91	Senegal	2.66	Burkina Faso	3.05
		Morocco	1.83	Morocco	3.32	Bangladesh	2.61	Bolivia	2.94
		Chile	1.66	China	2.44	Somalia	2.11	Tunisia	2.93
		Turkey	1.64	Niger	2.38	Kenya	2.00	Ethiopia	2.81
		India	1.20	Côte d'Ivoire	2.35	Tunisia	1.95	Kenya	2.72
Total	100	Total	94.24	Total	78.07	Total	64.92	Total	47.42

Table 7.2b Top aid recipients over time: Italy

Italy	1960		1970		1980		1990		2000	
Egypt	72.18	Indonesia	31.23	Somalia	57.70	Ethiopia	9.26	Uganda	24.71
Somalia	12.75	Egypt	23.76	Ethiopia	15.75	Zaire	7.94	Bosnia & Herzegovina	9.93
Ethiopia	7.31	Ethiopia	15.06	Libya	14.76	Somalia	6.09	Cameroon	8.12
Yugoslavia	4.71	Mexico	12.01	Indonesia	6.90	Mozambique	5.81	Ethiopia	7.82
India	3.53	Guinea	9.34	Mozambique	6.71	Tanzania	5.79	Zambia	7.23
Brazil	2.77	India	9.24	Zimbabwe	5.63	Egypt	4.74	Malta	6.27
Turkey	0.91	Tanzania	8.30	Thailand	4.28	Argentina	4.49	Yugoslavia	5.87
Chile	0.38	Somalia	8.14	Bangladesh	2.47	Peru	4.41	Honduras	5.74
Sudan	0.21	Sri Lanka	6.69	Brazil	2.47	Tunisia	3.57	Benin	5.74
Iran	0.12	Syria	3.99	Mexico	2.45	Kenya	2.93	Eritrea	5.60
Total	104.9	Total	127.8	Total	119.1	Total	55.05	Total	87.03

Table 7.2c Top aid recipients over time: The Netherlands

Netherlands	1960		1970		1980		1990		2000
Indonesia	88.31	Indonesia	34.06	India	13.29	Indonesia	11.92	Indonesia	11.90
Suriname	35.48	NL Antilles	17.59	NL Antilles	7.97	India	9.31	Tanzania	8.04
Chile	0.81	Suriname	16.40	Indonesia	7.84	Tanzania	5.93	Yugoslavia	5.91
NL Antilles	0.40	India	11.32	Tanzania	7.64	Bangladesh	4.48	Mozambique	5.10
		Pakistan	3.07	Suriname	6.95	Kenya	4.20	Zambia	4.23
		Chile	1.65	Bangladesh	4.88	Sudan	3.92	Uganda	3.58
		Nigeria	1.60	Kenya	4.36	NL Antilles	3.32	Bosnia & Herzegovina	3.58
		Kenya	1.31	Sudan	4.19	Suriname	2.85	Mali	3.51
		Colombia	1.04	Jamaica	3.15	Egypt	2.78	Yemen	2.85
		Tanzania	0.96	Peru	3.15	Zambia	2.70	Bolivia	2.75
Total	125	Total	89	Total	63.42	Total	51.42	Total	51.44

Table 7.2d Top aid recipients over time: Norway

Norway	1960		1970		1980		1990		2000
India	59.83	Pakistan	21.67	Tanzania	18.36	Tanzania	17.96	Yugoslavia	10.98
Korea	43.17	India	18.34	Bangladesh	9.74	Zambia	9.65	Mozambique	5.87
		Kenya	18.06	India	9.30	Mozambique	9.12	Tanzania	5.40
		Tanzania	9.84	Kenya	8.75	Bangladesh	7.67	Bosnia & Herzegovina	4.73
		Uganda	6.94	Pakistan	6.84	Nicaragua	6.12	Palestinian AA	4.29
		Zambia	4.89	Botswana	5.32	Ethiopia	4.45	Zambia	3.81
		Nigeria	3.61	Sri Lanka	4.74	India	4.37	Ethiopia	3.62
		Turkey	3.54	Turkey	4.46	Zimbabwe	4.21	Uganda	3.23
		Tunisia	2.05	Zambia	4.38	Sri Lanka	3.93	Somalia	3.09
		Madagascar	1.35	Mozambique	4.37	Kenya	3.93	Bangladesh	2.82
Total	100	Total	90.3	Total	76.26	Total	71.4	Total	47.85

Norway's total ODA each, nineteen more received between 0.025% and 0.1%, and seventeen countries received less than 0.025% (1/40 of 1%).[9] Not surprisingly, the countries at the bottom of these lists are rarely the subject of explicit deliberation, whether within the aid administration or in broader public debates. Indeed, as I argue below, the size of the flows to these countries is likely to reflect the cost of one or two 'token' projects sponsored there, rather than any explicit decision regarding the amount that different recipients ought to receive.

Aid frames and the recipient selection process

Table 7.3 combines the hypotheses from Chapter 2 with the information about frame salience presented in Chapter 3. In Belgium's case, given the salience of the obligation frame in the aid discourse, we can predict that aid flows will privilege former colonies, important trading partners and, to a lesser degree, countries that are popular targets of other donors. The dominant position of the wealth frame only serves to increase the predicted importance of commercial connections, and perhaps of the economic potential of recipient states. Congo/Zaire can be expected to be particularly important since it was a former colony, a major trading partner, *and* a country of considerable economic potential. Finally, the importance of the obligation frame also means that we expect aid allocations across recipients to remain relatively stable over time.

In Italy, as in Belgium, we expect to see aid flows targeted primarily at important trading partners and at states that have the potential to join that category. The salience of reputation should make prominent aid recipients attractive. The concern with enlightened self-interest and power during the late 1970s, finally, should result in an emphasis on large and unstable states, as well as in more widely dispersed aid. The importance of the power frame in the Netherlands leads to the expectation that former colonies will be favoured, along

---

[9] Nor is the pattern much different for other donors. Even Italy, in the throes of severe budget cutbacks, and with a degree of aid concentration on its top recipients considerably higher than that of the other three states considered here, gave aid to a total of eighty-one countries in 1997 (twenty-five received more than 1%, thirty-two 0.1–1%, twelve 0.025–0.1%, and twelve less than 0.025%).

Table 7.3 *Hypotheses about the relationship between frames and aid distribution*

Category	Salient when?	Recipient choice based on ...
Security	**Belgium** around 1960, around 1990 **Italy** 1960s **Netherlands** mid 1950s to 1960s **Norway** around 1960s	UN voting agreement, regime-type and location
Power	**Italy** late 1970s to early 1980s **Netherlands** throughout **Norway** mid 1990s	GDP, UN voting agreement, population, colonial status
Wealth	**Belgium** throughout early 1970s, 1980s **Italy** throughout 1990	Trade with recipient, GDP
Enlightened self-interest	**Belgium** mid 1980s, mid 1990s **Italy** late 1970s to 1980s, late 1990s **Netherlands** late 1980s to 1990s **Norway** around 1970, late 1980s, late 1990s	Population, stability, area
Reputation	**Belgium** second half of 1990s **Italy** throughout 1960, 1990s **Norway** 1960s, mid 1980s to mid 1990s	UN voting agreement, share of world aid receipts
Obligation	**Belgium** throughout, with occasional minor dips **Italy** early 1970s **Netherlands** 1970s (but emerging by mid 1960s) **Norway** mid 1960s throughout 1980	Total aid receipts, colonial status, trade with recipient
Humanitarianism	**Belgium** early 1990s **Netherlands** from mid 1970s **Norway** from early 1970s	GDP/capita, mortality, literacy, political and civil rights

with politically visible LDCs. The rising influence of humanitarianism from the mid 1970s leads us to expect that aid will become more widely dispersed from that time forward, and that a concern with the domestic conditions in recipient states will become more important.

Given the above-average importance of enlightened self-interest in Norway, we would expect the country to prioritize unstable and high-population states. During the 1960s and 1970s, the obligation frame predicts an emphasis on important trading partners. From 1970 humanitarianism takes over, and the poorest states should be favoured, as should those with relatively good governance. The interest in reputation throughout the early 1960s and again from the mid 1980s to the mid 1990s suggests that popular aid recipients will be targeted during those periods. Finally, the interest in power in the 1990s would suggest a greater interest in large states with economic potential. The salience of both enlightened self-interest and humanitarianism suggests that aid will be widely dispersed among recipients.

Belgium: cultural affinity and economic promise

Belgian bilateral aid initially focused on its former territories Congo, Rwanda and Burundi. Indeed, in 1960 and 1961 these were the only three countries receiving bilateral aid. In 1962, Brazil received a one-time commitment of US$2 million, equal to about 3 per cent of Belgian bilateral aid that year. Some other countries became regular recipients from 1963 on. The focus on the former colonies is in line with the importance of obligation as a motivation for aid among Belgian decision-makers. As Minister Scheyven noted, 'we provide aid specifically to three countries where we have moral and prior obligations: Congo, our former colony; Rwanda and Burundi, our former trust territories'.[10] Not until 1968 did aid to these three drop below 90 per cent of total bilateral aid.[11]

---

[10] *Kamer Documenten* 1969–70, nr 4-VIII, nr 5:10. See also a similar comment by Minister Brasseur some years earlier: *Parlementaire Handelingen*, 14 January 1964: 20.

[11] Even the selection of additional recipient countries occurred in the shadow of relations with Zaire. For example, Tunisia and Morocco were added in the mid 1960s because they were willing to accommodate Belgian development workers who had been active as teachers in Zaire but had left that country when its relations with Belgium became strained. *Parlementaire Handelingen*, 24 March 1971: 1199.

By 1972, a total of fifteen aid treaties had been signed with individual developing countries. Throughout this time, Zaire never received less than 50 per cent of total bilateral aid, even though it signed its own treaty only in 1968. Indeed, in Belgium, as in most donor states, aid flows often preceded – or proceeded independently of – officially negotiated aid treaties. For example, Turkey was the fourth ranked recipient for much of the 1960s, with no treaty in sight. Official criteria for entering into a formal development assistance relationship with a country closely reflected the Belgian aid discourse, with its joint emphasis on obligation and economic interest. They included 1) the presence of historical ties; 2) a desire to orient activities towards Latin America (an economically more advanced, and thus more promising, region than Africa); 3) the presence of Belgian development workers (including former colonial civil servants); and 4) Belgium's general desire to aid countries of above-average (economic) interest.[12]

The relative continuity from year to year in the distribution of aid flows is in line with our expectations for aid inspired by a sense of obligation. It also suggests, once again, that the political orientation of governments was not very influential, at least not in removing countries from the list or in adjusting their relative importance. By the late 1960s, Flemish groups became increasingly irritated at the enduring francophone bias in Belgium's aid programme. In part to placate the Flemish, the government added Indonesia, a former Dutch colony, as another target country in 1969. Minister Scheyven pointed out that 'the Dutch-language community would be able to find an opportunity for expression and original initiative there. This would nullify the argument that one of our two national communities is prevented from presenting itself internationally'.[13]

---

[12] Belgium, *Hulp door België verleend aan de ontwikkelingslanden, 1962–1963*, 8.

[13] Cited in Senate Committee Report 1969 nr 199:10. Most francophone representatives supported the initiative, agreeing that 'it is important to create a "neerlandophonie"' (Representative Bertrand. *Parlementaire Handelingen Senaat*, 6 March 1969: 501). The Flemish, on the other hand, were mostly insulted: 'I can assure you, Mr Minister, that the Flemish who wish to work in developing countries – and this in contrast to very many French speakers – speak more than one international language' (Representative Dewulf. *Parlementaire Handelingen*, 4 March 1969: 5). Many also suspected that Indonesia was actually added for economic reasons rather than to placate the Flemish. See Senator Bogaert's contribution, *Parlementaire Handelingen Senaat*, 24 March 1971: 1187.

Crises in Zaire during 1977–8 scared many Belgian firms out of their dependence on a single supplier of raw materials.[14] Zaire's reduced appeal to private economic interests was matched by a declining sense of obligation towards Mobutu's reprehensible regime. As a result, the dominance of Zaire within Belgium's development programme finally began to decline. By the end of the 1980s, the country accounted for 'only' 16 per cent of bilateral allocations.

Meanwhile, explicit references to economic interests in the selection of target countries continued unabated. For example, the government declared in 1984 that 'we have decided to initiate activities with respect to Gabon, a rich and promising country where we, oddly enough, had not yet established a presence'.[15] Such initiatives illustrate the difficulties of establishing the direction of causation between commercial ties and aid flows: aid may be used to develop new trade relations just as easily as trade relations may serve to increase a country's aid receipts. In fact, it was standard practice in Belgium to send an economic mission to a country prior to the signing of a new bilateral aid contract, 'to see whether there [were] any economic payoffs worth pursuing there'.[16] Almost all top aid recipients also conducted a considerable amount of trade with Belgium. For much of the 1980s, for example, there was rarely more than one country among the top-ten recipients whose imports from Belgium did not exceed its aid receipts by a factor of four or five.[17]

By the late 1980s, criteria for the selection of target recipients began to change, as first humanitarianism, and then enlightened self-interest and reputation became more important frames. In 1990, the government proposed a focus on the poorest states while continuing

---

[14] S. Marijsse and J. Debar, *Belgisch-Zaïrese economische relaties: Het effect van de Belgische tewerkstelling*. Nevertheless, many legislators still considered Zaire an 'attractive target' (Representative Colla, *Parlementaire Handelingen*, 17 May 1978: 2071).

[15] Guillot-Pingue, Chief of Staff for Development Cooperation under State Secretary Mayence-Goossens. Cited in Vaes, 'Het officiële Belgische beleid', 189.

[16] *Ibid.*, 495. Perhaps not surprisingly, Belgian exports to Gabon quadrupled between 1982 (when it first became an official target country) and 1986, while aid levels remained more or less steady.

[17] For many of the top recipients the ratio is closer to 10:1. In 1985, for example, the only exception was Bangladesh, which received nearly as much aid as it imported from Belgium.

Aid frames and the recipient selection process 185

to prioritize those countries with which Belgium had historical ties. Three years later, standards of living and human rights had become even more prominent in the list of published selection criteria. In addition, as the salience of humanitarianism and enlightened self-interest would predict, Belgium's aid became more widely and evenly dispersed. By 1994, the list of target recipients had expanded to include 114 countries![18] Nevertheless, the 'objective' criterion of existing historical and economic ties with recipients continued to play an important role.[19]

Both the selection of countries and the dispersion of aid in Belgium thus correspond to our general predictions. Economic interests – associated with the wealth and obligation frames alike – were dominant throughout. In addition, the strength of the obligation frame ensured that the emphasis on Belgium's former colonies remained considerable, even when other donor states had begun to phase out similar priorities.

Italy: post-colonial and regional interests

The marginal nature of Italy's aid policy throughout the 1970s is reflected in the lack of legislative and public discussion of the geographical allocation of aid flows. However, most legislators generally approved of a strong emphasis on the Mediterranean, on former colonies, and on areas where Italian colonists had settled. Particularly favoured were Somalia, Ethiopia, Libya and Argentina.[20] The degree to which Italy's early bilateral aid was shaped by export credits not targeted at any specific country is evident from the wide dispersion of that aid. In 1960, when most other donor states were still targeting their aid at a few priority recipients, thirty-seven countries received aid from Italy. Of those, nineteen received the minimum recorded by DAC ($10,000), suggesting that the money was used to support just a single export project. In addition, more than is the case for most other donors, the relative ranking of recipients fluctuated dramatically.

---

[18] OECD, *Development co-operation review series: Belgium*, 8.
[19] *Kamer Documents* 1992–3 nr 1164/13, 23 September 1993: 4.
[20] The government itself noted in its memorandum to the DAC in 1965: 'Italy is not, and does not consider herself, a global power. Hence, Italy concentrates its efforts in those regions where both historically and economically it has the biggest stakes.' Italy, *Examen annuel de l'aide, 1965*, 21.

Often, states jumped into the top ten when they received an important aid credit, only to disappear out of the top twenty-five the following year. For example, Egypt received 88 per cent of Italy's bilateral aid in 1960, nothing in 1961 or 1962, and 13 per cent in 1963 (making it the fourth recipient that year).

The two dominant aid recipients during the 1960s were Yugoslavia and Egypt. The former was important for the security and wealth frames alike, as it was both a socialist state on Italy's borders and a trading partner of considerable importance. It received about 30 per cent of Italy's aid, on average, during the early 1960s. In 1970, the top-four recipients were Indonesia, Egypt, Ethiopia and Mexico. Among these, only Ethiopia was one of the least developed countries, but it was also a major consumer of Italy's exports. The other three were among the more advanced LDCs, of considerable economic interest to Italian firms. Moreover, they were internationally prominent, and thus helped increase the visibility of Italy's aid efforts, in line with predictions deriving from the salience of the reputation frame. Indeed, aid distribution patterns throughout the early 1970s confirm our prediction that recipients would be selected primarily from among important trading partners and large, visible and popular LDCs.

We also predicted that aid would be particularly dispersed from the mid 1970s to the mid 1980s, as a result of the increased salience of the enlightened self-interest frame. If we count how many LDCs receive more than token amounts of aid,[21] we find the predicted increase over the course of the 1970s and early 1980s. There were thirty-seven such countries in 1970 and eighty-four in 1985. After that, enlightened self-interest fell in salience again, and the figure remained more or less constant for the next ten years.

The government continued to resist pressures to draw up an explicit list of recipients on which to concentrate aid during the early 1980s, hoping to maximize its freedom to follow changing economic interests. However, it finally did produce an official list of target countries in 1983,[22] in order to increase Italy's standing and influence within the aid community. The administration declared that it would favour as recipients countries that were 'problem states'; in particular those

---

[21] Token amounts are here defined as 0.025 per cent of total bilateral aid or less.
[22] Censis, *Libro bianco sulla cooperazione allo sviluppo, 1981–1984*.

that were both very poor and of interest to Italy economically or politically. However, its 'A-list' of states contained very few of the poorest 'problem' LDCs, although it did feature some of the most visible of the poorer LDCs, including Tanzania, Sudan and Angola.

More noticeable were a number of states of considerable interest to Italian exporters, such as Colombia, Ecuador and Jordan. On the whole, the list appeared primarily to serve as a rationalization of existing patterns. This was hardly surprising, since the wealth frame continued to dominate the aid discourse over the course of the 1980s. In fact, the share of bilateral aid allocated to those LDCs that were of the greatest commercial interest increased from about 20 per cent to about 35 per cent. As one study concluded: '[D]evelopment cooperation was considered as the driving force for all economic policy instruments towards developing countries.'[23]

In the early 1990s, Yugoslavia and its successor republics once more became important targets, a logical development given the fact that they were both important trading partners and a source of instability and refugees right on Italy's border. Indeed, the top seven source countries for immigrants and refugees all became official target countries for aid, and all repeatedly appeared near the top of the list of aid recipients. Their combined share of bilateral aid increased from 10% in 1983 to 17% in 1990, 23% in 1991 and 34% in 1992.[24] Finally, the 1990s also saw the power frame increase in salience again. As a result, Mediterranean recipients were prioritized, including the former Yugoslavia and Albania as well as Morocco, Tunisia, Egypt, Jordan and Turkey.

Over the years, the forces driving Italy's aid allocation have remained remarkably constant. Drastic changes in the list of most favoured recipients from year to year reflected an emphasis on funding individual projects rather than establishing an ongoing relationship with recipient governments. Important trading partners, countries where Italy's prestige was high,[25] and internationally visible countries

---

[23] Rhi-Sausi *et al.*, 'Italian bilateral aid policy', 3.
[24] *Ibid.*, 5.
[25] Indeed, one factor contributing strongly to the public disillusionment with Italy's aid policy in the 1990s was the extraordinarily hostile reception Italian troops received during the UN operation in Somalia. The Italian government had long claimed that Somalis viewed Italy as the most valued and admired of the industrialized states. Instead, it turned out to be the most widely despised. R. Fabiano, 'Avete sbagliato per venticinque anni'; see e.g. C. Valentini, 'Zero in diplomazia'.

were prioritized. Finally, regional considerations – including a concern with actual and potential refugee flows – implied a preference for Mediterranean states that dovetailed nicely with the commercial importance of these states.

The Netherlands: different ways to pursue influence

Dutch development aid was primarily a (post-) colonial proposition throughout the early 1960s. During the 1950s, between one-half and two-thirds of all aid went to Suriname, the Netherlands Antilles and Netherlands New Guinea. Indonesia, a state with enormous economic potential, benefited less, but this was by choice. Its independence struggle had been bitter, and it was reluctant to accept closer cooperation with its former ruler. By the early 1960s, however, Dutch aid initiatives began to broaden in scope.

Though the initial selection of countries to receive bilateral aid from the Netherlands has been termed 'arbitrary' by some,[26] it was decidedly more systematic than in Italy. Starting in the mid 1960s, the government began to put the choice of recipient countries on a more formal footing. Preliminary criteria for recipient selection were outlined in 1965: 'those countries where a suitable economic infrastructure is present' and where Dutch private industries were attempting to establish themselves.[27] The first official list of recipient countries was finalized in 1968, based on criteria including historical ties, development levels, existing aid relations and economic relations between the Netherlands and the recipient. Domestic groups almost immediately began to press for changes to this official list. Chile was added under pressure from Christian Democrats eager to support Frei's Christian Democratic regime. The Departments of Agriculture and Economic Affairs wanted to include at least one Middle Eastern state. Justice and Education, in contrast, were interested in including source countries

---

[26] Representative Ruygers in the 1969 aid debate: '[T]he selection [of target recipients] is a formalization of past, more or less accidental developments rather than a future-oriented vision of the best possible Dutch contribution to the cooperation with developing countries' (*Handelingen*, 12 June 1969: 3223). Cf. also the statement by Minister Bukman regarding recipient selection in the 1988 budget debates (*Handelingen*, 25 November 1987: 26–1266).

[27] Official government criteria, quoted in Hoebink, 'Geven is nemen', 54.

Aid frames and the recipient selection process 189

of migrant workers, apparently in hopes of being able to shift some of their expenditures to the development cooperation budget.[28]

In subsequent legislative debates, the Development Minister highlighted several additional criteria for selection, all following logically from considerations associated with the power frame: the economic size of the recipients, their language, a desire to have a recipient on every continent, privileging recipients targeted by other donors as well, and the political implications of the choice.[29] Despite the increasing formalization of selection criteria, however, established aid patterns were slow to change. In 1968, Indonesia, the Netherlands Antilles and Suriname still received 56% of Dutch bilateral aid; of the nine other official target recipients, only India, Pakistan and Nigeria received more than 1%. Interestingly, Turkey, not an official target until 1972 but a prominent source of migrant workers, received 5.8% in 1968, trailing only India among recipients without colonial ties to the Netherlands.

From the mid 1970s, humanitarianism became a salient part of the aid discourse, and Minister Pronk took pains to emphasize that 'economic relations do not affect the selection of recipients'.[30] Instead, he announced three criteria for selection: poverty, the actual need for foreign aid, and the extent to which the recipient's domestic policies improved the conditions of the poorest groups in society.[31] One of the most significant changes evident during Pronk's tenure was a considerable increase in the share of aid allocated to the least developed countries (LLDCs), which jumped from 7.5% of bilateral ODA in 1972 and 1973 to 15.8% the next year, and continued growing to almost 35% by 1978.

Symbolic and political considerations inspired by the power frame continued to play a role in recipient selection as well. Two countries that failed to meet the poverty criterion but had socialist, populist governments, Cuba and Jamaica, were added for political reasons (analogous to Chile's case earlier). Egypt, Sudan and North Yemen were selected to ensure a presence in the Middle East, and Upper Volta was added to include at least one French-speaking country. All these exceptions suggest that the influence of the official criteria was

[28] *Ibid.*, 54–5.
[29] Minister Boertien, *Handelingen*, 30 November 1971: 1402–3.
[30] Quoted in Hoebink, 'Geven is nemen', 59.
[31] Netherlands, *Bilaterale ontwikkelingssamenwerking*, 13–14.

less than that of the composite frame for aid, in which the influence frame was salient.[32]

During the 1980s, this same frame inspired an interest in taking the lead in implementing new international priorities such as democratic governance and emergency aid. As a result, in 1987, the list of target countries was expanded by fourteen LDCs that were suffering from particular emergencies or were tenuous 'young democracies', such as the Philippines. In other words, although our predictions for the power frame, as shown in Table 6.2, suggest concentration of aid on a few recipients, the Dutch interest in being present in all new initiatives actually had the opposite effect. This trend was reinforced by the growing salience of the humanitarian frame, which increased pressures to disperse aid ever more widely. It continued in the 1990s, with Pronk's return as Minister of Development Cooperation. Pronk resisted pressures to cut aid to countries with oppressive regimes, arguing that: 'It is important that we talk for as long as possible with countries with which we have established a long-term development cooperation relationship, in order to exercise an influence over their policy.'[33] This interest in influence required a substantial presence in as many LDCs as possible.

Pronk was succeeded in 1998 by Herfkens, whose stated main goal was a drastic reduction in the number of countries receiving substantial aid, to no more than twenty. However, she had trouble terminating aid to the poorest countries, given the salience of humanitarianism in the aid discourse. Since the power frame fits better with concentrated aid flows, Herfkens drew on its renewed salience in the late 1990s to defend her initiatives.[34] At the turn of the millennium, then, the two dominant themes in the Dutch aid discourse, power and humanitarianism, continued to shape the geographical distribution of aid.

However, the Dutch case also illustrates how the translation of these frames into policy choices can vary over time, depending on the

[32] See also Pronk's comments in the 1975 aid debate, *Handelingen*, 4 March 1975: 3197.
[33] Committee debate on *A World of Difference, Handelingen* UCV 22, 10 December 1990: 22–30. Not all countries welcomed Dutch attempts to exercise influence: as noted earlier, Indonesia terminated its aid relationship with the Netherlands in 1992, out of dissatisfaction with Pronk's continual criticism of its domestic human rights policies.
[34] See interviews with Herfkens in the *Volkskrant*, 31 October 1998, and in *Vrij Nederland*, 25 December 1999.

Aid frames and the recipient selection process 191

international context and on specific causal beliefs. Whereas Pronk emphasized influence through widespread presence and leadership in international initiatives, Herfkens aimed to maximize Dutch influence in a limited number of countries with which the Netherlands had long-standing relationships. Both, however, continuously emphasized the importance of humanitarian goals and initiatives, and both encountered problems suspending aid to the neediest LDCs, even when the salient power frame might have suggested doing so.

Norway: concentration or dispersion?

Norway's first bilateral aid recipient was India. It was a natural choice, as one of the first colonies to obtain independence after the Second World War. The other early aid project in which Norway was involved was a field hospital during the war in Korea, a joint Nordic effort whose appeal was due in part to the relative strength of the security frame at the time.[35] Throughout 1961, these two countries were Norway's only bilateral aid recipients. Both were also popular targets for other DAC countries, and it helped that they were of some economic interest to Norway. In the early 1960s, the government established an informal guideline for the concentration of bilateral aid on the Indian subcontinent and on Eastern Africa. Four East African countries were added to the recipient list over the course of the 1960s: Kenya, Tanzania, Uganda and Zambia. The choice of these countries appears to have been based on their regional propinquity, efforts at regional cooperation (which mirrored those among the Nordic states), and the fact that they spoke English, which facilitated communications. These priorities also explain the quotation opening the chapter, in which a legislator opposed adding a country that did not meet any of those criteria.[36]

Actual aid flows did not match this neat, concentrated picture, however. As was the case with other donor states, official recipient lists provide only part of the story. For example, in 1963 Algeria – not officially a target country – was the third most important aid

---

[35] Simensen, *Norsk utviklingshjelps historie*.
[36] For additional discussion of the considerations that entered into the selection of recipient countries, see H. Ø. Pharo, 'Reluctance, enthusiasm and indulgence: The expansion of bilateral Norwegian aid', 66–71; Ruud and Kjerland, *Norsk utviklingshjelps historie*, 229–59.

recipient, before Tanzania. By the next year, nineteen different countries received bilateral aid from Norway, and Turkey was now the third most important recipient. Five years later, in 1969, Nigeria was the second most important aid recipient, with 16.9 per cent of Norway's bilateral aid. In keeping with the prediction associated with the obligation frame that was salient at the time, all of these were of interest as trading partners.

The salience of the enlightened self-interest frame, and its emphasis on international (in)stability, led to a number of controversial recipient choices around 1970, as the government began aiding liberation movements in Southern Africa. Frelimo in Mozambique, the MPLA in Angola, and the PAIGC in Guinea Bissau and the Cape Verde Islands all received aid, even though this brought Norway into indirect conflict with NATO partner Portugal. Botswana was added to the list in 1972, 'to help it better to become independent from the domination of South Africa'.[37] In addition, the government supported liberation movements in Rhodesia, Namibia and South Africa. Despite the potential for controversy, the policy gained the support of most Norwegians, because it could be defended in terms of enlightened self-interest as well as humanitarianism.[38] The enlightened self-interest frame also inspired an emphasis on large, high-population states, reflected in the fact that the top two recipients in 1970 were India and Pakistan. The recipients that followed were smaller, but we have to go down to twentieth place to find a country with fewer than four million inhabitants. Even excluding India, the preceding eighteen countries had an average population of twenty-three million.

The government published specific criteria for the selection of aid recipients in 1972: first, status as one of the least developed countries (LLDCs), and second, the degree to which recipient governments followed a 'development-oriented and socially just policy ... especially for the worst-off groups of the population'. In addition, the government felt success required a stable, long-term relationship, even if serious political changes took place in the recipient state.[39] As a result, countries were rarely dropped from the list of recipients, a pattern

---

[37] Norway, *Stortingsmelding nr. 71*, 36.
[38] Norway, *Holdninger til Norsk utviklingshjelp 1974*; Norway, *Holdninger til Norsk utviklingshjelp 1977*.
[39] Norway, *Stortingsmelding nr. 29*, 22.

Aid frames and the recipient selection process 193

we encountered in Belgium and the Netherlands as well. In 1976, the two criteria were combined, and the government envisioned selecting those LLDCs 'following a development-oriented and socially just policy'.[40]

With the exception of Botswana, which was relatively well-off and remained a favoured recipient, the 1970s brought a humanitarianism-induced pattern of richer countries slowly moving down the list, diminishing in importance over time. Indeed, by 1985 the number of not-so-poor countries near the top was decidedly smaller than had been the case ten years earlier, with Pakistan falling to tenth place, whereas very poor countries such as Mozambique and Ethiopia had attained prominent positions in the top ten. In addition, from the mid 1980s the reputation frame produced an emphasis once again on large recipient countries. Thus, in 1985, most of the top recipients were quite large, with India in second place. Compared to 1970, however, smaller countries had moved up the list: Botswana, a country with a mere one million inhabitants, was in eighth place. Nonetheless, even excluding India, the average population for the other top nine countries was thirty-three million.

By the 1980s, aid had become dispersed across well over 100 recipients, a trend driven by the strength of the humanitarian frame. In fact, the number of countries receiving more than 0.025 per cent of Norway's bilateral aid rose over time from forty in 1975, to sixty-nine in 1985 and eighty in 1995. Dispersion thus increased considerably, as the salience of the humanitarian frame would predict. Still, the top-ten recipients of Norwegian bilateral aid in 1985 received an average of 1.7 per cent of total DAC aid, considerably more than one would expect in the absence of a preference for popular recipients. This suggests that reputational considerations continued to matter.

Comparing the four countries, several patterns emerge. First, in most countries it was easier to get added to the list of target recipients than to be taken off. Moreover, the motivations for adding or removing recipient states were clearly associated with the dominant themes in the aid discourse. In the Netherlands and Norway, humanitarian considerations such as per capita GDP and human rights concerns were the main reasons for taking such steps. In Belgium and Italy,

---

[40] Norway, *Innstilling S. nr. 192*, 3–6.

on the other hand, economic interests were more important. Second, political parties had at best a limited impact on geographical distribution. As I have argued repeatedly, this is because changes in political party strength were rarely accompanied by substantial shifts in the aid discourse. Given the constraining power of composite frames for aid, parties often were unable to introduce changes even had they wanted to do so. Moreover, even when official lists were adjusted to reflect party preferences, actual aid flows largely remained in line with the main themes of the aid discourse. A third finding is that the publication of official selection criteria and target lists was accelerated where humanitarianism, and to a lesser degree enlightened self-interest, were strong. Conversely, it was delayed where the wealth frame was strong, most notably in Italy.

Finally, we observed higher levels of aid dispersion than predicted in both Belgium and Italy, even though humanitarianism and enlightened self-interest were comparatively unimportant. This pattern was driven by the wealth frame. Since the aid administration in both countries was highly responsive to private industry, a newly independent country often received aid as soon as a domestic company became interested in a project in that country. However, the resulting dispersion was of a different nature than that in the Netherlands and Norway, as was especially evident in Italy. Dispersion inspired by humanitarian considerations was associated with relative stability from year to year in aid allocations; when driven by economic interests, however, it was associated with significant fluctuations over time, as projects in different countries started and finished.

A quantitative analysis of frames and aid allocation

The preceding section discussed how the main frames in the aid discourse in each country shaped patterns in the geographical distribution of aid flows. We saw that each donor state provides aid to a rather large number of recipients. Many of these are rarely explicitly discussed or even mentioned in legislative debates. It is worth examining, then, whether we can identify the factors that affect the selection of such less visible countries, as well as the decisions regarding the amount of aid they are to receive. In this section, I present a statistical model designed to answer these questions. Applied to the data on the geographical distribution of aid, it confirms the impact of the different aid frames on aid allocation patterns.

Statistical model

As noted at the start of the chapter, an extensive literature exists on the geographical allocation of development aid. Unfortunately, results often conflict, and the methodological validity – and hence the substantive results – of many are questionable. Many studies test separately for the influence of donor interests and recipient needs, introducing serious specification errors.[41] Others have considered only a specific subset of aid recipients (e.g. those from a particular region), without considering whether aid allocations to that subset are independent of those to other potential recipients.[42] With different studies taking different approaches, including different variables, and studying different cases, it is not surprising that the main conclusion of one recent survey of the field was a rather tepid 'not surprisingly, there is evidence that both [donor interests] *and* [recipient needs] play some role in the aid allocation by most donors'.[43]

Many aid allocation studies exclude countries receiving no aid at all. This means, however, that the first stage of the decision-making process is bypassed: we are no longer studying the geographical distribution of aid over all countries, but rather the distribution of aid over the subset that has *already* been selected to receive aid. Nonetheless, much of the aid literature has focused on this measure. In contrast, legislative debates on the geographical allocation of aid tend to concentrate on the *selection* of a limited number of states as target recipients, while distribution – the precise amount to be given to the each selected recipient – is rarely a bone of contention. In fact, empirical patterns suggest that each of these two decisions is significant: target recipients are selected first, and only then do donors decide how much each of those targets is to receive.

---

[41] E.g. Maizels and Nissanke, 'Motivations for aid'. A replication of this paper combining the two sets of variables suggests that its conclusions are tenuous at best (McGillivray and White, *Explanatory studies*, 38–9).
[42] E.g. Schraeder *et al.*, 'Clarifying the foreign aid puzzle'.
[43] E. Neumayer, *The pattern of aid giving: The impact of good governance on development assistance*, 20.

The group of countries receiving no aid at all is unlikely to be a random subset of all potential recipients. Hence, it is crucial to include them in our analysis. Since states cannot logically provide negative aid, it makes sense to treat aid receipts as a limited dependent variable truncated at zero.[44] It also seems likely that the decision whether or not to offer development assistance is correlated with the decision regarding the amount to provide. One possible model would be a Tobit estimator, which combines the selection and amount decisions into one. However, this approach imposes rather strong assumptions, requiring that the factors determining selection as a recipient are identical (and proportionally weighted) to those determining the amount of aid offered.[45] A better approach would be to model the two decisions as separate but correlated.[46] Lee and Maddala describe a two-equation model in this vein, using probit to model the selection decision, and a truncated linear regression to model the amount decision.[47] My model is derived from theirs.

As we saw earlier in the chapter, evidence suggests that a number of countries receive allocations that can best be described as token aid. These recipients do not warrant their own sections in the annual reports of a national aid administration, nor does the latter expend many administrative resources on the programme management of such aid flows. Instead, such flows may be associated with isolated diplomatic visits, or spring from a desire of the donor just to establish a 'presence' in the recipient. It appears likely that the exact sum allocated to such states will be less the result of an explicit decision by the

---

[44] Negative aid flows do get recorded on occasion, as a result of recipient state repayments on loans granted in previous years. However, such situations imply that the donor did not see fit to make a *net* allocation to the recipient, so it can be considered to have given zero aid.

[45] Cf. also Neumayer, *The pattern of aid*, 35.

[46] J. J. Heckman, 'The common structure of statistical models of truncation, sample selection and limited dependent variables and a sample estimator for such models'. See J. Meernik, E. L. Krueger and S. C. Poe, 'Testing models of U.S. foreign policy: Foreign aid during and after the Cold War', for an application of a Heckman model to US aid allocations.

[47] L.-F. Lee and G. S. Maddala, 'The common structure of tests for selectivity bias, serial correlation, heteroscedasticity and non-normality in the tobit model'. See also W. H. Greene, *Econometric analysis*, 706–14. M. McGillivray and E. Oczkowski ('A two-part sample selection model of British bilateral aid allocation') apply a slightly different version of this model to British aid flows.

donor than determined by the costs of the particular project(s) funded. Nevertheless, we can expect that donor states *do* distinguish between countries that deserve at least a token contribution, and those that do not. The decision to give token aid, then, lies on a continuum between no aid and substantial aid, suggesting the use of ordered probit. The introduction of a 'token aid' category is an innovation in the literature, and hence I derive a new estimator specific to the problem.

The second stage of the allocation decision concerns the amount of aid to provide to countries that have been selected to be recipients of substantial aid flows. This can be modelled using a truncated linear regression model. Rather than truncating at zero, however, truncation takes place at a level (T) below which aid is considered a 'token' contribution. One possible interpretation is that the donor state would never establish a substantial aid programme with a recipient unless it were planning to spend at least T.[48] In addition to the truncation at T, censoring takes place based on the first stage of the decision-making process. We observe the outcome of the amount decision only if the selection decision is to provide a substantial amount. Otherwise, we observe either 0 or a small, arbitrary amount below the threshold T. Given this formulation, we can derive the following log-likelihood function for maximum likelihood estimation:[49]

$$L = \sum_{i,y=0} \ln \Phi(-Z_i \gamma) + \sum_{i,y=1} \ln \left(\Phi(\tau - Z_i \gamma) - \Phi(-Z_i \gamma) \right) +$$

$$\sum_{i,y=2} \left\{ -\ln \sigma + \ln \Phi \left(\frac{Z_i \gamma - \tau - \rho J \left(\frac{w_i - x_i \beta}{\sigma} \right)}{\sqrt{(1 - \rho^2)}} \right) + \ln \varphi \left(\frac{w_i - x_i \beta}{\sigma} \right) - \ln \Phi \left(\frac{x_i \beta - T}{\sigma} \right) \right\}$$

Here z and x are the vectors of independent variables for the selection and amount decisions, respectively, and γ and β are their coefficients. σ is the standard deviation of the error term for the amount decision,

---

[48] One can think of it in terms of the administrative overhead of starting a new country programme. Such an additional cost is worth incurring only if the actual aid expenditure will be non-negligible.

[49] For the complete derivation of this function, see A. M. Van der Veen, 'Selecting the recipients of aid: A two-stage sample selection model'. Note that for the model to be identified it is important that there be a variable that affects the selection decision but not the amount decision, and which can be excluded from the estimation of the latter.

τ is the second ordered probit threshold (the first is set to 0), ρ is the correlation of the error terms between the two decisions, and T is the token threshold. Finally, φ and Φ are the standard univariate normal density and distribution functions, respectively, and J is the inverse normal distribution function. Maximum likelihood estimates are obtained by maximizing not only over the parameters for the selection and amount decisions (β and γ), but also over the three additional parameters: ρ, σ and τ.

Operationalization

To operationalize the quantity of aid received by a country, we need to take into account the fact that aid budgets rise and fall over time, independently of the characteristics of the recipient countries. Thus, an overall increase in a donor's aid budget may mean greater receipts for recipients across the board, regardless of any changes in their individual situations. With this in mind, I use the percentage of the donor's total bilateral aid disbursements received as the dependent variable. In addition, it stands to reason that many countries will receive relatively small aid shares, with just a few receiving a lot. Since we can expect a geometric distribution for the aid shares across recipients, I take the logarithm of the aid share to produce the actual dependent variable.

Turning next to the eligibility variable, the main issue to resolve is the choice of threshold for a token aid allocation. A reasonable choice seems to be an aid share of 0.025 per cent, which corresponds to roughly 1/25 of the amount each recipient would get if a donor were to divide its aid evenly across all potential aid recipients. Small though the amount might seem, a large number of countries receive only token aid by this standard. For example, in 1995 Belgium gave no aid to fifty-seven countries, token aid to forty, and substantial aid to eighty-five more. In other words, over one in five potential aid recipients received a share of less than 0.025 per cent each of Belgium's bilateral aid. In fact, the incidence of token aid donations has been increasing over time: they account for about 10 per cent of the entries in the entire dataset, but the figure has exceeded 15 per cent in recent years.

Finally, it is likely that the error terms in the equations will be correlated over time. Such a pattern may result from bureaucratic stickiness in budget allocations, for example, or from a prevalence

Table 7.4 *Independent variables that may affect the selection of aid recipients, with associated frames*

Variable	Measure	Frame
States encircling enemies	Dummy: border with Communist state	Security
Allied states, friendly regimes	UN voting agreement	Security, Influence, Reputation
Military/economic potential	GDP	Influence, Wealth
High-population states	Population	Influence, Reputation, Enlightened self-interest
Present or former colony	Dummy: former colony	Influence, Obligation
Exports to recipient	Exports	Wealth, Obligation
Imports from recipient	Imports	Wealth
Unstable states	Level of democracy	Enlightened self-interest
Environmental patrimony	Surface area	Enlightened self-interest
Popular and visible states	Share of total DAC aid receipts	Reputation, Obligation
Poverty	GDP per capita	Humanitarianism
Quality of health	Mortality rates, life expectancy	Humanitarianism
Quality of life	Illiteracy rates	Humanitarianism
Good governance	Civil and political rights	Humanitarianism

of multi-year aid projects. One solution would be not to include data from multiple years, but this would dramatically reduce the number of observations available for the statistical analysis. Instead, I include a lag of the dependent variable, which permits the pooling of data from multiple years.

Based on the general hypotheses listed in Table 7.3, I include a total of fifteen independent variables, some of which are associated with more than one frame, as shown in Table 7.4. Appendix C provides additional information about data sources and manipulations (including standardization). The quality of the data used is not always optimal, since reporting by developing countries tends to leave a lot to be desired. However, this problem does not hamper the present analysis; since we are studying the decision-making process of governments, our goal is to model the rules of thumb we expect them to apply, using the same data they have access to, regardless of the accuracy of these data.

Certain year-to-year changes in the variables do not affect the relative standing of different recipients. For example, economic growth generates a secular trend towards higher GDP per capita values and more international trade. Even logged, what was once a reasonably high GDP per capita might now seem low, and what once seemed like a significant amount of trade may now be almost negligible. Similarly, civil and political rights as well as the level of democracy have been on the rise in developing countries over the past few decades. However, there is no evidence to suggest that overall aid levels respond to greater injustice, better governance, or other global trends. In other words, it seems likely that donor states do not use such trends as an argument for increased (or reduced) aid. Instead, they appear to consider a recipient's position relative to other states. Accordingly, I standardize each of these variables on a year-by-year basis, over the universe of potential aid recipients (for details, see Appendix C).

Statistical analysis

The main results of the regression are shown in Table 7.5. A regression was run for each country individually as well as pooling the four countries together. For each specification, I systematically eliminated explanatory variables using a likelihood ratio test statistic. By reducing the number of estimated coefficients in a given model, this makes the results easier to interpret; more importantly, it permits the inclusion of additional observations (those with missing data for the eliminated variables but complete information for those remaining). Only three interacted variables were not statistically significant in any of the five analyses: Power × UN votes and Power × Population in the eligibility equation, and Wealth × GDP in the aid share equation.

Before analysing the substantive findings that emerge from Table 7.5, we first need to assess how well the interacted regressions perform overall. As discussed in the previous chapter, if my theoretical approach is correct, interacting measures of frame strength

Table 7.5a Selection: interacted regressions, all countries combined and each country separately

Eligibility	All	Belgium	Italy	Netherlands	Norway
Lag Dependent Variable	1.17 ***	1.02 ***	0.91***	1.18 ***	1.21***
Security * UN		2.23			
Security * Comm		−8.24 ***			
Power * GDP		14.01 ***			
Power * Colony				20.16**	
Wealth * GDP			1.88*		
Wealth * Exports	1.03***	−2.25 **			
Wealth * Imports	0.46**	0.75			
ESI * Population			−2.82***	−1.90***	3.13***
ESI * Democracy				0.75**	1.66***
ESI * Area			1.53***		
Reputation * Population	0.75***			3.85***	−1.39*
Reputation * UN					−1.10**
Reputation * DAC ODA	0.13***	0.24 ***	0.19	−15.33***	
Obligation * Colony	2.78*				
Obligation * DAC ODA		−0.14*			0.39**

Table 7.5a *(cont.)*

Eligibility	All	Belgium	Italy	Netherlands	Norway
Obligation * Exports		1.10*	1.21**		
Humanitarianism * GDP/cap.	−1.41***	−2.40***	−2.86***	−1.81***	−1.92***
Humanitarianism * Mortality	−0.61**	−1.35			
Humanitarianism * Literacy				0.70***	
Humanitarianism * Life Exp.	−0.56***	−2.83***			
Humanitarianism * Rights	−0.31***	−1.58***			
Constant	−0.49***	−0.21	−0.15	−0.28**	−0.72***

Significance levels: * < 0.1, ** < 0.05, *** < 0.01.

Table 7.5b *Aid share: interacted regressions, all countries combined and each country separately*

Aid share	All	Belgium	Italy	Netherlands	Norway
Lag Dependent Variable	0.30 ***	0.26 ***	0.12 ***	X	X
Security * UN	−1.81 *			−12.77 ***	
Security * Communism	4.64 ***			17.68 **	33.04 ***
Power * UN					11.58 **
Power * GDP		6.51 *	4.78		
Power * Population	2.33 ***				8.39 **
Power * Colony				14.62 ***	
Wealth * Exports	1.89 ***				
Wealth * Imports	−1.88 ***		−0.91	−2.55 **	−9.13 ***
ESI * Population				2.49 ***	−4.01 **
ESI * Democracy		−0.64	−0.79		1.54 *
ESI * Area	1.32 ***	2.30 ***	4.56 ***		2.09 *
Reputation * Population				3.62 ***	
Reputation * UN			0.79		−6.00 ***
Reputation * DAC ODA		0.44		0.65 ***	0.82 ***
Obligation * Colony	8.38 ***	9.27 ***	5.36 ***		
Obligation * DAC ODA	0.30 ***	0.44 ***	0.71 ***		
Obligation * Exports	2.66 ***	2.49 ***	8.59 ***	1.37 **	3.17 ***

Table 7.5b *(cont.)*

Aid share	All	Belgium	Italy	Netherlands	Norway
Humanitarianism * GDP/cap.	−2.16 ***	−2.60 ***	−3.86 ***	−1.46 ***	−2.73 ***
Humanitarianism * Mortality	−0.97 ***	0.97 *		−1.37 ***	−4.38 ***
Humanitarianism * Literacy		−0.02	0.27		−0.69 **
Humanitarianism * Life Exp.	−0.91 ***		1.35 **	−1.98 ***	−3.20 ***
Humanitarianism * Rights	−0.56	−0.88	−2.21	−1.33	0.30
Constant	−4.34	−4.19	−5.13	−5.82	−5.63 ***

Significance levels: * < 0.1, ** < 0.05, *** < 0.01.

A quantitative analysis of frames and aid allocation 205

Table 7.5c *Additional data: interacted regressions, all countries combined and each country separately*

	All	Belgium	Italy	Netherlands	Norway
Tau	−0.35***	−0.47***	−0.58***	−0.05	−0.53***
Sigma	0.34***	0.25***	0.38***	0.23***	0.40***
Rho	−0.73***	−0.33*	−0.42**	2.15***	0.88***
N	4964	973	974	976	824

Significance levels: * < 0.1, ** < 0.05, *** < 0.01.

with the relevant independent variables ought to increase the overall explanatory power of the model, as well as uncover patterns that would otherwise remain invisible. Both of these expectations are confirmed. For each of the five models, one or more patterns emerge in Table 7.5 involving variables that are not statistically significant if we run the corresponding uninteracted regressions.[50] For example, in the case of Belgium, UN voting agreement is important in the selection phase, but only when interacted with the security frame.

More importantly, the datasets used in this chapter are sufficiently large to compare the explanatory power of the interacted and uninteracted models directly. The most straightforward way to compare competing, non-nested specifications, given a specific model, is to generate a full specification including the variables of both models. The explanatory value of each of the competing specifications can then be assessed by way of a likelihood ratio test.[51] Quite often, this results in the conclusion that each specification provides at least some statistically significant explanatory leverage. Indeed, this turns out to be the case if we run a regression pooling all four countries. However, in the individual regressions, the interacted regression systematically contributes more explanatory power. Indeed, in the case of Belgium and the Netherlands, adding the uninteracted variables to the model provides no statistically significant additional explanatory power at all! In the

---

[50] In the interest of saving space, the results of these and other additional regressions are not presented here. They are available from the author upon request.
[51] R. Davidson and J. G. MacKinnon, *Estimation and inference in econometrics*, 381–8.

case of Italy, the added explanatory leverage is only slightly significant (one-tailed chi-squared probability of 0.06). Only in Norway do the plain variables contribute significantly (chi-squared probability 0.02). This constitutes strong support for the overall theoretical model.

Discussion

Table 7.5 is divided into three parts: the first shows the coefficient estimates for the eligibility (selection) decision, the second shows the estimates for the quantity (aid share) decision, and the third gives some auxiliary information for each regression. The results of these regressions underscore a number of the themes we encountered in the case studies, but they also bring to light several additional patterns. Almost all of the statistically significant coefficient estimates have the predicted sign, lending further support to the theoretical model. The few exceptions are discussed below.

Across all four countries, a salient wealth frame is associated with a preference for selecting aid recipients that are important trading partners (imports as well as exports). Interestingly, in the decision regarding the amount of aid a recipient receives, the sign on imports is negative, in the pooled analysis and in Italy, the Netherlands and Norway individually. Major sources of imports thus receive comparatively less aid. However, once one realizes that such developing countries are likely exporters of oil or minerals, this finding is not as surprising as it might seem at first.

As we predicted, a concern with reputation makes donors in general (and Belgium and Italy in particular) interested in selecting aid recipients that are popular aid targets for all OECD aid donors. Another strong pattern is that of generosity of support for former colonies; such countries receive far more aid than would otherwise be expected. Indeed, some of the largest estimated coefficients in Table 7.5 are those for Power * Colony (for the Netherlands) and Obligation * Colony (for Belgium and Italy). Humanitarian motivations also have the expected impact, in every single donor state. When the humanitarian frame is strong, donors demonstrate a preference for poorer countries (a negative coefficient for GDP/capita), as well as for countries with a lower life expectancy – such countries are comparatively worse off and hence in greater need. Taken as a whole, the data in Table 7.5 once again demonstrate the importance of non-material considerations as determinants of aid flows. The top part of each sub-table, where the security, power and wealth variables are listed, is clearly emptier than the bottom part of each sub-table, with reputation, obligation and humanitarianism.

In the selection (eligibility) phase, the only country where the security frame has any significance is Belgium. In the allocation (aid share) phase, the Netherlands and Norway appear too – indeed, when the security frame is salient, as it was in the early years of these aid programmes, sharing a border with a Communist country was a major advantage for a recipient of aid from one of these two countries. The influence frame is not particularly prominent, although it encourages the Netherlands to focus on its former colonies as aid recipients, while Norway privileges countries with large populations. The main patterns for the wealth frame have already been discussed. One puzzling finding here is for Belgium in the selection phase: the more Belgium exports to a developing country the less likely that country is to be selected as an aid recipient. As we saw earlier, this is a result of the deliberate Belgian policy of using aid as a way to create *new* export opportunities rather than to support existing exports.

The patterns for the enlightened self-interest frame are somewhat contradictory. This is almost certainly a result of the different ways in which enlightened self-interest can be interpreted (and is expressed in the coded debates). This frame makes both the Netherlands and Norway prefer democratic recipients, as one might expect. However, it also makes Norway more generous towards less populous countries. This puzzling finding may be associated with concerns about overpopulation, but that is not certain.

As we have already seen repeatedly, a concern with reputation makes Belgium and Italy, in particular, pay extra attention to the aid policies and programmes of other DAC countries. Interestingly, this pattern extends to the Netherlands and Norway too – not in the selection process, but in the decision about aid shares to be allotted. A concern with obligation also makes Belgium and Italy follow other DAC aid programmes more closely, but here the pattern is limited to those two countries only. All four countries, however, are more generous towards major export destinations when the obligation frame is salient. This is as predicted: if aid is seen simply as an obligation, many policy-makers will be inclined to use it to achieve other goals, such as export promotion.

Conclusion

The geographical distribution across recipient countries is the most widely studied dimension of foreign aid. This chapter investigated three different measures of this geographical distribution: the official choices of target recipients, the top recipients of actual aid flows, and the full spectrum of aid allocations, from the smallest to the largest sums. The case studies focused on the first two of these measures. Patterns in the selection of official targets, as well as in actual flows, agreed well with those predicted from the aid frames salient in each country.

In Belgium, the strength of the obligation frame translated into a strong emphasis on former colonies. At the same time, economic interests were dominant in the selection of new target recipients. In Italy, the dominance of the wealth frame was so strong that the country long avoided drawing up any list of target recipients at all. Instead, aid flows were largely determined by demand on the part of private firms, resulting in dramatic fluctuations from year to year in the relative rankings of different aid recipients. In the Netherlands, the power frame generated an interest in assuming a leadership position in new aid initiatives, as well as a desire to be present in as many LDCs as possible, so as to extend Dutch influence as widely as possible. The strength of the humanitarian frame ensured that the specific choice of initiatives and countries was shaped by humanitarian motivations. In Norway, finally, humanitarianism governed the selection of many aid targets, but the enlightened self-interest and reputation frames introduced a preference for disproportionately large and visible recipients.

The statistical analysis investigated the third measure of aid distribution. The analysis demonstrated that overall explanatory power increases when we interact measures of the strength of different frames with their associated variables. In addition, the interaction approach allowed us to uncover a number of patterns that would otherwise remain hidden. Both of these features were evident in Chapter 6 as well, but were attenuated there due to the smaller size of the dataset. The statistical analysis also indicated that the selection process of aid recipients is more idiosyncratic than the process of deciding how much aid to allocate to each of the selected countries, with fewer statistically significant coefficients for the first decision-making stage.

Conclusion

In substantive terms, the regressions underscored the connection between a preference for former colonies and the obligation frame, and they verified the humanitarian motivations underlying a preference for poor and needy recipient states. An interest in maximizing the visibility of aid by prioritizing popular aid recipients, associated with the reputation and obligation frames, was evident in several countries. The reputation frame also inspired a preference for states with large populations. Of course, not all patterns identified in the first part of the chapter emerged equally clearly in the statistical analysis, which cast a wider but simultaneously more superficial net. Nevertheless, the two parts of the chapter complemented one another well, with results that reaffirmed, one more time, the impact of aid frames on policy outcomes.

8 | Conclusion: frames and policy

The financial, political and emotional interests behind foreign aid will help to ensure that [the long list of] rationalizations [for aid] will persist and others will be put forward.

– Peter Bauer, *Reality and rhetoric*[1]

I do not have a model ... There are too many interacting variables to justify a model that would be both parsimonious and insightful.

– Carol Lancaster, *Foreign aid*[2]

Policy-making is rarely straightforward. No issue area stands alone, and multiple different goals and motivations may be relevant at any given time. Thus aid policy cannot be reduced simply to the expression of a 'moral vision',[3] nor to any particular 'national interest'.[4] It is, rather, governed by the interaction of many different frames for aid. As I have argued throughout this study, this makes it akin to a Swiss army knife: one tool, many functions. Or, as Italian legislator Grassi put it in 1995: aid is best seen simply as an 'instrument of which the large Western countries avail themselves today'. As such, even though Italians called into question one long-established frame for aid – economic self-interest – in the mid 1990s, Grassi argued that aid's value as an instrument for other frames implied a need to 'retain and safeguard our own development cooperation policy'.[5] At the same time, and contrary to the note of resignation that comes through in the quotation from Lancaster's valuable recent book on aid, this study has shown that it *is* in fact possible to develop a model that is both elegant and insightful, while remaining comparatively parsimonious.

---

[1] Bauer, *Reality and rhetoric*, 60.
[2] Lancaster, *Foreign aid*, 9.   [3] Lumsdaine, *Moral vision*.
[4] Hook, *National interest*.
[5] *III Commissione*, 22 February 1995: 284.

This concluding chapter is divided into three parts. The first section briefly reviews the material covered in the preceding chapters. Next, I provide some anecdotal evidence to demonstrate the relevance of the model to other aspects of aid policy as well as to the aid policy of other donor states. Finally, I suggest how the model might be applied to the analysis of other policy areas in foreign as well as domestic politics, and discuss the challenges inherent in applying a framework that requires measuring how decision-makers think about a particular policy.

Framing foreign aid

Foreign aid policy is often seen as puzzling because no single theoretical model has been successful in explaining the observed policy patterns. Numerous plausible explanations promise to explain individual pieces of the puzzle. Indeed, decision-makers themselves often call attention to both the breadth of possible goals and views associated with aid policy and the striking differences from one country to the next in terms of which goals are salient. Yet these various factors *can* be integrated into a single theoretical model. The theoretical framework adopted in this study is constructed on four claims. First, policy is shaped more by preferences than by structural constraints of various kinds, so we need to take preferences seriously.[6] Second, ideas matter for policy choices, and the ideas that matter most are frames, or ways of thinking about a particular policy area and its central purpose. Third, frames cannot be deduced simply from the socio-economic or political characteristics of policy-makers, their political parties or their country. They do not reduce to underlying variables; instead, if we are to understand policy choices, frames themselves need to be measured. Fourth, and finally, although the internal frames of individual policy-makers cannot be measured, records of policy debates among legislators provide a valuable proxy.

Analysing a variety of different aspects of aid policy from 1950–2000 in Belgium, Italy, the Netherlands and Norway abundantly demonstrates that a model built on these four claims does a better job of systematically explaining aid policy patterns than do prominent alternative models. To give but a few examples: the systematic impact

[6] Cf. Moravcsik, 'Taking preferences seriously'.

of political parties and government changes on aid policy has been minor at best. Richer states do not give more aid or privilege a noticeably different type of recipient state than do poorer states. Although smaller countries and consociational democracies do appear to be more generous donors, these correlations are weak and far from constant over time. Finally, there is little or no evidence that aid standards introduced by international institutions promote convergence in aid policies.[7]

The success of the empirical analyses is all the more gratifying given the fact that legislative debates provide a rather imperfect proxy for the true variable of interest: the composite aid frames in the minds of key decision-makers. Measuring the goals and preferences of particular individuals is fraught with difficulty, because we cannot (yet) identify the thought processes that take place within a person's head.[8] Fortunately, as Coleman reminds us, 'For corporate actors [such as states] the fact that the internal functioning is out in the open, in transactions between agents, allows a view of processes that are hidden for natural persons as actors'.[9] In democratic polities, among the most important such 'transactions' between agents are those among legislators. Legislators legitimize their policy preferences and attempt to convince their peers by deriving their decisions from the application of different frames to an issue area. Still, they are often not the final decision-makers, and the degree to which their arguments provide a good proxy depends in part on just how representative the ideas expressed by legislators are of the ideas held by those who take the key decisions. The analyses in this study suggest that the representation is in fact quite good.

Chapter 3 described the different arguments legislators use in debates and aggregated these arguments into seven broad frames: security, power, wealth, enlightened self-interest, reputation, obligation

---

[7] On the other hand, some impact on policy rhetoric is undeniable: witness continued promises to meet the target for aid volume of 0.7 per cent of GNP, for example in the 2002 Monterrey Consensus. United Nations, *Monterrey Consensus on financing for development*, paragraph 42.

[8] Intriguingly, recent advances in neuro-economics suggest that at some point it may become possible to identify different regions in the brain that are associated with different frames such as reputation, wealth or humanitarianism. A. G. Safey *et al.*, 'Neuroeconomics: Cross-currents in research on decision-making'.

[9] J. S. Coleman, *Foundations of social theory*, 513.

and humanitarianism. This aggregation process produced measures of the relative importance of each frame at any given time in a particular country. The most prominent frame in the debates overall was humanitarianism. However, it accounted for only a little more than a quarter of all arguments for aid, with considerable variation over time and across countries. The four case study countries fell into two groups based on the relative importance of both economic self-interest and humanitarianism, two ways of viewing aid that have also been central in the literature. The former was disproportionately strong in Belgium and Italy; the latter in Norway and the Netherlands. If that were the only difference, the academic literature's focus on these two factors might be justified. However, the empirical chapters showed that the other frames have had important policy implications as well.

In the case of Belgium, the frame that stood out most, after economic self-interest, was that of obligation, whereas in Italy it was reputation. In Italy, an interest in international influence was also evident for a while beginning in the late 1970s, whereas Belgian legislators never expressed a great interest in using aid to increase their country's international power. In both countries, considerations of enlightened self-interest became important on and off after the mid 1970s, although more consistently so in Italy than in Belgium. Norway and the Netherlands were similar in placing a greater emphasis on humanitarianism. However, the two countries differed considerably in the salience of additional frames. Whereas Dutch legislators focused disproportionately on the value of aid as an instrument for greater international influence, Norwegians emphasized reputational aspects, bringing influence into the picture only during the 1990s. Considerations of obligation were important in both countries during the 1970s. Enlightened self-interest, finally, played an important role in Norway both around 1970 and again during the 1990s, whereas in the Netherlands it emerged as a salient frame only in the latter period.

Chapter 4 discussed the sources of these various patterns. Salient frames initially arose from the national identities and historical experiences of different states. Moreover, the main features of the aid discourse established in those early years have proven strikingly durable over the decades that followed. The chapter also demonstrated that the constraints imposed by national traditions do not tell the full story.

The choice of frames governments choose to highlight in their communications with the public has implications for the shape of policy too. For example, the early discourses on aid in the Netherlands and Belgium diverged quite rapidly, despite the similar backgrounds of the two countries. Dutch elites emphasized the frames of international influence and humanitarianism, whereas Belgian elites placed more emphasis on obligation and economic self-interest. Their aid programmes soon diverged accordingly.[10]

The composite frames for a given policy are never unchanging. As Chapter 4 showed, international economic and political trends – stagnation, migration flows, etc. – may affect the salience of particular frames and the goals they specify, as was the case in Italy and Belgium with their emphasis on economic self-interest. More commonly, the pattern of prominent frames shifted gradually as a result of national experiences (as well as, to a lesser degree, international trends). Only serious crises in aid policy resulted in a substantial reshaping of the complexion of the aid discourse. Crises of this nature took place in Belgium and Italy when a growing body of evidence indicated that actual aid policy contradicted and undermined the policy's goals as specified by the dominant frames.

The evidence: from frames to policy

Chapters 5 to 7 documented the close relationship between the salient frames for aid in national debates and the policies chosen by decision-makers. In Chapter 5 we saw that frames dominant in the early years shaped the conversion from colonial administration to aid bureaucracy in Belgium, Italy and the Netherlands. The former used its aid programme as a place to park former colonial employees, feeling a sense of obligation both towards those employees and towards the economic actors left behind in the colonies. In the case of Italy, colonial economic interests were so negligible that the resulting aid programme was similarly minimal. The Netherlands, in contrast, tried to increase its international influence by setting up an aid programme with a much wider reach than its empire had had, as well as

---

[10] Lancaster makes a related point, noting that 'While values are slow to change, the way political elites frame aid-giving in terms of those values can have a visible impact on public support for aid'. Lancaster, *Foreign aid*, 6.

by seconding former colonial employees to international aid initiatives and organizations as much as possible.

The subsequent evolution of the aid programmes in these three countries and in Norway (which had no colonial administration to convert and thus set up a programme from scratch) similarly illustrated the influence of different frames. Although aid administrations underwent numerous reforms and reorganizations, these changes tended to remain largely cosmetic except when preceded by a substantial shift in the aid discourse, or widespread agreement that the current organization was inadequate to meet the goals specified by the most prominent frames. Apart from reorganizing the aid administration, new governments tried from time to time to reorient aid policy in different ways. However, such attempts were generally met by resistance both from within the administration and from the broader elite, underscoring the stable underlying complexion of the aid discourse. More often than not, governments gave in or were replaced before any real policy changes had taken effect.

Chapter 6 focused on the volume of aid provided by donor states. The evidence indicated that the correlation between the size of the welfare state and the size of a donor's aid programme, often noted in the literature, is specifically associated with a salient humanitarian frame. This explains the lack of correlation between these two variables in cases where humanitarianism is not prominent in the aid discourse. More generally, the chapter underscored the role of frames as selectors of explanatory variables: the welfare state serves as a significant explanatory variable only when the humanitarian frame is strong. International norms and standards introduced by the United Nations were important in the Netherlands and Norway primarily when the obligation frame was salient. Similarly, the aid performance of peer states was particularly important when reputation was a prominent frame, as was the case for Norway.

Donor-specific nuances in the emphasis of different frames also had a clear impact. For example, whereas obligation was cast as a responsibility to the global community in the Netherlands and Norway, it was more narrowly construed as a duty towards the former colonies in Belgium, with attendant implications for aid volume. Similarly, reputation was salient not only in Norway, but also in Italy. However, Italy was less concerned with beating its peers (as was Norway) than with providing enough aid not to be embarrassed internationally.

These findings show that although the classification of goals into seven broad rubrics is helpful, doing so may also obscure nuances that have important implications for policy choice.

In Chapter 7 the focus shifted to the distribution of aid across recipients as the dependent variable. The statistical analysis in this chapter confirmed, among others, the connection between a preference for former colonies and a prominent obligation frame, as well the link between humanitarian motivations and a preference for poor and needy recipients. Qualitatively, Chapter 7 showed that patterns both in the selection of official targets and in actual aid flows can be predicted from the aid discourse in each country just as other aspects of aid policy can. In Belgium, the strength of the obligation frame resulted in a strong emphasis on former colonies, whereas economic interests were dominant in the selection of new target recipients. In Italy, the dominance of the wealth frame was so strong that the country long avoided even drawing up lists of target recipients. Instead, aid flows were largely determined by the contracts obtained by private firms, and we saw a dramatic fluctuation from year to year in the relative rankings of different aid recipients. In the Netherlands, the influence frame generated an interest in assuming a leadership position in new aid initiatives, as well as a desire to be present in as many LDCs as possible. The strength of the humanitarian frame ensured that the choice of initiatives and countries was largely inspired by humanitarian motivations. In Norway, finally, humanitarianism governed the selection of many aid targets, but the enlightened self-interest and reputation frames introduced a preference for disproportionately large and visible recipients.

Extending the explanatory value of aid frames

Other aspects of aid policy[11]

Chapters 5 to 7 did not exhaust the features of aid programmes one might wish to explain.[12] One dimension not discussed much in this study is the type of projects selected for funding. One reason

---

[11] The discussion in this section draws on the detailed case studies in Van der Veen, 'Ideas and interests in foreign policy', Chapters 6–9.
[12] Cf. Easterly and Pfutze, 'Where does the money go?'.

for this omission is that the DAC's project category definitions are too vague and unstandardized to allow us to make any more specific predictions. Nevertheless, what little evidence is available strongly suggests that here, too, frames shape policy choice. For example, economic infrastructure and industrial projects tend to be favoured more when the economic self-interest frame is salient, whereas social infrastructure, education and humanitarian relief tend to be prioritized when the humanitarian frame becomes prominent.

Moreover, where humanitarian considerations are stronger, we tend to find a greater number of programmes explicitly targeting humanitarian goals, ranging from a concern with basic human needs to supporting the role of women in development. The growing salience of humanitarian motivations over the past few decades has also brought about a greater focus on emergency relief for famines and other disasters. Conversely, where economic considerations are stronger, we find more programmes explicitly targeted at supporting domestic economic actors, such as the construction and infrastructure industries in Italy.

Another variable of some interest is the funding of domestic NGOs active in development assistance. As is the case with multilateral organizations, the literature often assumes that such NGOs are comparatively less self-interested and hence more likely to pursue the well-being of recipient groups. However, plenty of NGOs appear to be interested primarily in their own economic fortunes. During the 1970s and 1980s, for example, many Italian legislators had their own NGOs, whose main function was to funnel aid funds into their own pockets and those of their supporters.[13] When corruption scandals broke in the early 1990s, many of these NGOs quickly disappeared, and the number of Italian NGOs active in development assistance fell precipitously.

Generally speaking, government decision-makers are interested in development-oriented NGOs for two reasons: 1) they may be more effective at pursuing particular (usually humanitarian) goals, and 2) by their orientation and emphasis they make it possible for governments to express particular values and beliefs. This suggests that funds ought to be channelled disproportionately through those

---

[13] Rhi-Sausi *et al.*, 'Italian bilateral aid policy', 19.

NGOs whose activities signal a particular identity or value orientation on the part of decision-makers.[14] Moreover, on balance more aid should be channelled through NGOs as the humanitarianism frame gets stronger in a country.

Indeed, this is largely what we observe. The two countries where the humanitarian frame was strongest, the Netherlands and Norway, were also the ones that supported NGO activities most generously. The Dutch government began funding NGOs as early as 1965, with allocations in proportion to the main religious and secular denominations represented in Dutch society. This was seen as a way both to promote public involvement in aid policy and to express Dutch and Christian values.[15] In Norway, NGO funding began around the same time. The share of the aid budget received by NGOs fluctuated over time, ranging as high as 25 per cent of total bilateral aid. Indeed, during the early 1970s, NGOs frequently were unable to spend the sums made available by the Norwegian government. As in the Netherlands, the government's motives for funding NGOs were twofold. First, NGOs were thought to be particularly adept at administering grassroots projects of the type favoured by Norwegian frames for aid. Second, NGO involvement was deemed to have positive effects on public opinion on foreign aid.[16]

Conversely, Belgian and Italian governments appear to have used NGO funding primarily in a – not very successful – attempt to reassure sceptical populations about the humanitarian inspiration behind their aid programmes. Neither Belgium nor Italy even began funding NGOs until the 1970s. Funding of NGOs in Belgium did not pick up significantly until the early 1990s, when the humanitarian frame became more important and corruption scandals induced the government to signal its good intentions by channelling more aid through humanitarian organizations. In Italy, regular funding of NGOs also began rather late and never amounted to much. Here, too, its main

---

[14] One current example of the latter is the so-called 'global gag rule' used by recent Republican presidents to prohibit US aid funds from going to NGOs anywhere that discuss abortion in any way. This rule can be seen as the international expression of deeply-held values on the part either of the main decision-makers or of particular domestic constituencies that are being accommodated.

[15] See e.g. statements by State Secretary Diepenhorst, cited by Vondeling, *Handelingen*, 6 October 1964: 115.

[16] Stokke, 'Norwegian development-cooperation policy', 134.

function was to alleviate public suspicions about a policy beholden to corrupt economic interests. Neither in Belgium nor in Italy did NGOs account for more than about 1 per cent of the total aid budget for any extended period of time.[17]

Aid frames in other countries

Ample empirical evidence indicates that the link between frames and aid policy choices exists in all donor states, not just in those studied in detail here. For example, publications by the US government regarding foreign aid nearly always frame aid in terms of national security and, to a lesser degree, general self-interest.[18] Nor is the salience of national security limited to official publications only: an important book critical of US aid policy published in 1987 bore the telling title *Betraying the national interest*.[19]

When President Carter came into office, he attempted to increase the prominence of the humanitarian frame. However, he failed to have much of an impact, and neither the aid discourse among members of Congress nor aid policy itself changed much during his term in office.[20] In this respect, Carter's experience resembled that of Dutch Development Minister Schoo, who tried to push aid discourse and policy away from humanitarianism around the same time, but was, as we have seen, equally unsuccessful in her efforts.

With national security and (economic) self-interest as the dominant frames for aid in the United States, it becomes clear why US aid volume has been so low in comparative terms. Most decision-makers feel that the United States – a military superpower as well as the largest economy in the world – has several other, more promising, avenues for the pursuit of both security and wealth. This emphasis on security as a frame for aid also explains why the terrorist attacks of 9/11 had a considerable impact on aid policy, much more so than in other states where national security is less prominent as a frame for aid.

---

[17] Van der Veen, 'Ideas and interests in foreign policy'.
[18] Agency for International Development, *Why foreign aid*; Congressional Budget Office, *Enhancing U.S. security through foreign aid*.
[19] F. M. Lappé, R. Schurman and K. Danaher, *Betraying the national interest*.
[20] A. M. Van der Veen, 'Reframing the purpose of U.S. foreign aid: The impact of Carter's emphasis on human rights'.

Studies of Japanese aid policy suggest that aid frames are influential there as well. Consider, for example, Rix's analysis of Japan's aid programme from 1993, which highlights the reputation frame, along with economic self-interest and obligation, while ignoring humanitarianism almost entirely:

Japan is less interested in the economic welfare effects at the recipient end than in choosing projects which meet Tokyo administrative criteria, such as projects which take large volumes of funds, can advertise Japan's presence or can achieve easily measured targets

...

[Aid] shows the Japanese people that their country is indeed a major player on the world scene fulfilling its international responsibilities, and doing well as a result: 'Japan as top donor' is a common headline.[21]

Other observers of Japan's aid programme have similarly identified these patterns in Japan's aid discourse and policy alike.[22]

In her recent study on foreign aid Lancaster provides insightful case studies of the two countries just discussed, but also of France, Germany and Denmark.[23] While she explicitly shies away from elaborating a single, integrated model of aid policy, her descriptions of national aid policies – and of the factors shaping them – lend valuable support to the argument presented here. Her analysis of US and Japanese aid is in line with the brief assessments offered above. For Denmark, her discussion highlights the importance of humanitarianism, and of an obligation to help the poor – a picture that in its broad outlines closely resembles that for Norway presented here. In light of the extensive shared history of Denmark and Norway, and my argument that national identity and values have a crucial impact on aid frames in a country, this should come as no surprise. Lancaster also highlights the role of governments as norm entrepreneurs, and of government funding for NGO activities, with conclusions that match those in this study.[24]

---

[21] A. Rix, *Japan's foreign aid challenge: Policy reform and aid leadership*, 168, 178.
[22] E.g. R. M. Orr, *The emergence of Japan's foreign aid power*.
[23] Lancaster, *Foreign aid*.
[24] Ibid., p. 210.

Aid frames and policy advocacy

A frame-based model of aid policy also offers important suggestions for those who wish to promote and strengthen development assistance policies. Very little has been said in this study about whether aid 'works', in the sense that it durably improves the fortunes of aid recipients. The question of the efficiency and effectiveness of aid has been the subject of a large literature.[25] The most prominent recent work in this area has been Easterly's critical *White man's burden*.[26] However, Easterly does not offer a particularly new argument (nor does he claim to do so). Two decades earlier Myint already noted the challenges involved in making aid work: 'I am still skeptical as to how far official aid is capable of reaching the poor after it has gone through the double filter of the governments of the aid-giving and the aid-receiving countries, each naturally pursuing its own political and economic goals.'[27]

For those who believe that these challenges can be overcome, and that the potential benefits of aid outweigh the pitfalls, the present study offers insights into the best way to go about promoting different types of aid policy. Taking into account national foreign policy traditions, leaders can try to shape the conceptions of aid held by their constituents through development education, both in the schools (a long-term policy) and in the media, as we saw in Chapter 4. In addition, if obligation or reputation are prominent frames, it may make sense to try to change the set of states that are considered peer states. For Belgium, for example, whether France or the Netherlands is seen as the more logical referent makes a considerable difference. Or, to offer a more extreme example, imagine if Italy felt obliged to do as least as much as the Nordic countries!

Those who wish to reduce the risk of aid policy being captured by rent-seeking private interests can also work to increase the public

---

[25] E.g. R. Cassen, *Rich country interests and Third World development*; C. Jepma, *On the effectiveness of development aid*; T. M. Tsikata, *Aid effectiveness: A survey of the recent empirical literature*; World Bank, *Assessing aid: What works, what doesn't, and why*.

[26] Easterly, *The white man's burden*.

[27] G. M. Meier and D. Seers, *Pioneers in development*, 172. Similarly, Bolkestein, a prominent Dutch politician who has often been critical of aid, argued in 1995 that aid tends to work best in situations where it is least needed, and it is most likely to fail where it is most needed. (Interviewed in the *Volkskrant*, 14 December 1995.); cf. also P. T. Bauer, 'The disregard of reality'.

visibility of legislative deliberations. Chapter 4 illustrated the implications of low transparency and accountability for aid policy. The Italian government for many years was able to pursue an aid policy that was at considerable odds with the wider public's ideas about aid by systematically withholding factual information about policy implementation. Other governments have followed a similar approach. For example, foreign aid appropriations are often attached as 'riders' onto other bills in the US Congress, allowing them to pass with minimal public scrutiny. However, the Italian experience also illustrates the risks of such a policy for governments: ideas become rather unstable and the public can rapidly turn against the government when the contradictions between the former and the latter become obvious. This latter possibility suggests intriguing opportunities for political entrepreneurs opposed to their government's policies.

Framing and policy-making: beyond aid

Although the focus in this study was on foreign aid, the theoretical building blocks of the model are not specific to aid, and the general model can easily be applied to other policy areas, in foreign as well as domestic policy. Indeed, the theoretical discussion in Chapter 2 did not rely on any specific features of aid policy to develop the model. As I argued there, the model is most applicable in contexts where a policy can be seen as a Swiss army knife, or multitool – one policy with multiple plausible goals and associated strategies. Conversely, where there is complete agreement as to the goal of a policy – or where the material constraints on policy choice are severe – the model has little to say about the sources of remaining variation in observed policy choices.[28]

---

[28] This does not mean that framing becomes irrelevant in those cases; instead, the nature of the framing changes. As prospect theory experiments show, for example, even when a policy is seen through a single frame it matters whether choices are seen (i.e. framed) as involving gains or losses. However, Kahneman and Tversky themselves concede that if there is variation in framing at the goal level, there is little point in even considering the framing of the payoffs in terms of gains and losses. The variation in outcomes driven by different policy frames dwarfs that introduced by different ways of framing gains and losses within a frame. D. Kahneman and A. Tversky, 'Choices, values, frames'.

In fact, it is exceedingly rare for a policy to have a single, unambiguous goal. For example, many people think of monetary policy as being close to an ideal, single-relevant-and-obvious-goal policy. Nevertheless, in a study of European monetary integration, McNamara found that how decision-makers framed this policy area was crucial to their decisions.[29] Monetary policy *does* differ from aid policy, however, in that there are fewer relevant frames: the range of different plausible goals is narrower than is the case for aid. The more widely the possible goals range, or the more divergent the policy prescriptions that can logically be associated with them, the greater the potential contribution of the theoretical framework presented in this study. Conversely, the narrower the range of possible goals, or the greater their overlap in terms of associated policies, the greater the predicted impact of other sources of variation, such as structural and institutional constraints.

Applying a frame-based model of policy-making does present some particular challenges. I will consider three important issues in turn: 1) specifying the relevant frames for the issue area, 2) measuring the salience of different frames independently from the policy choices observed, and 3) deriving observable implications to associate with each frame (and combinations thereof). Of course, these three issues cannot be cleanly separated, as the specification of frames has implications for measurement approaches as well as for the types of implications we can derive. Conversely, constraints on our ability to measure may affect which frames can be identified empirically, and limits to the available data on policy outcomes may have implications for our ability to distinguish the impact of different frames.[30] Nevertheless, it will be helpful to consider the three issues in turn.

In this study, the set of relevant frames was derived from a consideration of two sources: the theoretical literature on the determinants of foreign aid, and the political discourse within the donor states on foreign aid. Not surprisingly, given the interaction between academic experts and political entrepreneurs in many issue areas, both sources suggested the same broad set of frames, although an initial

---

[29] K. R. McNamara, 'Consensus and constraint: Ideas and capital mobility in European monetary integration', 457.

[30] In other words, it is futile to specify frames whose implications cannot be empirically distinguished.

examination of the discourse revealed more nuances than the literature would have led one to expect. In many policy areas, arriving at a set of relevant frames will be fairly straightforward, as long as the literature or discourses consulted are not limited to a single case or time period.

However, it will often be important to consider carefully the specificity of the frames we choose to use. The empirical chapters of this study occasionally brought to light the limitations inherent in using rather broad frames. Such frames may well be so general as to give rise to very similar predictions about aid policy, making it difficult to distinguish their empirical influence. For this reason alone, it is valuable to investigate as many different aspects of a policy area as possible.

Second, and more importantly, broad aggregations often result in the loss of nuances that might well have given rise to very different predictions. For example, it might have been valuable, if possible, to keep separate three types of perceived obligation encountered in this study: that arising from a debt to former colonies, that associated with a general sense of international responsibility, and that inspired by a sense that it is necessary to support specific international initiatives one has helped introduce. Some of those nuances were captured in the qualitative case studies, but data limitations imply that aggregation into a single, broader category often cannot be avoided if one wishes to do any form of quantitative analysis.

More generally, some degree of aggregation is probably advisable. After all, we can be certain that there will be some slippage between the mental frames used by public officials and their public expressions of those frames, both because they themselves may not express their ideas quite accurately, and because they may strategically shape their statements, as discussed in Chapter 3. In an ideal world, measurability would not be an issue. In the real world, however, we simply have to accept both that ideas tend to be fuzzy around the edges, and that the potential measures of them are fuzzier still. Nevertheless, the evidence presented in this study amply demonstrates that even noisy measures of frames can add significant explanatory power to our inquiries.

This brings us to the issue of measuring the frames that are to be included in a model. Several considerations come into play here: the potential accuracy of the measures, limitations to the available data, and the costs of measurement. In this study, I measured frames by coding legislative debates on aid. As discussed in Chapters 2 and 3, this may introduce some additional sources of distortion or mismeasurement. The quality of the measures was likely helped by the fact that all four case study countries were parliamentary democracies with an electoral system of proportional representation. This means that legislators constitute a representative cross-section of the political elite, and that the legislatures have more actual decision-making power than is the case in presidential systems, which might make their debates less superficial or strategic.

However, this advantage is almost certainly smaller than one might expect. In fact, recent research suggests that governments in majoritarian democracies are in fact quite 'representative' in their policy attitudes.[31] Moreover, elected officials often display what Mansbridge has labelled 'gyroscopic' representation, in which they draw on their own values and principles rather than making strategic, possibly party-based, calculations.[32] It is worth recalling, moreover, that this study focused on legislative debates in order to extract a *proxy measure* for the salient aid frames in the minds of those who make the actual decisions. Most specific aid policy decisions, after all, are made by bureaucrats, not by either the legislature or the executive. It is, of course, possible that legislative debates will offer a poorer proxy for the beliefs of decision-makers in presidential or majoritarian systems. However, this is an empirical more than a theoretical question; what evidence we have suggests that there is little reason to believe legislative debates in such systems offer fewer valuable insights into the reigning policy frames.[33]

A focus on legislative debates does introduce some other potential pitfalls. In particular, on issues that are not extensively debated, there may be too few statements regarding a particular policy to get a reliable measure of the balance of different frames. One solution to this problem is to combine observations over multiple debates, as I did in this study. In addition, the number of legislators present at a debate may

---

[31] Golder and Stramski, 'Ideological congruence'; cf. G. B. Powell, 'The ideological congruence controversy: The impact of alternative measures, data, and time periods on the effects of election rules'.
[32] Mansbridge, 'Rethinking representation'.
[33] G. Mucciaroni and P. J. Quirk, *Deliberative choices: Debating public policy in Congress*; Van der Veen, 'Reframing the purpose'.

vary for exogenous (and arbitrary) reasons, particular current events may colour the debate, and so on. Since ideas about aid tend to be relatively stable, I used a moving average in presenting the data. However, this came at the cost of ignoring potentially meaningful short-term fluctuations, and may be less appropriate in other policy areas.

An alternative would be to turn to a different source for the measures of frames. For example, general foreign policy debates in a country, while less focused, also tend to be rather more extensive. This may allow us to measure the frames that are relevant to a particular foreign policy issue with more precision than if we looked at specific debates on that issue only. Indeed, as we saw in the case studies, the initial constellation of ideas about aid derived to a large extent from general foreign policy traditions in the donor state. General beliefs about the goals and values of foreign policy might, therefore, serve as a suitable proxy for the particular motivations relevant to aid. However, the payoff of such an approach depends on the degree to which policy-specific frames correspond to broader foreign policy frames. Foreign aid policy, for example, is unusual in the number of different possible justifications one can adduce, some of which have little to do with broader foreign policy goals. For my purposes in the present study, therefore, specific aid debates were more valuable than general foreign policy debates.

Another approach would be to move beyond legislative debates to a different source altogether. After all, coding debates is very resource-intensive, and it is difficult to generate measures of frames for a large number of countries or years. If, therefore, we can find more cost-effective ways to extract roughly the same information, even when doing so means accepting somewhat higher levels of noise in the data, the potential payoff would be considerable. The two obvious alternative sources are media and public opinion. Reports in the media are often biased, possibly sensationalist, and irregular in the frequency and depth of their coverage. Nevertheless, it might be possible to extract valuable data using some form of automatic coding based on keywords, and applying this to a sufficiently broad sample of a nation's media would mitigate some of these problems.[34]

[34] Cf. D. Hopkins and G. King, 'A method of automated nonparametric content analysis for social science'. Given the obvious promise of theoretical models incorporating measures of ideas and identity, juxtaposed with the relative cost of obtaining such measures compared to data on other variables, quite

Compared to media reports, most public opinion surveys have the great benefit of being more representative. However, they tend not to be performed at sufficiently regular intervals, often do not ask the right questions, and are only sporadically available prior to the mid 1970s, severely limiting their relevance to the study of policies going back to the 1960s or before. Moreover, survey results are notoriously subject to distortions due to different ways of phrasing a question, another form of framing which – ironically but not surprisingly – makes it more difficult to get at the underlying frames people use to arrive at decisions. Surveys also ask for respondent opinions in the absence of a budget constraint, which leads to exaggeratedly high levels of public support for policies that sound appealing to the average respondent. Finally, opinion polls primarily survey the public, whose relative ranking of different policy frames may diverge from that of the decision-making elite.

In sum, each possible source for the measurement of frames has its own strengths and weaknesses, and the optimal source for a particular application will depend on availability, resources and the particular questions one wishes to ask. Now that we have briefly considered the first two issues associated with operationalizing a frame-based model of policy-making – the choice of which frames to use, and how to measure them – it is time to turn to the third issue: moving from measures of frame salience to policy predictions. A first consideration here is that of calibration: how strong should a frame be before we can expect it to have an impact? In this study, I focused on frames whose relative salience exceeded the overall dataset average by 25 per cent or more. This threshold is obviously arbitrary, since the dataset average would likely change if we were to add additional data, especially from additional countries. Nevertheless, some kind of comparison is crucial. The broader the dataset, the better we will be able to identify the characteristics that make an individual observation stand out. After all, if aid debates looked the same in every country, we would have no grounds for predicting variation in policy outcomes. It may be interesting that 30 per cent of all arguments for

---

a few researchers have become interested over the past few years in ways to facilitate and automate the derivation of such measures (R. Abdelal *et al.*, 'Identity as a variable'), so it is not unreasonable to hope for considerable progress in this area in the near future.

aid are humanitarian in a given year in country X, but this figure only becomes substantively interesting once we know whether 30 per cent is above or below the average across all countries and years (and by how much).

It is also important to think about the speed with which ideas about aid can change. Some authors have argued that public discourse is so easily manipulable as to have no independent predictive value. For example, in his classic study on imperialism, Hobson makes an argument similar to mine regarding the government's interest in shaping public opinion, but he is much more sceptical about the stability of the latter:

> It is difficult to set any limit upon the capacity of men to deceive themselves as to the relative strength and worth of the motives which affect them ... It is precisely in this falsification of the real import of motives that the gravest vice and the most signal peril ... reside. When, out of a medley of mixed motives, the least potent is selected for public prominence because it is the most presentable, when issues of a policy which were not present at all to the minds of those who formed this policy are treated as chief causes, the moral currency of the nation is debased.[35]

However, the data presented in this study strongly indicates that 'the capacity of men to deceive themselves' is not as great as Hobson perceives it to be. Other studies support this finding. For example, Inglehart has found that broad orientations – comparable in some sense to frames – are quite stable on the whole.[36]

A more important issue is that of the relationship between frame salience and its impact on policy formation. Predicting policy from frame strength requires two additional assumptions: that policymakers consider the goal associated with a frame important, and that they consider the policy in question a valuable instrument for the pursuit of that goal. For example, a legislator might declare that aid is primarily useful for the purposes of pursuing international status, while at the same time arguing that this international status is of no

---

[35] J. A. Hobson, *Imperialism: A study*, 209. The parallels with foreign aid are obvious. Aptly, Hobson also wrote: 'Most serious of all is the persistent attempt to seize the school system for Imperialism masquerading as patriotism' (*ibid.*, 229).

[36] R. Inglehart, *Culture shift in advanced industrial society*, 104–29.

value at all. Alternatively, he might argue that international status *is* valuable, but that there are more cost-effective ways to pursue the same goal. There is some evidence in the case of Norway that the emergence of another policy area more promising in terms of international status – mediation of enduring conflicts, such as between Israel and Palestine (the Oslo Accords) – resulted in a reduction in the importance assigned to foreign aid. Similarly, in the case of the United States, policy-makers often argued that aid was primarily an instrument for the pursuit of security and geopolitical interests, and that since the United States had more effective policies at its disposal to pursue those same goals, it was not worth allocating many resources to aid.

The second of these two problems is more easily tractable than the first, as the examples already suggest. In most cases, it is not too difficult to obtain measures of the degree to which policy-makers perceive alternative policy tools (or issue areas) to be more or less apposite – for a particular frame – compared to the issue area under consideration. The two examples given above nicely illustrate the importance of doing so if we are to make accurate predictions of policy choice. It will usually be more difficult to get a good sense of the relative importance overall of a particular goal. One possible source here was already mentioned earlier: overall (non-issue-specific) foreign policy debates or, more generally, general debates on the broad issue area encompassing the policy in question. The more stable the valuation of overall goals – i.e. divorced from particular policy areas – the easier it will be to get good measures of that valuation. The broader case study literature can be quite helpful here, as suggested in the discussion of the sources of frames in Chapter 4.

Another important consideration in the derivation of specific hypotheses is the influence of causal beliefs. Different causal beliefs, when coupled with identical indicators of frame strength, may result in quite different policy predictions. For example, we saw in the discussion of multilateral aid in Chapter 5 that the causal belief usually assumed in the literature – multilateral aid is less biased and thus more purely humanitarian than bilateral aid – was not shared by some Dutch and Norwegian policy-makers. As a result, the Netherlands gave less multilateral aid than the salience of the humanitarian frame in their discourse would suggest, given the conventional assumption about such aid. Similarly, we saw that when it became clear to Italians that aid was not, in fact, contributing to Italy's international reputation, aid policy changed considerably. In other words, a change in the causal belief linking aid and reputation led to a change in aid policy, even as reputation remained a salient goal for aid.

Moreover, it is not only the case that different causal beliefs coupled with the same frames lead to different policy outcomes. It is also possible for different frames coupled with different causal beliefs to produce the same policy outcomes. Thus we saw in Italy's case, too, that multilateral aid has been argued to serve the purpose of increasing Italy's status. Given the salience of the reputation frame, this has been one of the factors contributing to high levels of multilateral aid in Italy.[37]

All of the above issues are ideational in nature. The issue of calibration highlights the importance of placing ideas in a comparative context rather than just considering them by themselves in isolation. If there is no variation in the salience of an idea across observations (over time or across countries), it will not be possible to demonstrate empirically the impact of the idea. The need to consider policy-specific frames in a broader context – a context which makes clear the overall importance of the frame across policy areas and the potential alternative policy tools that might pursue the same goal – underscores the relevance of broader, underlying attitudes, as well as the potential importance of policy substitutability, a topic that has been attracting growing attention in recent years.[38] Finally, the importance of causal beliefs as an intervening factor between goals and choices reminds us that frames by themselves provide only an incomplete guide to policy choice, which accounts for some of the challenges faced by studies of the impact of ideas in international relations.

There are, of course, institutional factors to be considered as well. For example, the more institutionalized a set of frames is, the more resistance there will be to changing policies in accordance with changes in the salience of frames among the political elite. The structure of a government is likely to have an impact too in certain contexts, as is the political composition of the government. On the other hand, it is

---

[37] Rhi-Sausi *et al.*, 'Italian bilateral aid policy', 5.
[38] See G. Palmer, S. B. Wohlander and T. C. Morgan, 'Give or take: Foreign aid and foreign policy substitutability', for an application of this insight to the study of foreign aid.

worth recalling that differences in the relative salience of frames for aid almost never align well with party-political divisions. In other words, in the issue area of aid, institutional structure is unlikely to matter all that much. This gives rise to two intriguing predictions deserving of further investigation: 1) the more frame strength is correlated with political affiliation (i.e. the more party-political divisions align with differences in emphasis on different frames), the greater the expected impact of institutional structure; and 2) the greater the electoral salience of an issue, the more likely electoral institutions and outcomes will matter for policy choice. In other words, it seems plausible that one of the reasons foreign aid policy is not greatly affected by elections or electoral structures is that it is rarely the central issue people use to decide their vote.

Conclusion

The literature on official development assistance is a curious one. On the one hand, many authors emphasize the moral and (enlightened) self-interested aspects of aid, and extol its positive results. On the other hand, involvement in ODA is a bit like working in a restaurant: one realizes how unappealing reality often is once one scrapes away the veneer of official statements, glossy brochures and rigorously culled anecdotes. The result is often disillusionment or cynicism. Interestingly, the divide between those who emphasize the moral and positive features of aid and those who highlight its problems does not map neatly onto political affinities. On the left-hand side of the political spectrum one finds both optimistic works such as Lumsdaine's *Moral vision in international politics* and highly critical studies such as Hancock's *Lords of poverty*; analogously, the right-hand side features both Bauer's cynical *Reality and rhetoric* and Liska's positive *The new statecraft: Foreign aid in American foreign policy*.[39] Such combinations offer yet another reminder of the lack of explanatory power of measures of the strength of particular political currents.

The pull of these two branches of the aid literature – dedicated and disgusted – is strong: those who endeavour simply to explain aid policy frequently find their arguments coloured by one side or the other.

---

[39] Bauer, *Reality and rhetoric*; Hancock, *Lords of poverty*; Liska, *The new statecraft*; Lumsdaine, *Moral vision*.

Lumsdaine believes aid is morally good, and works hard to show that moral visions on the part of decision-makers shape aid policy; Bauer's experiences convinced him that aid was counterproductive, and he argued that aid is inspired by a host of different motives, most of which are morally suspect, as the quotation opening this chapter suggests. The temptation to let the normative analysis affect its positive counterpart has weakened the aid literature as a whole.

This study has shown that a better approach is to take the preferences and goals of decision-makers seriously, rather than simply to assume them (or wish them) to be of one kind or another. Measuring the frames specifying the goals and purposes of aid makes it possible to demonstrate their strong and systematic impact on the aid policies we observe. Moreover, the study has also shown that these ideas cannot be reduced either to simple material interests or to a struggle between the latter and altruism, reinforcing the importance of measuring rather than imputing goals. Ideas related to a donor state's identity, such as reputation, obligation and a belief in the value of policies pursuing international public goods (enlightened self-interest), play an important role in determining national implementations of development assistance.

In a 1998 interview, Max van den Berg, the chairman of NOVIB, the most prominent Dutch development NGO, fulminated against the subversion of development cooperation by other goals:

We are very conscious to avoid turning aid into a goal in itself, like an industry offering employment. There are, indeed, those who offer aid without the goal of fighting poverty. USAID [the US aid agency] has been messing everything up. It often uses aid for completely different purposes, such as the war on drugs ... [Americans] often have geopolitical goals that introduce serious distortions into the aid 'market'.[40]

This study has shown that similar criticisms could be made for any donor state, including the Netherlands itself. All aid programmes are shaped to a considerable degree by goals other than the humanitarianism that van den Berg wanted to see as the sole motivation. It is not particularly fruitful to deplore or deny the reality of aid as a policy with multiple goals, not all of which are aimed at the well-being of

[40] H. Koch, 'NOVIB: Interview Max van den Berg'.

the recipients. Instead, those who are interested, as van den Berg is, in shaping in national choices regarding aid policy ought to take the findings presented in this study into account as they design their strategies. We have seen that governments can affect the salience of frames by providing domestic development education as well as manipulating the political visibility of aid. But governments are not the only actors that can provide information about (and affect the visibility of) development cooperation; NGOs have long been active in this area as well, with varying success.

The last part of this chapter discussed some of the issues that arise in generalizing my theoretical model to other issue areas. Even issue areas where the variety of goals appears to be less wide-ranging can benefit from analyses that pay more attention to the goals and preferences of different actors. This study not only introduces a promising theoretical framework for doing so, but also presents important findings showing that non-material goals, such as considerations of reputation and obligation, can be quite important in shaping policy. Although operationalizing and generalizing a frame-based approach to policy-making presents many challenges, the potential payoff is considerable. Moreover, some of the issues discussed in the third part of this chapter may well be less severe in issue areas where the competing frames are more constrained and more easily distinguishable than they are in foreign aid, as might be the case in areas of trade and finance, for example.

The theoretical framework presented in this study is more synthetic than many found in the international relations literature. If one allows for a wider range of preferences and goals, it becomes impossible to make very specific predictions in the absence of frame measures. There are, of course, constraints on the distribution of frames. As Chapter 4 showed, international experiences and history strongly shape the initial distribution of frames when new policies are introduced. This allows us to make some general predictions about frame strength, for example about the presence of an obligation frame in former colonial powers. However, the central feature of my theoretical framework is its emphasis on measuring rather than assuming preferences and goals. Indeed, I would argue that its relative dearth of policy-specific predictions is not a weakness but rather an unavoidable implication of its main insight.

Moreover, it appears unlikely that a less synthetic argument will be able to explain policy patterns as nicely. Indeed, many have tried to do so in the area of foreign aid, and their insistence on assuming goals is a key cause of the weakness of this literature. Too often, models that intend to be more rigorous instead end up being more simplistic, or even disingenuous, ignoring important policy features or adding ad hoc explanations that sneak additional goals back in. I would argue that it is more fruitful to pursue theoretical elegance at a level above that of state goals. We may not be able to make simple predictions about what states want, because their goals are often neither material nor straightforward. However, armed with an independent measure of what it is they want, we *can* make clean and straightforward predictions about their likely choices, and about the additional factors we would expect to affect those choices. In the study of foreign aid, in particular, that is more than we have been able to do until now.

Appendix A: Legislative debates coded

This appendix lists the parliamentary aid debates coded in each country. The main source of the data for each year is the debate about that year's development cooperation budget. Sometimes additional debates were coded in the same year, such as general debates on the overall development assistance programme of the government. Occasionally, additional debates for the preceding year were included in order to get a slightly larger sample of speaking turns. This was useful particularly for Belgium and Italy, where aid debates have been both less extensive and more legalistic than in the Netherlands or Norway. As a result, each data point is less a snapshot than an average impression of the discourse over a two to three year period.

Belgium

Belgian budgets are debated in parliamentary committee first, before being reviewed and voted on in a plenary session. Both the Senate and the Chamber of Representatives have to approve the budget in a plenary session, but one Committee does the bulk of the work, preparing a report for the full session. In even years, the committee of the Chamber has this duty; in odd years, it falls to the Senate. The locus of initial discussion tends to feature more in-depth policy debates. For consistency's sake, however, only debates of the Chamber or its committees were coded. The Minister or State Secretary in charge usually opens the committee debates, then takes a series of questions by committee members, and (usually, but not always) answers these. The plenary discussion features a brief report by the committee chair, followed by statements on the budget and on aid policy in general by representatives from all of the major parties, together with some additional questions for the Minister or State Secretary.

Table A.1 *Debates coded for Belgium*

Year	Debate(s)	Date(s)
1955	1954 Budget – Foreign Affairs and Foreign Trade	4 and 10 February 1954
	1955 Budget – Foreign Affairs and Foreign Trade	23 February and 15 March 1955
1958	1956 Budget – Foreign Affairs and Foreign Trade	23, 29 and 30 November and 1 December 1955
	1958 Budget – Foreign Affairs and Foreign Trade	23 January 1958
	1958 Budget – Colonial Affairs	23 April 1958
1960	1960 Budget – Foreign Affairs and Foreign Trade	26–7 January and 9–10 February 1960
	1960 Budget – Colonial Affairs	7 June 1960
1962	1962 Budget – Agriculture	6–7 December 1961
	1962 Budget – Foreign Affairs, Foreign Trade, and Technical Assistance	20–1 and 27–8 February 1962
1965	1965 Budget – General discussion	10 December 1964
	1965 Budget – Foreign Affairs and Foreign Trade	30 March and 6–7 April 1965
1968	1968 Budget – Foreign Affairs and Foreign Trade	4 and 9 July 1968
1970	1970 Budget – Foreign Affairs, Foreign Trade, and Development Cooperation	11–12 and 17–18 February 1970
1972	Interpellation – Restructuring Aid Administration	10 February 1971
	1972 Budget – Foreign Affairs, Foreign Trade, Development Cooperation	31 May and 7–8 and 14 June 1972
	1972 Budget – Defence	21 June 1972
1975	1975 Budget – Foreign Affairs, Foreign Trade, Development Cooperation	5–6 February 1975
1978	1978 Budget – Development Cooperation	17 May 1978
1980	1980 Budget – Foreign Affairs, Foreign Trade, Development Cooperation	19–20 November 1980

Belgium 237

Table A.1 *(cont.)*

Year	Debate(s)	Date(s)
1982	1982 Budget – Foreign Affairs, Foreign Trade, Development Cooperation	26–7 October 1982
1985	1985 Budget – Development Cooperation (Discussion in Foreign Affairs Committee)	20 June 1985
	1985 Budget – Foreign Affairs (Committee)	1 July 1985
	Interpellation – Language equality	8 May 1985
1988	1988 Budget – Foreign Affairs, Foreign Trade, Development Cooperation (in Committee)	19 May 1989
	1988 Budget – *ibid.* (plenary session)	25 May 1989
	Interpellation – Development Cooperation in Zaire	30 June 1989
1990	1990 Budget – Development Cooperation (in Committee)	(no date)
	1990 Budget – *ibid.* (plenary session)	22 December 1989
	Interpellation – Development Cooperation in Zaire (I)	30 May 1990
	Interpellation – Development Cooperation in Zaire (II) (both interpellations in Committee)	12 July 1990
1992	1992 Budget – Development Cooperation (Committee)	5 May 1992
1995	1994 Budget – Development Cooperation (Committee)	13 October 1993
	1995 Budget – Development Cooperation (Committee)	26 October 1994
1998	Debate – Reorganization of Development Cooperation Administration (Committee)	5 November 1997
	1998 Budget – Development Cooperation (Committee)	19 November 1997

238   *Legislative debates coded*

Table A.1 *(cont.)*

Year	Debate(s)	Date(s)
2000	New Law on Development Cooperation (Committee)	5 March 1999
	New Law on Development Cooperation (plenary)	9 March 1999
	2000 Budget – Development Cooperation (Committee)	30 November 1999
	2000 Budget – Development Cooperation (plenary)	22 December 1999
	Policy Paper on Development Cooperation (Committee)	14 July 2000

Throughout the early 1980s, plenary discussions in the Chamber of Representatives featured a relatively thorough discussion of aid policy. However, the need to discuss all major legislation twice (once in each house), made for a procedural nightmare, and budget debates took place further and further into (and even beyond!) the year covered by the budget. In an attempt to bring this process under control and to increase legislative oversight – which was minimal, given that budgets were often already completely spent by the time they were discussed – plenary discussions became increasingly sporadic and limited; I was forced to rely primarily on Committee records from 1985 on.

The disadvantage of these, for coding purposes, is that in most years only summary accounts are available, making it difficult to find and code explicit statements for aid, and to get a sense of the length of individual speaking turns. Although different arguments are still attributed to individual representatives, sometimes their contributions are combined, and usually the summary emphasizes specific policy discussions over general statements of goals and motivations. For such summary accounts, all speaking turns are assigned the same length, and individual arguments are attributed to particular speakers where possible.

In the main body of this study, citations to Belgian parliamentary debates are given as *Parlementaire Handelingen*, <date>: <page>, whereas citations of committee meetings are given as *Kamer Documents*, <doc. nr> <session> <item nr>: <page>.

Italy

Parliamentary procedure in Italy is similar to that in Belgium, with the Senate and the Chamber of Representatives taking turns initiating legislative discussion. The Chamber goes first in odd years.[1] Unfortunately, there have been few debates on development assistance policy in full plenary sessions of either chamber. Most of the work, including approval of the budget, takes place within the Third Committee, which handles Foreign Affairs. In years when the Chamber debates second, the Committee discussion tends to be both shorter and more legalistic. Nevertheless, only Chamber debates were coded, as in the case of Belgium.

Coding the legislative aid discourse is made more difficult in Italy by the fact that, until the mid 1980s, the various expenditure categories associated with development assistance were not combined under a single budgetary heading. In particular, contributions to multilateral development agencies were almost always discussed separately, and thus rarely entered into the debates covering the technical assistance and bilateral aid budgets. Nor were they covered by the successive laws dealing with development assistance policy. The raw material for the coding primarily covers bilateral aid allocations, and debates over appropriations to specific multilateral development agencies are underrepresented. Until the 1980s, extensive discussion of Italy's development aid policy was reserved for the revision of the specific laws covering development assistance. The debates over those laws have been included in the coding, as they usually enjoyed broader participation and interest than the annual budget debates. In recent years, there have been a number of Committee hearings on Italy's aid policy, and these have been included where relevant.

References to parliamentary debates are given by date and the location of the debate: *Atti Parlamentari* for plenary sessions, and *III Commissione* for committee meetings. Where relevant, the document number is cited. Whenever possible, references are to the *Resoconto*

---

[1] Prior to 1960, the Chamber went first in legislative years beginning in an odd year, e.g. 1957–8.

Table A.2 *Debates coded for Italy*

Year	Debate	Date(s)
1950	Interpellation on failure of colonial policy	24 September 1948
	1948–9 Budget – Foreign Affairs	24 and 28 September 1948
	1950–51 Budget – Foreign Affairs (Committee report)	Doc. C.1310A (date unknown)
1952	1952–53 Budget – Foreign Affairs	14 October 1952
	1953–54 Budget – Foreign Affairs	30 September and 2 and 6 October 1953
1955	1955–6 Budget – Foreign Affairs	22 and 27 September 1955
1958	1957–8 Budget – Foreign Affairs (Committee)	10, 15 and 16 October 1957
	1958–9 Budget – Foreign Affairs (Committee)	23, 25 and 28 October 1958
1960	1959–60 Budget – Foreign Affairs (Committee)	19 and 25 June 1959
1962	1961–2 Budget – Foreign Affairs (Committee)	4 May 1961
	Law 1594 of 1962: Technical Cooperation (Committee)	12 July 1962
	1962–3 Budget – Foreign Affairs (Committee)	2 August 1962
1965	1965 Budget – Foreign Affairs	3 December 1964
	Presentation by Undersecretary on Technical Cooperation (Committee)	20 January 1966
1968	1968 Budget – Foreign Affairs (Committee)	21 December 1967
	Law 380 of 1968: Technical Cooperation (Committee)	23 February 1968
1970	1970 Budget – Foreign Affairs (Committee)	19 November 1969
1972	Law 1222 of 1971: Development Cooperation (Committee)	11 November 1971
	1972 Budget – Foreign Affairs (Committee)	1 March 1972

Table A.2 (*cont.*)

Year	Debate	Date(s)
1975	1974 Budget – Foreign Affairs (Committee)	28 November and 11 December 1973
	1975 Budget – Foreign Affairs (Committee)	11 and 18 December 1974, and 15 and 22 January 1975
	1976 Budget – Foreign Affairs (Committee)	12, 26 and 27 November 1975
1978	1978 Budget – Foreign Affairs (Committee)	6, 11 and 12 April 1978
1980	1980 Budget – Foreign Affairs (Committee)	25 March and 24 April 1980
1982	1982 Budget – Foreign Affairs (Committee)	15, 21 and 22 April 1982
1985	1985 Budget – Foreign Affairs (Committee)	10 and 11 October 1984
1988	Law 49 of 1987: Development Cooperation (Committee)	9–10 and 18 December 1986, and 19 February 1987
	1988 Budget – Foreign Affairs (Committee)	16 and 18 December 1987
1990	1990 Budget – Foreign Affairs (Committee)	22, 23 and 28 November 1989
	Presentation on Development Cooperation by MFA (Committee)	7 December 1989
1992	Presentation on Development Cooperation by MFA (Committee)	28 May and 12 June 1991
	1992 Budget – Foreign Affairs (Committee)	26–7 November and 3–4 December 1991
1995	1995 Budget – Foreign Affairs (Committee)	12–13 and 19 October 1994
	Presentation on Development Assistance by DG (Committee)	22 February 1995
1998	1997 Budget – Foreign Affairs (Committee)	8–10 and 15 October 1996
	1998 Budget – Foreign Affairs (Committee)	25–6 and 29 November 1997

Table A.2 (*cont.*)

Year	Debate	Date(s)
2000	2000 Budget – Foreign Affairs (Committee)	17 and 23 November 1999
	New Law on Development Cooperation – 6413 (Committee)	1, 15, 22 and 29 February, 1 March and 19 July 2000
	New Law on Development Cooperation – 6413 (Plenary)	18 December 2000

Abbreviations: MFA: Minister of Foreign Affairs; DG: Director General for Development Cooperation.

Stenografico (verbatim parliamentary record), as opposed to the *Resoconto Sommario* (the summary version).

The Netherlands

In the Netherlands, important policy initiatives have at times been debated in Committee meetings, but most of the relevant discussion occurs in full sessions of the Chamber of Representatives, or Second Chamber. The budget for development cooperation falls under Foreign Affairs, but is usually debated separately, either just before or just after the main Foreign Affairs budget. The Senate is much less influential in day-to-day legislative activities than is the case in Italy and Belgium.

Dutch budget debates are structured in the form of an extended question-and-answer session with the Minister of Development Cooperation. Discussion begins with representatives from every party expressing their basic position on development cooperation. The Minister in charge then makes a lengthy presentation, in which she discusses her policy initiatives and answers any specific questions the representatives may have asked. A second round of questions and answers follows. Occasionally, if necessary, a third round finishes the debate. References in the text to Dutch debates are given as: *Handelingen*, <date>: <page>. Unless otherwise indicated, this refers to the Chamber's parliamentary record. Committee meetings are cited with the name of the Committee and the meeting number.

Table A.3 *Debates coded for the Netherlands*

Year	Debate	Date(s)
1950	1950 Budget – Economic Affairs	29 November 1949
1952	1951 Budget – Foreign Affairs	16 January 1951
	1951 Budget – Education	10 May 1951
	1952 Budget – Foreign Affairs	20–21 November 1951
1955	1954 Budget – Foreign Affairs	16–17 December 1953
	1955 Budget – General debate	5 and 7–8 October 1954
	1955 Budget – Economic Affairs	17–18 November 1954
	1955 Budget – Foreign Dependencies	9 December 1954
	1955 Budget – Foreign Affairs	21–2 December 1954
1958	Interpellation about aid budget	12 June 1957
	1958 Budget – General debate	15–16 October and 12–13 November 1957
	1958 Budget – Foreign Affairs	4–6 February 1958
1960	1960 Budget – General debate	29–30 September and 27–8 October 1959
	1960 Budget – Foreign Affairs	2–3 and 9 February 1960
1962	1962 Budget – General debate	3–5 October and 8 November 1961
	1962 Budget – Economic Affairs	15 November 1961
	1962 Budget – Finance	20 December 1961
	1962 Budget – Foreign Affairs	4 and 9–11 January 1962
	Debate on 1962 White Paper on Aid	2 and 6 November 1962
1965	1965 Budget – General debate	6–8 October 1964
	1965 Budget – Foreign Affairs (in Committee)	9 December 1964
	1965 Budget – Foreign Affairs	2 February 1965
1968	1968 Budget – Foreign Affairs (Development Cooperation) (in Committee)	16 November 1967
	1968 Budget – Foreign Affairs	7 and 13 February 1968
1970	Debate on White Paper on Assessing Aid Policy	12 June 1969
	1970 Budget – Foreign Affairs (Development Cooperation)	11–12 and 17 February 1970

Table A.3 (*cont.*)

Year	Debate	Date(s)
1972	1972 Budget – Foreign Affairs (Development Cooperation)	25 and 30 November and 2 December 1971
1975	1975 Budget – Foreign Affairs (Development Cooperation)	26–7 February and 4 March 1975
1978	1978 Budget – Foreign Affairs (Development Cooperation)	15 and 22 February 1978
1980	1980 Budget – Foreign Affairs (Development Cooperation)	19–21 February 1980
1982	1982 Budget – Foreign Affairs (Development Cooperation)	2–3 December 1981
1985	1985 Budget – Foreign Affairs (Development Cooperation)	7–8 November 1984, and 22 January 1985
1988	1988 Budget – Foreign Affairs (Development Cooperation)	24–5 November 1987
1990	1990 Budget – Foreign Affairs (Development Cooperation)	23–4 January and 7 February 1990
	Debate on White Paper on Development Cooperation (Committee)	3 December 1990
1992	1992 Budget – Foreign Affairs (Development Cooperation)	26–7 November 1991
1995	1995 Budget – Foreign Affairs (Development Cooperation)	23–4 and 30 November 1994
1998	1998 Budget – Foreign Affairs (Development Cooperation)	9 and 11 December 1997
2000	2000 Budget – Foreign Affairs	7–9 December 1999

Norway

In Norway, development assistance often accounts for over 90 per cent of the foreign affairs budget (about 94.5 per cent in 1999), and hence tends to dominate the budget discussion. All aid debates take place in the main chamber of parliament, the Storting, or in one of its committees. Among the four countries studied, only Norway regularly debates reports of the previous year's development cooperation

Norway

activities. This adds to the scope of material available. However, sometimes the previous year's report and next year's budget are debated in quick succession, with the result that one or the other will be rather meagre. I also coded a few general debates on aid policy, where relevant. References to Norwegian debates are given as *Stortingstidende*, <date >: <page>.

Table A.4 *Debates coded for Norway*

Year	Debate	Date(s)
1952	Development aid debate	5 May 1952
	1952–3 Budget – Foreign Affairs: Aid	25 June 1952
1955	1955–6 Budget – Foreign Affairs: Aid	25 April 1955
1958	1958–9 Budget – Foreign Affairs: Aid	10 June 1958
1960	July–December 1960 Budget – Foreign Affairs	29 February 1960
1962	1962 Budget – Foreign Affairs: Aid	17 November 1961
	Debate on aid policy and creation of aid administration	8 February 1962
	Debate on annual report on aid policy (over 1960–61)	1–2 June 1962
1965	1965 Budget – Foreign Affairs: UN aid programmes	26 November 1964
	1965 Budget – Foreign Affairs: IDA	3 December 1964
1968	1968 Budget – Foreign Affairs: Aid	6 December 1967
	Debate on expanding aid policy	21 May 1968
1970	Interpellation on principles of aid policy	25–6 February 1970
	Debate on annual report on aid policy (over 1969)	2–3 June 1970
1972	1972 Budget – Foreign Affairs	15 November 1971
1975	1975 Budget – Foreign Affairs	14 November 1974
1978	1978 Budget – Foreign Affairs	21 November 1977
1980	1980 Budget – Foreign Affairs	15 November 1979
1982	1982 Budget – Foreign Affairs	23 November 1981
1985	1985 Budget – Foreign Affairs	26 November 1984
1988	1988 Budget – Foreign Affairs and Aid	30 November 1987

Table A.4 (*cont.*)

Year	Debate	Date(s)
1990	1990 Budget – Foreign Affairs and Aid	4 December 1989
1992	1992 Budget – Foreign Affairs	25 November 1991
1995	1995 Budget – Foreign Affairs	1 November 1994
	Debate on annual report on aid policy (over 1993)	21 February 1995
1998	1998 Budget – Foreign Affairs	9 December 1997
	Debate on Minister's Development Policy Speech	14 May 1998
2000	Debate on Minister's Development Policy Speech	2 December 1999
	2000 Budget – Foreign Affairs	10 December 1999
	Debate on Minister's Development Policy Speech	16 May 2000

Appendix B: Debate coding examples

This appendix gives sample quotations for each of the forty-four different arguments for aid that were coded. Arguments are listed under the general frame to which they were allocated. Note that certain arguments were allocated to several frames, as described in Chapter 3. However, each argument is listed only once here. For each quotation, I list the legislator, his or her country, and the date and location in the parliamentary record.

Table B.1 Motivations for aid, with sample quotations, by general frame

	Sample quotation	Source
Security		
General self-interest (shared with power, wealth, enlightened self-interest)	1. 'We must give aid because we feel it is necessary, and because, in the final analysis, it is necessary for our own interests.' 2. '[We must take] into account the indispensable considerations of present and future Belgian interests.'	1. Pettersen, Norway, Stortingstidende, 8 February 1962: 1796 2. De Grauw, Belgium, Parlementaire Handelingen Senaat, 3 March 1964: 947
Struggle against Communism	Norway's aid project in India is 'a practical initiative in the war against Communism'.	Strom, Norway, Stortingstidende, 21 May 1953: 1162
Geopolitics and security more generally	Aid is 'a defense initiative'	Haugland, Norway, Stortingstidende, 6 May 1954: 1131[1]
Burden-sharing	'that which is essential, is to do something. We should not always rely on the Americans: Belgium, too, has its role to play.'	Scheyven, Belgium, Parlementaire Handelingen, 30 November 1955: 14
A better alternative to military expenditures	'The resources that are currently used for military purposes, ought to be reduced ... and the sums recuperated in this way could be used for the development of the Third World.'	De Facq, Belgium, Parlementaire Handelingen, 31 May 1972: 1348

Supporting allied regimes	'I believe it is right and important that we do not forget our own family of nations when we help others. Turkey and Portugal have a lot of problems, and it would be deplorable if we denied two allied nations this practical form of solidarity.'	Thyness, Norway, *Stortingstidende*, 15 November 1979: 793
Power		
Influence	1. 'The greater our contribution, the greater becomes our need [and ability] to exercise … greater influence in the international context.'	1. Værno, Norway, *Stortingstidende*, 23 November 1981: 683
	2. 'If Europe wants to continue to play a role in the world, it is necessary that the European countries occupy themselves not only with their own problems, but also with the problems of other countries.'	2. Le Hodey, Belgium, *Parlementaire Handelingen*, 23 November 1955: 15
Obtaining a voice in international institutions	1. 'It does not seem to me that Belgium can stay outside this movement. A political problem of peace has been posed and, even if it were only with a modest participation, I would like us to take our place in the group of countries that are allowed to provide input into this issue.'	1. Bohy, Belgium, *Parlementaire Handelingen*, 29 November 1955: 11

Table B.1 (cont.)

Power	Sample quotation	Source
	2. '[O]ur country could play a significant role in international institutions, by adopting a position as an advocate of human solidarity, rather than as a representative of the rich countries.'	2. Cudell, Belgium, *Parliamentary Documents Kamer*, 4-VIII, nr. 6: 3
Leadership (shared w. reputation)	1. 'We are in a position today to assume this role of progress, peace, and justice, to take up the torch in order to be at the vanguard of tomorrow's world.' 2. 'I believe that [a reduction in aid] would gravely undermine the leading position that the Netherlands has until now assumed internationally with respect to the issue of less developed areas.'	1. Baudson, Belgium, *Parlementaire Handelingen*, 17 February 1970: 13 2. Ruygers, Netherlands, *Handelingen*, 12 June 1957: 949
Example (shared w. reputation)	'I believe that such an initiative on our part ... will contribute strongly to a feeling among other countries that they have to follow our example.'	Gustavsen, Norway, *Stortingstidende*, 8 February 1962: 1783
International presence (shared w. wealth)	'[B]ecause a supranational character is increasingly evident in the picture of the social and political development of peoples, the presence of Italy in this international arena is all the more important.'	Italy, Montini, *III Commissione*, 4 May 1961: 8

Wealth

Economic self-interest	'[T]echnical assistance provides a great way to participate in the development of a country and in investments and consumption in its market.'	Pedini, Italy, *III Commissione*, 23 February 1968: 261
Promote exports	Aid 'has to serve to open markets for us'.	Van Offelen, Belgium, *Parlementaire Handelingen*, 30 March 1965: 41
Secure imports	Italy 'should aim at … those [developing countries] which produce primary materials for industry, especially minerals and metals'.	Cardia, Italy, *III Commissione*, 27 November 1975: 16
Job creation	1. '[A]gricultural engineers and technicians … returned from the Congo, for whom nothing has been done until now, could serve in the administration of technical assistance.'	1. Saintraint, Belgium, *Parlementaire Handelingen*, 7 December 1961: 23
	2. 'One of the attractive aspects of contributing to the [UN] Children's Fund … is that the purchase and shipment of goods happens here at home, so that in this way we provide a certain amount of job creation to Dutch industry.'	2. Schmal, Netherlands, *Handelingen*, 2 February 1960: 627

Table B.1 (*cont.*)

Enlightened self-interest	Sample quotation	Source
Global instability	1. 'If we do not do this with a feeling that time is of the essence, the whole world's peace and stability will be in the greatest possible danger.' 2. '[We are] faced with the choice, either to provide development aid, in order to improve the standard of living of the local population, or to leave those countries to their own fates and contribute to the creation of conflagrations that sooner or later will turn into revolutions, which can endanger our Western world.'	1. Moe, Norway, *Stortingstidende*, 21 May 1968: 3761 2. Colla, Belgium, *Parlementaire Handelingen*, 31 May 1972: 1347
Mutual dependence	'[B]y now it is clear to the Norwegian people that the developing countries' destiny is our destiny.'	Bergesen, Norway, *Stortingstidende*, 8 February 1962: 1790
Strengthening the United Nations	'Multilateral aid through the UN has the great advantage that it strengthens the UN, and creates interest and confidence in the UN. This helps the UN pursue its goals, and that is extremely important.'	Røiseland, Norway, *Stortingstidende*, 21 May 1968: 3781
Environmental protection	'[We] propose … a strong increase in the allocation to the climate fund, which are resources we believe we ought to be allocated over and above normal aid, so that the developing countries can address the threatening environmental situation with our assistance, and so that they can invest in technologies and means of production that will allow us to avoid – or at least limit – the environmental disasters that are rapidly approaching.'	Chaffey, *Stortingstidende*, 25 November 1991: 1108

International justice (shared w. humanitarianism)	'[O]ur foreign policy aims at … bringing about just economic and political relations in the world.'	Schlingemann, Netherlands, *Handelingen*, 11 February 1970: 2198
Distributive justice (shared w. humanitarianism)	1. Aid is 'the core of a global welfare policy'.	1. Schuijt, Netherlands, *Handelingen*, 7 February 1968: 1111
	2. Aid policy should be seen 'in terms of an international system of taxation'.	2. Pronk, Netherlands, *Handelingen*, 19 February 1980: 3115
Support democratization (shared w. humanitarianism)	In countries with human rights problems, 'various human rights initiatives form an important part of our now limited engagement'.	Nordheim-Larsen, Norway, *Stortingstidende*, 21 February 1995: 2287
Reputation		
Prestige and status	'I feel that the authorities would do well to be more concerned with our country's reputation.'	Moe, Norway, *Stortingstidende*, 21 May 1968: 3762
National identity	'Belgium as a small country, with a particular history and a particular tradition, and with a broad "humanistic" ideology, has to be able to provide this type of humanitarian aid.'	Coens, Belgium, *Parlementaire Handelingen*, 17 May 1978: 2068

Table B.1 (cont.)

	Sample quotation	Source
Reputation		
Symbolic value of aid	Recent EC aid is good 'not so much because of the sum of 10 billion [Dutch guilders] but because we as the EEC have taken an important step in our development policy'.	Franssen, Netherlands, *Handelingen*, 26 February 1975: 3051[2]
Others do less	'Even with these reductions Norway will be the global leader where aid is concerned.'	Petersen, Norway, *Stortingstidende*, 25 November 1991: 1096
Noble and glorious task (shared w. obligation)	1. 'Europe, conscious of its civilizing mission, has a duty to respond to the deserving calls of those who sincerely request aid.'	1. Lahaye, Belgium, *Parlementaire Handelingen Senaat*, 16 February 1967: 736
	2. Norwegian legislators ought to be grateful for the opportunity to 'take the lead where it concerns a task which talks to the deepest and best instincts of our own people'.	2. Hambro, Norway, *Stortingstidende*, 25 June 1952: 2242
Obligation		
Responsibility as a rich nation	1. 'Development policy ... should not be considered in terms of solidarity, but in terms ... of collective responsibility.'	1. Dewulf, Belgium, *Parlementaire Handelingen*, 4 March 1969: 5
	2. '[A] number of countries, such as ours, are "obligated" to provide bilateral aid, simply because they have duties and responsibilities.'	2. Scheyven, Belgium[3]

Role in the international system	'It is exactly to us, small countries, that it falls to create ways to escape from the noose that is slowly tightening around us.'	Baudson, Belgium, *Parlementaire Handelingen*, 17 February 1970: 11
'Repayment' for aid received from others	1. 'Is it that special, that we who received assistance from others, give a little of the same kind of assistance ourselves?'	1. Pedersen, *Stortingstidende*, June 25, 1952: 2244
	2. 'We have in the past had the opportunity to benefit from the benevolence of America and therefore we ought now to supplement the efforts of this country, now that it is falling short for various reasons.'	2. Aarden, Netherlands, *Handelingen*, 7 February 1968: 1137
Colonial guilt	'We have committed an error and a mistake with respect to the population of the former colony. We have a debt to this country.'	Dehousse, Belgium, *Parlementaire Handelingen Senaat*, 6 March 1963: 789
Shared history and culture	Aid is a way to strengthen ties with Third World countries that share 'our languages and our cultures.'	Bertrand, Belgium, *Parlementaire Handelingen*, 6 March 1969: 50
International standards	'If one applies the by now generally accepted norm that the most developed countries should transfer at least 1% of their national income, the Netherlands lags far behind.'[14]	Burger, Netherlands, *Handelingen*, 4 October 1961: 90

Table B.1 (*cont.*)

Obligation	Sample quotation	Source
Others do more	'We really ought to be ashamed that in Belgium, in contrast to the Netherlands and the Scandinavian countries, we have made cuts in the development cooperation budget.'	Caudron, Belgium, *Parlementaire Handelingen*, 19 November 1980: 313
Continuity	'Continuity is important. If a county has been included in the list [of favoured recipients], then that has to remain the case for a longer period of time … Once you start something, you must give the policy in question a lot of time to succeed.'	Pronk, Netherlands, *Handelingen*, Development Cooperation Commission, Session 22, 10 December 1980: 67
Support structural adjustment	Aid is important because it provides 'resources among others for the structural adjustment policy'.	Bukman, Netherlands, *Handelingen*, 25 November 1987: 1274
Public opinion	'Society is willing to provide quite a significant sum for development cooperation, at a time that other areas of the government budget experience serious cuts.'	Van Leijenhorst, Netherlands, *Handelingen*, 24 November 1987: 25–1222
Humanitarianism		
Humanitarianism	1. 'The ever-increasing gap between the less developed countries and the Western capitalist countries … presents itself in a dramatic fashion to humanity's conscience.'	1. Cardia, Italy, *III Commissione*, 19 November 1969: 27
	2. Italy's new law for development cooperation has an 'extraordinary humanitarian content'.	2. Sarti, Italy, *III Commissione*, 18 December 1986: 39

Solidarity	'We shall strengthen our solidarity with all people, wherever they may live in this small world of ours, through our initiative and increased efforts.'	Pettersen, Norway, *Stortingstidende*, 8 February 1962: 1772
Because there is a gap between rich and poor	1. '[T]he determining objective of development aid is to reduce the gap between the rich countries and the developing countries.' 2. 'It is human solidarity that pushes us to this initiative.'	1. Petersen, Norway, *Stortingstidende*, 21 May 1978: 3795 2. Willot, Belgium, *Parlementaire Handelingen*, 20 March 1963: 7
Morally right	'[W]e have no moral or any other right to push [this problem] away from us.'	Strøm, Norway, *Stortingstidende*, 5 May 1952: 1217
Christian charity	1. 'Among those who are listening now are Catholic colleagues, who for that very reason are particularly sensitive to this human problem.' 2. 'I believe that we must consider development cooperation from a biblical standpoint.'⁵	1. Cardia, Italy, *III Commissione*, 19 November 1969: 27 2. Van Rossum, Netherlands, *Handelingen*, 25 November 1971: 1369
Support admired regimes	'[We] welcome the activities of the Norwegian and Swedish social democracies with respect to the national revolution [in Portugal] … We are ready to support the proposal for wide-ranging bilateral aid and increased cooperation.'	Kielland, Norway, *Stortingstidende*, 14 November 1974: 935–6

Table B.1 (*cont.*)

Humanitarianism	Sample quotation	Source
Promote human rights	'It is especially important to support states attempting to lay the basis for a democratic regime, both economically and politically, in order to help them retain what they have achieved and develop further towards real democracy.'	Lied, Norway, *Stortingstidende*, 26 November 1984: 1186

[1] In fact, Haugland wanted to include development aid as part of the defence budget, 'as a demonstration of our interest in peace and of our way of practising international politics' (*ibid.*). Interestingly, in this second quotation, the reputation frame takes the upper hand.
[2] Similarly, five years earlier, Franssen had argued that the symbolic value of East–West cooperation in development assistance was more important than the sum of resources flowing to the developing countries, or even than the needs or interests of the developing countries (*Handelingen*, 12 February 1970: 2239).
[3] Cited in Gedopt, 'Belgisch buitenlands beleid', 59.
[4] References to international standards were tallied only when the speaker explicitly concluded from her nation's shortfall that more aid ought to be given, so as to come closer to meeting the standard.
[5] Van Rossum proceeded to cite Isaiah 3, verses 14–15, which read: 'The spoil of the poor is in your houses. What do you mean by crushing my people, by grinding the face of the poor?' He concluded: 'I think that these verses very clearly illustrate our Christian obligation and that we should use them as our guiding principles' (*ibid.*).

Appendix C: Aid distribution: data and sources

Data for the dependent variable was derived from the aid database of the OECD's Development Assistance Committee (DAC), both in CD-ROM format and online (www.oecd.org/dac).[1] As discussed in Chapter 7, the aid measure selected was net disbursements. Occasionally countries repay earlier development loans, which makes it appear as though they receive negative aid. However, we are concerned with a recipient's share of a donor's total aid in a given year. Since negative aid is equivalent to a zero share, negative values are truncated to 0. For every recipient-year, I calculated the aid share of that recipient from each of our four case study countries, as well as its aid share from the DAC as a whole. Often, a few countries get most of the aid, while a much larger number gets comparatively little. In order to generate a more meaningful ranking, therefore, I take the log of these aid shares.[2]

Data for the independent variables was drawn from a number of different databases. Basic country indicators – GDP, area and population, as well as literacy, life expectancy and mortality rates – are from the World Bank's *World Development Indicators* CD-ROM (2004 edition).[3] Trade data were taken from Gleditsch's trade and GDP

---

[1] Through an error on the part of the DAC, no data is listed for the Netherlands in 1966. Instead, the information was taken from the DAC's printed annual records for 1966–7. In addition, the CD-ROM has entries of '-' as well as 0. Comparison to printed records indicates that '0' refers to aid amounts too small to be rounded up to the smallest unit in the CD-ROM database (0.1), i.e. less than 0.05. I have assumed that the average actual aid disbursed in entries with '0' is 0.02, and replaced these zeroes accordingly.

[2] This means that the dependent variable has values below 0 (log(1) = 0), which may be a bit confusing at first glance, but does not pose substantive problems. On the other hand, countries receiving no aid at all would be assigned a value of negative infinity. To eliminate this problem, a tiny value is added to each aid share (0.0000000001).

[3] Most World Bank indicators are only available at sporadic intervals for any given country. Since I am concerned with the data available to decision-makers,

dataset.[4] Data on political similarity is provided by Gartzke's Affinity of Nations dataset, which provides an indicator of voting agreement at the United Nations.[5] Data on the quality of democracy (or autocracy) in a country were taken from the Polity IV dataset, and information about political and civil rights came from the Freedom House dataset.[6]

Finally, two variables were coded by hand: the variable for contiguity with a Communist state, and that for status as a former colony of one of our donor states. Former Belgian colonies are Zaire/Congo, Rwanda and Burundi. Coded as former Italian colonies are Eritrea, Ethiopia, Libya and Somalia. Former Dutch colonies are Indonesia, Suriname, the Netherlands Antilles and Aruba. Norway did not own any colonies.[7] Contiguity with a Communist state was coded with the use of an atlas (see Table C.1).

A number of variables were rescaled in order to generate a more even distribution and to allow pooling. Variables that are distributed with geometrically decreasing densities (i.e. their histogram resembles a graph of e^{-x}) were transformed by logging ($\log_{10}$). This was done to the variables for trade, GDP, population, GDP/capita and area. In addition, the World Bank, trade, Polity IV and Freedom House data were all standardized (mean 0, standard deviation 1) on an annual basis. Unless this is done, variables that trend over time – such as ever rising trade levels, or falling mortality rates – will cause difficulties. Moreover, since we wish to explain aid shares, which are by definition calculated for a given year, standardizing makes good sense even without any secular trends.[8]

---

not the (unknown) actual values of these variables, it is not problematic to fill in missing data based on the available information. I chose to interpolate between or extrapolate from the closest available figures, on the assumption that decision-makers are likely to impute continued progress (or deterioration, during crises) in these variables, even when no new data is available.

[4] Gleditsch, 'Expanded trade and GDP data'.
[5] E. Gartzke, 'The affinity of nations index, 1946–2002'; C. S. Signorino and J. M. Ritter, 'Tau-b or not tau-b: Measuring the similarity of foreign policy positions'.
[6] M. G. Marshall and K. Jaggers, 'Polity IV project: Political regime characteristics and transitions, 1800–2002' and www.freedomhouse.org/template.cfm?page=439 (accessed 15 December 2010), respectively.
[7] Italy had colonist settlements in Libya, but it never formally claimed Libya as a colony.
[8] Standardization is performed on all the data available in a given year, i.e. not just on the subset of observations for which all explanatory variables are present. This has implications for the mean and standard deviation values used in the standardization process, although the effects are small.

Aid distribution: data and sources

Table C.1 *Data used to generate Communist-border variable*

State	Period	Neighbours
Afghanistan	1979–92	Iran, Pakistan
Angola	1976–91	Namibia, Zaire, Zambia
Cambodia	1973–92	Laos, Thailand, Vietnam
China	1949–	Bhutan, India, Myanmar, Nepal, Pakistan, Taiwan
Laos	1975–	Cambodia, Myanmar, Thailand, Vietnam
Mozambique	1975–89	Malawi, South Africa, Tanzania, Zambia, Zimbabwe
Nicaragua	1979–89	Costa Rica, Honduras
North Korea	1948–	South Korea
(North) Vietnam	1954–	Cambodia, Laos
USSR	1945–91	Afghanistan, Iran, Turkey

Since we are trying to predict aid shares based on current values of the independent variables, the explanatory variables need to be lagged. Those explanatory variables that are based on general judgements, for example regarding democracy or political and civil rights, need only a one-year lag, as they will be based on assessments at the time policy is being set. Variables that rely on the collection of data need to be lagged by an additional year. This includes trade, UN voting, aid receipts from other donors, and the human development data from the World Bank. Lagging variables also helps eliminate the potential problem of simultaneity between the dependent and independent variables – and, substantively, of mistaking the true direction of the causal arrow. For example, total ODA receipts by a recipient state – a measure of popularity – include those provided by the donor state being studied. Moreover, exports from the donor to the recipient are likely to be funded in part by aid funds, and figures for GDP per capita are boosted by aid receipts. Fortunately, since current aid cannot affect any of these factors in previous years, lagging prevents problems.

The dataset covers 176 countries and seventeen years, at the two to three year intervals determined by the debate codes over the period 1960–2000 (1960, 1962, 1965, 1968, 1970, etc.). A number of independent variables have missing values, however. In particular, Freedom

Table C.2. *Summary statistics for non-donor-specific explanatory variables, after processing (interpolate/extrapolate, log, standardize, lag)*

Variable	Mean	Std. Dev.	Min	Max
Communist border	0.0824	0.275	0	1
GDP	−0.284	0.834	−2.774	1.960
Population	0.0271	0.918	−2.640	2.599
Former colony	0.0158	0.125	0	1
Democracy	−0.225	0.892	−1.956	1.710
Area	0.0297	0.981	−3.028	1.778
DAC aid share	−7.457	4.620	−23.026	−1.471
GDP/capita	−0.346	0.829	−2.835	2.273
Mortality	0.344	0.951	−1.309	3.135
Illiteracy	−0.229	0.946	−3.807	1.908
Life expectancy	−0.348	0.937	−2.844	1.357
Rights	0.211	0.889	−1.736	1.774

House's rights data begins only in 1972. In addition, a number of aid recipients have no information available in the World Bank's dataset on the human development variables (mortality, literacy, life expectancy), and some aid recipients are not present in the Polity IV dataset. Table C.2 provides summary data for the non-donor-specific variables, and Table C.3 provides summary data for the dyadic variables (in four parts, for each of the case study countries).

In closing, it is worth saying a word about collinearity in the data. A common test is to see whether any bivariate correlations exceed 0.7 to 0.8. There are a few such high correlations in the data: GDP is highly correlated with population, exports and imports (and the last two are also correlated). Area and population are highly correlated, as are rights and democracy. Finally, per capita GDP, mortality, literacy and life expectancy have a several high bivariate correlations amongst them. Fortunately, paring down the specifications using likelihood ratio tests results in the elimination of nearly all situations where highly correlated variables occur in the same model, so additional steps were unnecessary.

Table C.3a *Summary statistics for explanatory variables: Belgium*

Variable	Mean	Std. Dev.	Min	Max
Eligibility	0.945	0.946	0	2
Aid share	−14.318	8.431	−23.026	−0.167
UN voting	−0.210	0.739	−1.940	3.263
Exports	−0.314	0.806	−2.910	1.655
Imports	−0.282	0.845	−3.034	2.019

Table C.3b *Summary statistics for explanatory variables: Italy*

Variable	Mean	Std. Dev.	Min	Max
Eligibility	0.875	0.9417	0	2
Aid share	−14.844	8.549	−23.026	−0.659
UN voting	−0.192	0.750	−2.216	3.315
Exports	−0.283	0.878	−3.228	1.810
Imports	−0.267	0.910	−3.777	1.798

Table C.3c *Summary statistics for explanatory variables: the Netherlands*

Variable	Mean	Std. Dev.	Min	Max
Eligibility	1.041	0.938	0	2
Aid share	−13.325	8.362	−23.026	−0.268
UN voting	−0.187	0.731	−2	3.281
Exports	−0.319	0.802	−3.399	1.604
Imports	−0.272	0.885	−3.210	2.059

Table C.3d *Summary statistics for explanatory variables: Norway*

Variable	Mean	Std. Dev.	Min	Max
Eligibility	0.771	0.946	0	2
Aid share	−15.957	8.553	−23.026	−0.442
UN voting	−0.148	0.724	−2.0631	3.452
Exports	−0.333	0.785	−2.878	1.776
Imports	−0.351	0.814	−2.596	1.855

Bibliography

Abdelal, R., Y. M. Herrera, A. I. Johnston and R. McDermott, 'Identity as a variable', *Perspectives on Politics* Vol. 4, No. 4 (2006).

Achten, H., *Ontstaansgeschiedenis van de wet van 10 augustus 1981 tot oprichting van een fonds voor ontwikkelingssamenwerking. Overzicht van de parlementaire standpunten en verklaringen* (Brussels: ABOS, 1981).

Agency for International Development, *Why foreign aid?* (Washington, DC: US Government Printing Office, 1992).

Ajzen, I. and M. Fishbein, *Understanding attitudes and predicting social behavior* (Englewood Cliffs: Prentice Hall, 1980).

Alesina, A. and D. Dollar, 'Who gives foreign aid to whom and why?', *Journal of Economic Growth* Vol. 5, No. 1 (2000).

Aliboni, R., 'Italian aid policy in the 60's', *Lo Spettatore Internazionale* Vol. 7, No. 2 (1972).

   'Italy and Africa: The aid policy', *The International Spectator* Vol. 4, No. 3–4 (1969).

Anderson, B., *Imagined communities: Reflections on the origin and spread of nationalism* (London: Verso, 1983).

Ardesi, L., 'L'impatto della cooperazione allo sviluppo sulla società italiana', *Politica Internazionale* No. 1 (1987).

Armingeon, K., M. Gerber, P. Leimgruber and M. Beyeler, 'Comparative political data set 1960–2006' (Berne: Institute of Political Science, University of Berne, 2008).

Austen-Smith, D., 'Strategic models of talk in political decision making', *International Political Science Review* Vol. 13 (1992).

Baehr, P. R., P. P. Everts, J. H. Leurdijk, F. M. Roschar, A. van Staden, C. P. van den Tempel, W. H. Vermeulen and R. M. M. de Vree, *Elite & buitenlandse politiek in Nederland* (The Hague: Staatsuitgeverij, 1978).

Ball, R., 'Cultural values and public policy: The case of international development aid', *Quarterly Journal of Economics and Finance* Vol. 50, No. 1 (2010).

Balsvik, R., 'U-landsdebatt i det Norske Storting, 1952–1966' (1969).

Banfield, E. C., 'American foreign aid doctrines', in R. A. Goldwin (ed.), *Why foreign aid?* (Chicago: Rand McNally, 1963).
Barnett, M. N., 'Culture, strategy and foreign policy change: Israel's road to Oslo', *European Journal of International Relations* Vol. 5, No. 1 (1999).
Bauer, P. T., 'The disregard of reality', *Cato Journal* Vol. 7, No. 1 (1987).
  Reality and rhetoric: Studies in the economics of development (Cambridge, MA: Harvard University Press, 1984).
Beck, N. and J. N. Katz, 'What to do (and not to do) with time series-cross section data', *American Political Science Review* Vol. 89, No. 3 (1995).
Belgium, *ABOS jaarverslag 1983* (Brussels: ABOS, 1983).
  Hulp door België verleend aan de ontwikkelingslanden, 1962–1963 (Brussels: Advisory Council for Development Cooperation, 1964).
Berlage, L. and R. Renard, *Evaluatie van ontwikkelingshulp in België en Nederland*, Research paper in economic development nr 24 (Leuven: Departement Economie, Katholieke Universiteit Leuven, 1993).
Berthélemy, J.-C. and A. Tichit, 'Bilateral donors' aid allocation decisions – A three-dimensional panel analysis', *International Review of Economics and Finance* Vol. 13 (2004).
Bleich, E., *Race politics in Britain and France: Ideas and policy-making since the 1960s* (Cambridge University Press, 2003).
Bloom, W., *Personal identity, national identity, and international relations* (Cambridge and New York: Cambridge University Press, 1990).
Botcheva, L. and L. L. Martin, 'Institutional effects on state behavior: Convergence and divergence', *International Studies Quarterly* Vol. 45, No. 1 (2001).
Bowles, P., 'Recipient needs and donor interests in the allocation of EEC aid to developing countries', *Canadian Journal of Development Studies* Vol. 10, No. 1 (1989).
Brandt, W. and the Independent Commission on International Development Issues, *Common crisis North–South: Cooperation for world recovery* (Cambridge, MA: MIT Press, 1983).
  North–South: A programme for survival (Cambridge, MA: MIT Press, 1980).
Breuning, M., 'Words and deeds: Foreign assistance rhetoric and policy behavior in the Netherlands, Belgium, and the United Kingdom', *International Studies Quarterly* Vol. 39 (1995).
Brundtland, G. H. and the World Commission on Environment and Development, *Our common future* (New York: Oxford University Press, 1987).

Bueno de Mesquita, B. and A. Smith, 'Foreign aid and policy concessions', *Journal of Conflict Resolution* Vol. 51, No. 2 (2007).
'A political economy of aid,' *International Organization* Vol. 63, No. 2 (2009).
Busini, G. and E. Taviani, 'Italy', in I. Smillie and H. Helmich (eds.), *Public attitudes and international development* (Paris: OECD, 1998).
Cassen, R., *Rich country interests and Third World development* (New York: St Martins Press, 1982).
Censis, *Libro bianco sulla cooperazione allo sviluppo, 1981–1984* (Rome: Ministero degli Affari Esteri, 1985).
Chong, A. and M. Gradstein, 'What determines foreign aid? The donors' perspective,' *Journal of Development Economics* Vol. 87, No. 1 (2008).
Chong, D. and J. N. Druckman, 'Framing public opinion in competitive democracies', *American Political Science Review* Vol. 101, No. 4 (2007).
'Framing theory', *Annual Review of Political Science* Vol. 10 (2007).
Cleymans, B., 'Ronde tafel gesprek' (Ontwikkelingssamenwerking 1983).
Coleman, J. S., *Foundations of social theory* (Cambridge, MA: Harvard University Press, 1990).
Congressional Budget Office, *Enhancing U.S. security through foreign aid* (Washington, DC: Congressional Budget Office, 1994).
Coolsaet, R., *Buitenlandse zaken* (Leuven: Kritak, 1987).
Cooper, C. and J. Verloren van Themaat, 'Dutch aid determinants, 1973–85: Continuity and change', in O. Stokke (ed.), *Western middle powers and global poverty. The determinants of the aid policies of Canada, Denmark, the Netherlands, Norway, and Sweden* (Uppsala: The Scandinavian Institute of African Studies, 1989).
Crabb, Jr, C. V. and J. Savoy, 'Hans J. Morgenthau's version of realpolitik', *Political Science Reviewer* Vol. 5 (1975).
Dassù, M. and M. De Andreis, 'Italian foreign and development cooperation policy', in A. P. Hewitt (ed.), *Crisis or transition in foreign aid?* (London: Overseas Development Institute, 1994).
Davidson, R. and J. G. MacKinnon, *Estimation and inference in econometrics* (New York: Oxford University Press, 1993).
De Coninck, D., *Witte olifanten: De miljardenschandalen van de Belgische ontwikkelingssamenwerking* (Leuven: van Halewyck, 1996).
De Jong, J. J. P., 'Onder ethisch insigne: De origine van de Nederlandse ontwikkelingssamenwerking', in J. Nekkers and P. A. M. Malcontent (eds.), *De geschiedenis van vijftig jaar Nederlandse ontwikkelingssamentwerking 1949–1999* (The Hague: SDU, 1999).

De Schaetzen, Y., 'L'Italie et l'Afrique: La volonté politique conjuguée avec le dynamisme des entrepreneurs', *Afrique Industrie*, No. 358 (1986).

Derrida, J., *Positions* (University of Chicago Press, 1981).

de Saussure, F., C. Bailly, A. Sechehaye and A. Riedlinger, *Cours de linguistique générale* (Paris: Payot, 1916).

Dessler, D. and J. Owen, 'Constructivism and the problem of explanation: A review article', *Perspectives on Politics* Vol. 3, No. 3 (2005).

Doucouliagos, H. and M. Paldam, 'The aid effectiveness literature: The sad results of 40 years of research', *Journal of Economic Surveys* Vol. 23, No. 3 (2009).

Druckman, J. N., L. R. Jacobs and E. Ostermeier, 'Candidate strategies to prime issues and image', *Journal of Politics* Vol. 66 (2004).

Dudley, L. and C. Montmarquette, 'A model of the supply of bilateral foreign aid', *American Economic Review* Vol. 66, No. 1 (1976).

Easterly, W., *The white man's burden: Why the West's efforts to aid the rest have done so much ill and so little good* (New York: Penguin Press, 2006).

Easterly, W. and T. Pfutze, 'Where does the money go? Best and worst practices in foreign aid', *Journal of Economic Perspectives* Vol. 29, No. 2 (2008).

Entman, R. M., *Projects of power: Framing news, public opinion, and U.S. foreign policy* (University of Chicago Press, 2004).

Epstein, W. M., 'Response bias in opinion polls and American social welfare', *Social Science Journal* Vol. 43, No. 1 (2006).

Fabiano, R., 'Avete sbagliato per venticinque anni', *L'Espresso*, 27 December 1992.

Finnemore, M. and K. Sikkink, 'International norm dynamics and political change', *International Organization* Vol. 52, No. 4 (1998).

'Taking stock: The constructivist research program in international relations and comparative politics', *Annual Review of Political Science* Vol. 4 (2001).

Forte, F., 'Il programma di aiuti economici ai paesi arretrati', *Il Mulino* Vol. 10, No. 9 (= 107) (1961).

Foucault, M. and C. Gordon, *Power/knowledge* (New York: Pantheon Books, 1980).

Foy, C. and H. Helmich, eds., *Public support for international development* (Paris: OECD, 1996).

Frank, Jr., C. R. and M. Baird, 'Foreign aid: Its speckled past and future prospects', *International Organization* Vol. 29, No. 1 (1975).

G-8, 'The Gleneagles Communiqué' (Gleneagles: G-8, 2005).

Gamson, W. A., *Talking politics* (Cambridge University Press, 1992).

Gartzke, E., 'The affinity of nations index, 1946–2002' (New York: Columbia University, 2006).
Gedopt, M., 'Belgisch buitenlands beleid inzake ontwikkelingssamenwerking. Houding regering – parlement' (Licentiaatsverhandeling, Katholieke Universiteit Leuven, 1974).
George, J., *Discourses of global politics: A critical (re)introduction to international relations* (Boulder: Lynne Rienner, 1994).
Giordano, P., 'Intervista a Pannella: "Quale crisi? La gente ci segue"', *Paese Sera*, 24 July 1982.
Gleditsch, K. S., 'Expanded trade and GDP data', *Journal of Conflict Resolution* Vol. 46, No. 5 (2002).
Goffman, E., *Frame analysis: An essay on the organization of experience* (Cambridge: Harvard University Press, 1974).
Golder, M. and J. Stramski, 'Ideological congruence and electoral institutions', *American Journal of Political Science* Vol. 54, No. 1 (2010).
Goldstein, J. and R. O. Keohane, *Ideas and foreign policy: Beliefs, institutions, and political change* (Ithaca: Cornell University Press, 1993).
Gounder, R., *Overseas aid motivations: The economics of Australia's bilateral aid* (Aldershot: Avebury, 1995).
Greene, W. H., *Econometric analysis* (New York: Macmillan, 1993).
Griffin, K. B., 'Foreign aid after the Cold War', *Development and Change* Vol. 22, No. 4 (1991).
Griffin, K. B. and J. L. Enos, 'Foreign assistance: Objectives and consequences', *Economic Development and Cultural Change* Vol. 18 (1970).
Grilli, E. and F. Daveri, 'Italia e terzo mondo', *Relazioni Internazionali* Vol. 56, No. 17 (1992).
Hagen, K. A., '"Poenget er at dette skal være utviklingshjelp." En analyse av ordningen med "statsgaranti på særlige vilkår ved eksport til og ved investeringer i utviklingsland", og denne ordningens tilknytning til Norsk utviklingshjelp i perioden 1963–1984' (Universitetet i Bergen, 1986).
Hall, P., 'Conclusion', in P. Hall (ed.), *The political power of economic ideas: Keynesianism across nations* (Princeton University Press, 1989).
  'Policy paradigms, social learning and the state: The case of economic policy-making in Britain', *Comparative Politics* Vol. 25, No. 3 (1993).
Hancock, G., *Lords of poverty: The power, prestige, and corruption of the international aid business* (New York: Atlantic Monthly Press, 1989).
Hayter, T., *Aid as imperialism* (Harmondsworth: Penguin, 1971).

Heckman, J. J., 'The common structure of statistical models of truncation, sample selection and limited dependent variables and a sample estimator for such models', *Annals of Economic and Social Measurement* Vol. 5 (1976).

Hjertholm, P. and H. White, 'Foreign aid in historical perspective', in F. Tarp (ed.), *Foreign aid and development: Lessons learnt and directions for the future* (New York: Routledge, 2000).

Hoadley, J. S., 'Small states as aid donors', *International Organization* Vol. 34, No. 1 (1980).

Hobson, J. A., *Imperialism: A study* (London: James Nisbet & Co., 1902).

Hoebink, P., *The comparative effectiveness and the evaluation efforts of EU donors* (The Hague: National Advisory Council for Development Cooperation, 1995).

De effectiviteit van de hulp: Een literatuuroverzicht van macro- naar micro-niveaus, Focus op ontwikkeling nr. 1 (The Hague: Ministry of Foreign Affairs, 1995).

'Geven is nemen: De Nederlandse ontwikkelingshulp aan Tanzania en Sri Lanka' (Universiteit van Nijmegen, 1988).

Hoffmann, S., *Primacy or world order? American foreign policy since the Cold War* (New York: McGraw-Hill, 1978).

Holdar, S., 'The study of foreign aid: Unbroken ground in geography', *Progress in Human Geography* Vol. 17, No. 4 (1993).

Holsti, K. J., 'National role conceptions in the study of foreign policy', *International Studies Quarterly* Vol. 14, No. 3 (1970).

Hommes, E. W., 'Evaluaties van een evaluatie: I. Commentaar van een socioloog', *Economisch-Statistische Berichten* Vol. 54, No. 2695 (1969).

Hook, S. W., *National interest and foreign aid* (Boulder: L. Rienner Publishers, 1995).

Hopkins, D. and G. King, 'A method of automated nonparametric content analysis for social science', *American Journal of Political Science* Vol. 54, No. 1 (2010).

Hopkins, R. F., 'Political economy of foreign aid', in F. Tarp (ed.), *Foreign aid and development: Lessons learnt and directions for the future* (New York: Routledge, 2000).

Hout, W., 'European development aid: A cross-national analysis of competing explanations', *Acta Politica* Vol. 26, No. 4 (1991).

Huber, E., C. Ragin, J. D. Stephens, D. Brady and J. Beckfield, 'Comparative welfare states data set' (Chapel Hill: Department of Political Science, 2004).

Hurwitz, J. and M. Peffley, 'How are foreign policy attitudes structured? A hierarchical model', *American Political Science Review* Vol. 81, No. 4 (1987).

Hveem, H., *International relations and world images. A study of Norwegian foreign policy elites* (Oslo: Universitetsforlaget, 1972).

Imbeau, L.-M., *Donor aid – The determinants of development allocations to Third World Countries: A comparative analysis* (New York: Peter Lang, 1989).

Inglehart, R., *Culture shift in advanced industrial society* (Princeton University Press, 1990).

Istituto Ricerche Studi Economici e Sociali, *Emergenza, fame e cooperazione allo sviluppo: Analisi, documentazione, proposte* (Milano: Franco Angeli, 1987).

Italy, *Examen annuel de l'aide, 1965*, Pub. no. (65)1/12 (Paris: OECD/ Ministero degli Affari Esteri, 1965).

   La politica di cooperazione dell'Italia con i paesi in via di sviluppo: Indagine conoscitiva della 3a Commissione Permanente (Affari Esteri, Emigrazione): Raccolta di atti e documenti (Rome: Ufficio di Segreteria, 1991).

   Raccolta di atti della Commissione Parlamentare d'Inchiesta sull'attuazione della politica di cooperazione con i paesi in via di sviluppo (Rome: Ufficio di Segreteria, 1996).

Jepma, C., *On the effectiveness of development aid* (The Hague: Ministry of Foreign Affairs, 1995).

   The tying of aid (Paris: OECD Development Centre, 1991).

Jervis, R., *The logic of images in international relations* (Princeton University Press, 1970).

   Perception and misperception in international politics (Princeton University Press, 1976).

Jobert, B., 'Europe and the reshaping of national forums: The French case' (paper presented at the Ideas, discourse, and European integration, European Union Center, Harvard University, Cambridge, MA, 2001).

Johnson, J., 'Is talk really cheap? Prompting conversation between critical theory and rational choice', *American Political Science Review* Vol. 87, No. 1 (1993).

Johnston, A. I., 'Realism(s) and Chinese security policy in the post-Cold War period', in E. B. Kapstein and M. Mastanduno (eds.), *Unipolar politics: Realism and state strategies after the Cold War* (New York: Columbia University Press, 1999).

Kahneman, D. and A. Tversky, 'Choices, values, frames', *American Psychologist* Vol. 39 (1989).

Kato, M., 'A model of U.S. foreign aid allocation: An application of a rational decision-making scheme', in J. E. Mueller (ed.), *Approaches to measurement in international relations: A non-evangelical survey* (New York: Appleton-Century-Crofts, 1969).

Katzenstein, P. J., 'Introduction: Alternative perspectives on national security', in P. J. Katzenstein (ed.), *The culture of national security: Norms and identity in world politics* (New York: Columbia University Press, 1996).

Keck, M. E. and K. Sikkink, *Activists beyond borders: Advocacy networks in international politics* (Ithaca: Cornell University Press, 1998).

Keohane, R. O., 'Political influence in the General Assembly', *International Conciliation* Vol. 36, No. 557 (1966).

Khong, Y. F., *Analogies at war: Korea, Munich, Dien Bien Phu, and the Vietnam decisions of 1965* (Princeton University Press, 1992).

Kinder, D. R. and L. M. Sanders, *Divided by color: Racial politics and democratic ideals* (University of Chicago Press, 1996).

King, G., R. O. Keohane and S. Verba, *Designing social inquiry: Scientific inference in qualitative research* (Princeton University Press, 1994).

Kingdon, J., *Agendas, alternatives and public policies* (New York: HarperCollins, 1995).

Kirschen, E. S., 'Objectifs et determination de l'aide aux pays sous-développés', *Cahiers Economiques de Bruxelles* No. 24 (1964).

Knutsen, T. L., 'Norsk utenrikspolitikk som forskningsfelt', in T. L. Knutsen, G. M. Sørbø and S. Gjerdåker (eds.), *Norges utenrikspolitikk* (Oslo: Cappelen, 1997).

Koch, H., 'NOVIB: Interview Max van den Berg', *Trouw*, 17 January 1998.

Kogan, N., *The politics of Italian foreign policy* (New York: Praeger, 1963).

Kossmann, E. H., *In praise of the Dutch republic: Some seventeenth century attitudes* (London: Lewis, 1963).

Kratochwil, F. V., *Rules, norms, and decisions: On the conditions of practical and legal reasoning in international relations and domestic affairs* (New York: Cambridge University Press, 1989).

Lagerberg, C. S. I. J. and J. Vingerhoets, 'Ontwikkelingssamenwerking: De moeizame weg naar een nieuw beleid', *Internationale Spectator* Vol. 27, No. 20 (1973).

Lancaster, C., *Foreign aid: Diplomacy, development, domestic politics* (University of Chicago Press, 2007).

Lappé, F. M., R. Schurman and K. Danaher, *Betraying the national interest* (New York: Grove Press, 1987).

Larson, D. W., 'Problems of content analysis in foreign-policy research: Notes from the study of the origins of Cold War belief systems', *International Studies Quarterly* Vol. 32 (1988).

Lebovic, J. H., 'National interest and U.S. foreign aid: The Carter and Reagan years', *Journal of Peace Research* Vol. 25, No. 2 (1988).

Lee, L.-F. and G. S. Maddala, 'The common structure of tests for selectivity bias, serial correlation, heteroscedasticity and non-normality in the tobit model', *International Economic Review* Vol. 26, No. 1 (1985).

Lembke, H. H., *Norway's development cooperation* (Berlin: German Development Institute, 1989).

Levitt, M. S., 'The allocation of economic aid in practice', *Manchester School of Economics and Social Studies* Vol. 36, No. 2 (1968).

Liland, F. and K. A. Kjerland, *Norsk utviklingshjelps historie, bind 3: 1989–2002. På bred front* (Oslo: Fagbokforlaget, 2003).

Liska, G., *The new statecraft: Foreign aid in American foreign policy* (University of Chicago Press, 1960).

Lumsdaine, D. H., *Moral vision in international politics: The foreign aid regime, 1949–1989* (Princeton University Press, 1993).

Maas, P., 'Kabinetsformaties en ontwikkelingssamenwerking', in A. Melkert (ed.), *De volgende minister. Ontwikkelingssamenwerking binnen het cabinet: 1965 tot?* (The Hague: NOVIB, 1986).

McGillivray, M. and E. Oczkowski, 'A two-part sample selection model of British bilateral aid allocation', *Applied Economics* Vol. 24 (1992).

McGillivray, M. and H. White, *Explanatory studies of aid allocations among developing countries: A critical survey*, Pub. no. 148 (The Hague: Institute of Social Studies, 1993).

McKinlay, R. D. and A. Mughan, *Aid and arms to the Third World: An analysis of the distribution and impact of U.S. official transfers* (New York: St. Martin's Press, 1984).

McNamara, K. R., 'Consensus and constraint: Ideas and capital mobility in European monetary integration', *Journal of Common Market Studies* Vol. 37, No. 3 (1999).

Maizels, A. and M. K. Nissanke, 'Motivations for aid to developing countries', *World Development* Vol. 12, No. 9 (1984).

Mansbridge, J., 'Rethinking representation', *American Political Science Review* Vol. 97, No. 4 (2003).

Marijsse, S. and J. Debar, *Belgisch-Zaïrese economische relaties: Het effect van de Belgische tewerkstelling* (Antwerp: UFSIA, 1982).

Marshall, M. G. and K. Jaggers, 'Polity IV project: Political regime characteristics and transitions, 1800–2002' (College Park: Center for International Development and Conflict Management, University of Maryland, 2002).

Marullo, S., R. Pagnucco and J. Smith, 'Frame changes and social movement contraction: U.S. peace movement framing after the Cold War', *Sociological Inquiry* Vol. 66 (1996).

Mason, E. S., *Foreign aid and foreign policy* (New York: Harper & Row (for the Council on Foreign Relations), 1964).

Maurizio, R., 'I prossimi tre anni di cooperazione', *Cooperazione* Vol. 19, No. 37/38 (1984).

Meernik, J., E. L. Krueger and S. C. Poe, 'Testing models of U.S. foreign policy: Foreign aid during and after the Cold War', *Journal of Politics* Vol. 60, No. 1 (1998).

Meier, G. M. and D. Seers, eds., *Pioneers in development* (New York: Oxford University Press, 1984).

Menichini, D., *Cooperazione Italiana allo sviluppo: Analisi e proposte* (Rome: Osservatorio della Cooperazione (Gruppo Parlamentare Verdi), 1993).

Millikan, M. F., 'The political case for development aid', in R. A. Goldwin (ed.), *Why foreign aid?* (Chicago: Rand McNally, 1963).

Milliken, J., 'The study of discourse in international relations: A critique of research and methods', *European Journal of International Relations* Vol. 5, No. 2 (1999).

Monti, A., *Economia e politica dell'aiuto pubblico allo sviluppo. Il sistema italiano di cooperazione con i paesi in via di sviluppo: Un'analisi critica*, Pub. no. 28–9 (Rome: Istituto di Studi per la Programmazione Economica, 1983).

Moravcsik, A., 'Taking preferences seriously: A liberal theory of international politics', *International Organization* Vol. 51, No. 4 (1997).

Moravcsik, A. and J. W. Legro, 'Is anybody still a realist?', *International Security* Vol. 24, No. 2 (1999).

Morgenthau, H. J., 'Preface to a political theory of foreign aid', *American Political Science Review* Vol. 56, No. 2 (1962).

Morgenthau, H. J. and N. Chomsky, 'The national interest and the Pentagon papers', *Partisan Review* Vol. 39 (1972).

Mosley, P., *Overseas aid: Its defence and reform* (Brighton: Wheatsheaf Books, 1987).

Moyo, D., *Dead aid: Why aid is not working and how there is a better way for Africa* (New York: Farrar, Straus, Giroux, 2009).

Mucciaroni, G. and P. J. Quirk, *Deliberative choices: Debating public policy in Congress* (University of Chicago Press, 2006).

Muller, P., 'Les politiques publiques comme construction d'un rapport au monde', in A. Faure, G. Pollet and P. Warin (eds.), *La construction du sense dans les politiques publiques: Débats autour de la notion de référentiel* (Paris: L'Harmattan, 1995).

Mureddu, G., 'Obiettivi espliciti e impliciti degli aiuti allo sviluppo', *Sviluppo – Development* No. 2 (1994).
Nadelmann, E. A., 'Global prohibition regimes: The evolution of norms in international society', *International Organization* Vol. 44 (1990).
'Nei rapporti Italia-Somalia uno scandalo da 1.500 miliardi', *Il Secolo*, 11 January 1991.
Netherlands, *Beweging gewogen. Impactsstudie NCO* (The Hague: SDU, 1992).
   Bilaterale ontwikkelingssamenwerking: Om de kwaliteit van de Nederlandse hulp (The Hague: Staatsuitgeverij, 1976).
   Een wereld in geschil (The Hague: SDU, 1993).
   Een wereld van verschil. Nieuwe kaders voor ontwikkelingssamenwerking in de jaren negentig (Tweede Kamer document 21 813) (The Hague: SDU, 1991).
   Hulp in uitvoering: Ontwikkelingssamenwerking en de herijking van het buitenlandse beleid (The Hague: SDU, 1995).
   Jaarverslag over 1951 (The Hague: Ministerie van Buitenlandse Zaken/ Commission for International Technical Assistance, 1952).
   Nota betreffende de bijdrage aan het programma der Verenigde Naties voor technische hulp aan economisch laag ontwikkelde landen, Pub. no. 1734, #1–4 (The Hague, 1950).
   Nota: Hulpverlening aan minder ontwikkelde landen (The Hague: Staatsuitgeverij, 1966).
   Nota inzake de hulpverlening aan minder ontwikkelde gebieden (The Hague: Ministerie van Buitenlandse Zaken, 1956).
   Ontwikkelingssamenwerking en werkgelegenheid: Nota (The Hague: Staatsuitgeverij, 1984).
Neumayer, E., *The pattern of aid giving: The impact of good governance on development assistance* (New York: Routledge, 2003).
Noël, A. and J.-P. Thérien, 'From domestic to international justice: The welfare state and foreign aid', *International Organization* Vol. 49, No. 3 (1995).
Norbye, O. D. K. and A. Ofstand, *Norwegian development aid experiences: A review of evaluation studies 1986–92*, Pub. no. 2.96 (Oslo: Utenriksdepartmentet, 1996).
Norway, *Budsjett Innstilling S. nr. 4* (Oslo: Stortinget, 1959).
   Engen-utvalget: Instilling fra utvalget for utredning av spørsmålet om Norges hjelp til utviklingslandene (Oslo: Utenriksdepartementet, March 1961).
   FN-sambandet i Norge (Evalueringsrapport nr 2.95) (Oslo: Utenriksdepartementet, 1995).

Bibliography

Holdninger til Norsk utviklingshjelp 1974, Pub. no. 32 (Oslo: SSB, 1975).

Holdninger til Norsk utviklingshjelp 1977, Pub. no. 46 (Oslo: SSB, 1978).

Holdninger til Norsk utviklingshjelp 1983, Pub. no. 83/35 (Oslo: SSB, 1983).

I. Om den videre utbygging av Norges bistand til utviklingslandene. II. Om opprettelse av 'Direktoratet for utviklingshjelp', Pub. no. 109 (Oslo: Utenriksdepartementet, April 1967).

Innstilling S. nr. 186 (1986–1987) (Oslo: Stortinget, 1987).

Innstilling S. nr. 192 (Oslo: Stortinget, 1975).

Innstilling S. nr. 255 (Oslo: Stortinget, 1981).

Stortingsmelding nr. 29 (Oslo: Stortinget, 1972).

Stortingsmelding nr. 71 (Oslo: Stortinget, 1972).

OECD, *Development co-operation: Efforts and policies of the members of the Development Assistance Committee: 1971 report* (Paris: OECD/DAC, 1972).

Development co-operation: Efforts and policies of the members of the Development Assistance Committee: 1977 report (Paris: OECD/DAC, 1978).

Development co-operation report 2006: Summary (Paris: OECD/DAC, 2007).

Development co-operation report 2007 (Paris: OECD/DAC, 2008).

Development co-operation report 2010 (Paris: OECD/DAC, 2010).

Development co-operation review of Belgium (Paris: OECD/DAC, 2001).

Development co-operation review of Italy: Main findings and recommendations (Paris: OECD/DAC, 2000).

Development co-operation review series: Belgium, Pub. no. 7 (Paris: OECD/DAC, 1995).

Development co-operation review series: Norway, Pub. no. 14 (Paris: OECD/DAC, 1996).

Development co-operation review series: Norway, Pub. no. 36 (Paris: OECD/DAC, 1999).

Geographical distribution of financial flows to aid recipients. 1998 report (Paris: OECD/DAC, 1999).

ODA steady in 2000; other flows decline (Paris: OECD/DAC, 2001).

Twenty-five years of development co-operation, a review: Efforts and policies of the members of the Development Assistance Committee, 1984 report (Paris: OECD/DAC, 1985).

Ohlin, G., *Foreign aid policies reconsidered* (Paris: OECD, 1966).

Oppewal, J. and D. Seroo, 'De moraal van Réginald Moreels: "Als ethiek ten koste gaat van effectiviteit, dan moet dat maar"', *Internationale Samenwerking* Vol. 14, No. 4 (1999).

Orr, R. M., *The emergence of Japan's foreign aid power* (New York: Columbia University Press, 1990).

Otter, M., 'Domestic support for foreign aid: Does it matter?', *Third World Quarterly* Vol. 24, No. 1 (2003).

Palmer, G., S. B. Wohlander and T. C. Morgan, 'Give or take: Foreign aid and foreign policy substitutability', *Journal of Peace Research* Vol. 39, No. 1 (2002).

Pearson, L. B. and Commission on International Development, *Partners in development* (New York: Praeger, 1969).

'Per la fame 350 miliardi. Pannella ne chiede 3 mila', *La Stampa*, 4 August 1982.

Pharo, H. Ø., 'Reluctance, enthusiasm and indulgence: The expansion of bilateral Norwegian aid', in H. Ø. Pharo and M. P. Fraser (eds.), *The Aid Rush: Aid Regimes in Northern Europe During the Cold War* (Oslo, Norway: Unipub (Oslo Academic Press), 2008).

Poe, S. C., 'Politieke partijen en de Derde Wereld', *De Wereld Morgen*, No. 6 (1977).

'United States aid allocation: The quest for cumulation', *International Interactions* Vol. 16 (1991).

Porter, D., *U.S. economic foreign aid: A case study of the United States Agency for International Development* (New York: Garland Publishing, 1990).

Powell, G. B., 'The ideological congruence controversy: The impact of alternative measures, data, and time periods on the effects of election rules', *Comparative Political Studies* Vol. 42, No. 12 (2009).

Pratt, C., ed., *Internationalism under strain: The North–South policies of Canada, the Netherlands, Norway, and Sweden* (University of Toronto Press, 1989).

Price, R., 'Reversing the gun sights: Transnational civil society targets land mines', *International Organization* Vol. 52 (1998).

Price, R. and C. Reus-Smit, 'Dangerous liaisons? Critical international relations theory and constructivism', *European Journal of International Relations* Vol. 4, No. 3 (1998).

Ramirez, F. O., Y. Soysal and S. Shanahan, 'The changing logic of political citizenship: Crossnational acquisition of women's suffrage rights, 1890–1990', *American Sociological Review* Vol. 62 (1997).

Randel, J. and T. German, eds., *The reality of aid 1996* (London: Earthscan, 1996).

The reality of aid 1997/1998 (London: Earthscan, 1997).

The reality of aid 1998/99 (London: Earthscan, 1998).

Rein, M. and D. Schön, 'Reframing policy discourse', in F. Fischer and J. Forester (eds.), *The argumentative turn in policy analysis and planning* (Durham, NC: Duke University Press, 1993).

Reus-Smit, C., *The moral purpose of the state: Culture, social identity, and institutional rationality in international relations* (Princeton University Press, 1999).

Rhi-Sausi, J. L., M. Dassù, D. Fanciullacci and Å. Torkelsson, 'Italian bilateral aid policy, 1983–1993', in J. L. Rhi-Sausi and M. Dassù (eds.), *Coordinating the development aid policies of European countries* (Rome: CESPI, 1994).

Riker, W. H., 'Heresthetic and rhetoric in the spatial model', in J. M. Enelow and M. J. Hinich (eds.), *Advances in the spatial theory of voting* (Cambridge University Press, 1990).

Risse, T., '"Let's argue!" Communicative actions in world politics', *International Organization* Vol. 54, No. 1 (2000).

Riste, O., 'The historical determinants of Norwegian foreign policy', in J. J. Holst (ed.), *Norwegian foreign policy in the 1980s* (Oslo: Universitetsforlaget, 1985).

Rix, A., *Japan's foreign aid challenge: Policy reform and aid leadership* (London: Routledge, 1993).

Romano, S., 'La cultura della politica estera italiana', in S. Romano and R. J. B. Bosworth (eds.), *La politica estera italiana, 1860–1985* (Bologna: Il Mulino, 1991).

Round, J. I. and M. Odedokun, 'Aid effort and its determinants', *International Review of Economics and Finance* Vol. 13 (2004).

Ruge, M. H., 'Technical assistance and parliamentary debates', *Journal of Peace Research* Vol. 1, No. 2 (1964).

Ruud, A. E. and K. A. Kjerland, *Norsk utviklingshjelps historie, bind 2: 1975–1989. Vekst, velvilje og utfordringer* (Oslo: Fagbokforlaget, 2003).

Sabatier, P., 'The advocacy coalition framework: Revisions and relevance for Europe', *Journal of European Public Policy* Vol. 5, No. 1 (1998).

Sachs, J., *The end of poverty: Economic possibilities of our time* (New York: Penguin Press, 2006).

Safey, A. G., G. Loewenstein, S. M. McClure and J. D. Cohen, 'Neuroeconomics: Cross-currents in research on decision-making', *Trends in Cognitive Sciences* Vol. 10, No. 3 (2006).

Samset, K., K. Forss and O. Hauglin, *Learning from experience: A study of the feedback from evaluations and reviews in Norwegian bilateral aid*, Pub. no. 1.93 (Oslo: Utenriksdepartementet, 1993).

Scheufele, D. A., 'Framing as a theory of media effects', *Journal of Communication* Vol. 49, No. 1 (1999).

Schimmelfennig, F., 'The community trap: Liberal norms, rhetorical action, and the Eastern enlargement of the European Union', *International Organization* Vol. 55, No. 1 (2001).

Schmidt, V. A., 'Democracy and discourse in an integrating Europe and a globalising world', *European Law Journal* Vol. 6, No. 3 (2000).

Schön, D. and M. Rein, *Frame reflection: Toward the resolution of intractable policy controversies* (New York: Basic Books, 1994).

Schoultz, L., 'U.S. foreign policy and human rights violations in Latin America: A comparative analysis of foreign aid distribution', *Comparative Politics* Vol. 13, No. 2 (1981).

Schraeder, P. J., S. W. Hook and B. Taylor, 'Clarifying the foreign aid puzzle: A comparison of American, Japanese, French, and Swedish aid flows', *World Politics* Vol. 50, No. 2 (1998).

Schweller, R. L., 'Realism and the present great power system: Growth and positional conflict over scarce resources', in E. B. Kapstein and M. Mastanduno (eds.), *Unipolar politics: Realism and state strategies after the Cold War* (New York: Columbia University Press, 1999).

Shepsle, K. A., 'Comment', in R. Noll (ed.), *Regulatory policy and the social sciences* (Berkeley: University of California Press, 1985).

Signorino, C. S. and J. M. Ritter, 'Tau-b or not tau-b: Measuring the similarity of foreign policy positions', *International Studies Quarterly* Vol. 43, No. 1 (1999).

Simensen, J., *Norsk utviklingshjelps historie, bind 1: 1952–1975. Norge møter den tredje verden* (Oslo: Fagbokforlaget, 2003).

Sniderman, P. M., 'The new look in public opinion research', in A. W. Finifter (ed.), *Political science: The state of the discipline* (Washington, DC: American Political Science Association, 1993).

Sniderman, P. M. and S. M. Theriault, 'The structure of political argument and the logic of issue framing', in W. E. Saris and P. M. Sniderman (eds.), *Studies in public opinion* (Princeton University Press, 2004).

Snow, D. A. and R. D. Benford, 'Ideology, frame resonance, and participant mobilization', in B. Klandermans, H. Kriesi and S. Tarrow (eds.), *International social movement research: Volume 1* (London: JAI Press, 1988).

Snyder, R. C., H. W. Bruck and B. Sapin, *Foreign policy decision-making: An approach to the study of international politics* (New York: Free Press, 1962).

Speelman, B., 'Tussen droom en daad...? Ontwikkelingssamenwerking als politiek instrument in België' (Licentiaatsverhandeling, Handelshogeschool, 1995).

Stapel, J., 'Onderzoek 26 mei 1981', *Acta Politica* Vol. 17, No. 1 (1982).

Stokke, O., 'The determinants of aid policies: Some propositions emerging from a comparative analysis', in O. Stokke (ed.), *Western middle powers and global poverty. The determinants of the aid policies of Canada, Denmark, the Netherlands, Norway and Sweden* (Uppsala: The Scandinavian Institute of African Studies, 1989).
'The determinants of Norwegian foreign aid policies', in O. Stokke (ed.), *Western middle powers and global poverty. The determinants of the aid policies of Canada, Denmark, the Netherlands, Norway and Sweden* (Uppsala: The Scandinavian Institute of African Studies, 1989).
'The evaluation policy and performance of Norway', in O. Stokke (ed.), *Evaluating development assistance: Policies and performance* (London: Frank Cass, 1991).
'Norwegian development-cooperation policy: Altruism and international solidarity', in J. J. Holst (ed.), *Norwegian foreign policy in the 1980s* (Oslo: Universitetsforlaget, 1985).
'Spenningen mellom egeninteresse og altruisme i Norsk bistandspolitikk', in O. Stokke (ed.), *Norsk utenrikspolitisk årbok 1981* (Oslo: NUPI, 1982).
Stokke, O., ed., *Western middle powers and global poverty. The determinants of the aid policies of Canada, Denmark, the Netherlands, Norway and Sweden* (Uppsala: The Scandinavian Institute of African Studies, 1989).
Surel, Y., 'The role of cognitive and normative frames in policy-making', *Journal of European Public Policy* Vol. 7, No. 4 (2000).
Tamnes, R., *Norsk utenrikspolitikks historie. Bind 6: Oljealder 1965–1995* (Oslo: Universitetsforlaget, 1997).
Tana, F., 'Tangenti sugli aiuti? Per i Somali, "un'offesa"', *Il Messaggero*, 9 April 1988.
'Terzo Mondo e opinione pubblica: Le responsabilità della stampa – intervista a Italo Pietra', *Politica Internazionale* Vol. 14, No. 7 (1986).
Tarp, F., C. F. Bach, H. Hansen and S. Baunsgaad, 'Danish aid policy: Theory and empirical evidence', in K. L. Gupta (ed.), *Foreign aid: New perspectives* (Boston: Kluwer Academic Publishers, 1999).
Terlinden, C. and L. Hilditch, *Untie aid: Towards effective partnership* (Brussels: ActionAid Alliance, 2003).
Thérien, J.-P. and A. Noël, 'Political parties and foreign aid', *American Political Science Review* Vol. 94, No. 1 (2000).
Thomas, G., J. W. Meyer, F. O. Ramirez and J. Boli, eds., *Institutional structure: Constituting state, society and the individual* (Newbury Park: Sage Publications, 1987).

Tingley, D., 'Donors and domestic politics: Political influences on foreign aid effort', *Quarterly Journal of Economics and Finance* Vol. 50, No. 1 (2010).

Trumbull, W. N. and H. J. Wall, 'Estimating aid-allocation criteria with panel data', *Economic Journal* Vol. 104, No. 425 (1994).

Trygstad, S. E., 'U-hjelpsdebatten i Stortinget, 1965–74' (Universitetet i Trondheim, 1978).

Tsikata, T. M., *Aid effectiveness: A survey of the recent empirical literature* (Washington, DC: International Monetary Fund, 1998).

Tyrangiel, J., 'Bono's mission', *Time* (2002).

UNIOP, *De onderontwikkeling in de Derde Wereld en de geldinzamelingen* (Brussels: NCOS, 1972).

United Kingdom, *Ministerial round table on trade and poverty in least developed countries* (London: Department for International Development, 2001).

United Nations, *Doha Declaration on financing for development* (Doha: United Nations, 2008).

Monterrey Consensus on financing for development (Monterrey: United Nations, 2003).

United States Department of Agriculture, 'Are revolving loan funds a better way to finance rural development?', Pub. no. 724–05 (Washington, DC, 1996).

Vaes, R., 'Het officiële Belgische beleid inzake ontwikkelingssamenwerking: Een beleidsanalyse' (Licentiaatsverhandeling, Vrije Universiteit Brussel, 1984).

Valentini, C., 'Zero in diplomazia', *L'Espresso*, 27 December 1992.

Van Bilsen, A. A. J., *Structurele aspecten van de ontwikkelingssamenwerking. Deel I: Donorbeleid* (Brussels: ABOS, 1987).

Van Dam, F., *Onbehagen rond de ontwikkelingshulp* (Groningen: Wolters, 1964).

Van den Dool, R. J., ed., *Normverva(n)ging: Een bijdrage aan de discussie over de budgetaire norm voor internationale samenwerking* (The Hague: Voorlichtingsdienst Ontwikkelingssamenwerking, 1993).

Van der Heijden, H., 'Evaluaties van een evaluatie: II. Commentaar van een economist', *Economisch-Statistische Berichten* Vol. 54, No. 2695 (1969).

Van der Veen, A. M., 'Ideas and interests in foreign policy: The politics of official development assistance' (Dissertation, Harvard University, 2000).

'Not whether but why: Using public opinion to explain foreign policy' (paper presented at the Annual meeting of the American Political Science Association, San Francisco, 2001).

'Reframing the purpose of U.S. foreign aid: The impact of Carter's emphasis on human rights' (Athens, GA: University of Georgia, 2007).

'Selecting the recipients of aid: A two-stage sample selection model' (Philadelphia, 2001).

Van Soest, J., *The start of international development cooperation in the United Nations, 1945–1952* (Assen: Van Gorcum, 1978).

Van Staden, A., R. A. H. Schipper, K. J. Silverstrone *et al.*, 'Role conceptions in the post-war foreign policy of the Netherlands', in J. H. Leurdijk (ed.), *The foreign policy of the Netherlands* (Alphen aan den Rijn: Sijthoff & Noordhoff, 1978).

Vandommele, M., 'Twintig jaar Belgisch ontwikkelingsbeleid. Op zoek naar een visie en naar een houding', *Internationale Spectator* Vol. 36, No. 9 (1982).

Vandommele, M. and D. Barrez, 'Interview met L. Tindemans: "Stapsgewijs naar 0,70% van het BNP tegen 1989"', *De Wereld Morgen* No. 4 (1986).

Vangi, C., *Cooperazione con i paesi in via di sviluppo: criteri pratici orientativi per l'applicazione delle norme della legge n. 38 del 9 febbraio 1979* (Milan: F. Angeli, 1982).

Verloren van Themaat, J., 'Loopt Nederland achter met de organisatie van zijn ontwikkelingshulp?', *Internationale Spectator* Vol. 32, No. 9 (1978).

'Waarom geven landen hulp?', *Economisch-Statistische Berichten* Vol. 65, No. 20 (1982).

Vertzberger, Y., *The world in their minds: Information processing, cognition, and perception in foreign policy decision-making* (Stanford University Press, 1990).

Voorhoeve, J. J. C., *Peace, profits and principles: A study of Dutch foreign policy* (The Hague: Martinus Nijhoff, 1979).

Wabl, M. G., 'A "Monterrey consensus" might replace the Washington consensus', *United National Chronicle, Online Edition* (2002).

Wallace, W., 'Foreign policy and national identity in the United Kingdom', *International Affairs* Vol. 67, No. 1 (1991).

Waltz, K. N., 'Reflections on *Theory of international politics*: A response to my critics', in R. O. Keohane (ed.), *Neorealism and its critics* (New York: Columbia University Press, 1986).

Theory of international politics (Reading: Addison-Wesley, 1979).

Weldes, J., *Constructing national interests: The U.S. and the Cuban missile crisis* (Minneapolis: University of Minnesota Press, 1999).

Wendt, A., *Social theory of international politics* (Cambridge University Press, 1999).

White, H., 'Trends in the volume and allocation of official flows from donor countries', *International Review of Economics and Finance* Vol. 13 (2004).

Winham, G. R., 'Developing theories of foreign policy making: A case study of foreign aid', *Journal of Politics* Vol. 32, No. 1 (1970).

Wittkopf, E. R., 'Foreign aid and the United Nations votes', *American Political Science Review* Vol. 67 (1973).

Western bilateral aid allocations: A comparative study of recipient state attributes and aid received (Beverly Hills: Sage, 1972).

World Bank, *Assessing aid: What works, what doesn't, and why* (New York: Oxford University Press, 1998).

World development report 1990: Poverty (New York: Oxford University Press, 1990).

Zaller, J. R., *The nature and origins of mass opinion* (Cambridge University Press, 1992).

Index

Africa, 21, 65, 80, 91, 117, 175, 183, 191, 192
African Development Bank, 105
aid allocation, *see* aid policy: distribution
aid debates, 77
aid discourse, 16, 17, 19, 48, 131, 137, *see also* aid frames
   stability/change over time, 108, 109, 110, 194, 213
aid distribution, *see* aid policy: distribution
aid fatigue, 8, 90
aid frames, x, 4, 5, 10, 21, 59, 95, 210, 212, 248
   cross-national variation, 4, 5, 16, 18
   dataset, viii, ix, 58, 59, 60, 61, 62, 64
   economic self-interest, *see* aid frames: wealth
   enlightened self-interest, 10, 12, 17, 56, 60, 97, 109, 132, 151, 181, 194, 207, 232
   government influence on, 77, 96, 101, 102, 104, 109, 214, 221, 228, 233
   humanitarianism, 5, 9, 10, 12, 16–18, 56, 61–4, 76, 97, 103, 109, 128, 132, 148, 151, 167, 169, 181, 194, 206–7, 209, 212–13, 215, 216–18, 228, 232
   international influences on, 96, 108, 214
   measurement, 18, 22, 73, 74, 76
   obligation, 10, 13, 16, 18–19, 56, 60–1, 63, 76, 128, 132, 151, 167, 181, 207, 209, 215–16, 221, 224, 232, 233
   origins, 16, 77, 78
   political ideology and, 231
   political parties and, 50
   power/influence, 10, 11, 60, 63, 97, 128, 132, 151, 181, 207
   reputation, 10, 13, 18, 56, 60–1, 63, 75–6, 103, 128, 132, 151, 167, 169, 181, 206–7, 209, 212, 215, 221, 228, 232
   salience, 15, 108, 140
   security, 5, 10, 11, 18, 60, 62, 76, 132, 151, 181, 207
   stability/change over time, 5, 16, 17, 214, 226, 228
   wealth, 10, 11, 19, 60–3, 97, 103, 109, 111, 128, 132, 151, 167, 181, 194, 206–7, 212–13, 217
aid policy
   administration, 19, 40, 110, 111, 114, 136, 137, 196, 214, 215
   arguments for, 53, 55, 56, 59, 76, 210, 211, 212, 247
      religious, 53
   distribution, x, 4–5, 16, 20, 40–5, 171, 173–5, 194–5, 197–8, 201, 203, 205–6, 208, 212, 216
      dispersion, 17, 175, 194
      legislative debates on, 195
      stability/change over time, 175, 194
   donor states, *see* donor states
   economic interests, 8
   frames, *see* aid frames
   government influence on, 87, 88
   history, 6
   humanitarian relief, 8
   legislative debates, 5, 15, 18, 109, 211, 225, 235

283

aid policy (*cont.*)
  measurement
    commitment vs disbursement, 172
    overall vs per capita, 173
  motives, 2, 4, 7, 9, 11, 12, 13, 48, *see also* aid frames
    self-interest, 9
  multilateral aid, ix, 19, 41–4, 110–11, 126, 131–2, 137, 229
  NGO funding, 217, 218, 220
  political parties and, 106, 149, 194, 212, 215
  project selection, 4
  public information, 17, 97, 101, 103, 109, 221, 233
  quality, 7, 40, 41, 42, 43, 44, 110
  recipient dependence on, 6
  salience of, 78
  theory of, 2, 36, 39
  tied aid, ix, 42, 43, 44, 110, 111, 126, 127, 128, 131
  to former colonies, 39, *see also* colonies/former colonies
  volume, viii, x, 2–5, 8, 13, 19, 40–1, 43–5, 139, 140–3, 145–6, 149, 162, 165, 167–8, 200, 212, 215
    international norm, 3, 4, 7, 9, 43, 139, 141, 144, 145–7, 153, 156, 160, 212, 215
    trends, 8, 9
aid recipients
  characteristics, 199, 200, 206–9, 216
  popular, 180, 182, 186, 191, 193, 206, 208, 209
  token aid, 196, 197, 198
aid volume, *see* aid policy: volume
Albania, 187
Algeria, 191
analogies, 38
Anderson, Benedict, 27
Angola, 187, 192
Argentina, 185
Aruba, 260
Asia, 175
Australia

aid policy
  volume, 147

Bangladesh, 175, 183
basic human needs, 8
Bauer, Peter, 6, 210, 231, 232
Belgium, 4
  aid debates, 58, 59, 90
  aid frames, viii, ix, 18, 48, 63, 65, 66, 67, 75, 104
    enlightened self-interest, 65, 91, 96, 97, 100, 120, 133, 134, 153, 184, 213
    humanitarianism, 64, 65, 133, 153, 184
    obligation, 64–5, 79, 84–5, 90, 112, 115, 120, 133, 140, 150, 152, 169, 171, 180, 183–5, 206–8, 213, 214, 216
    origins, 78
    reputation, 64, 65, 152, 184, 207
    security, 65
    wealth, 64–5, 79, 85, 90, 112, 115, 120, 131, 133, 140, 150, 152–3, 171, 180, 183–5, 193, 194, 208, 213, 214, 216
  aid policy, 17, 19, 102
    ABOS (administration), 120, 127, 133
    administration, 19, 90, 104, 110, 112, 115, 119, 120, 137, 194
    arguments for, 63
    corruption, 90, 91, 104, 120, 153
    distribution, x, 20, 175, 176, 182–5, 193, 198, 205–8, 216
    dispersion, 185, 194
    stability/change over time, 183
    evaluation, 105, 108
    history, 84, 111, 115
    legislative debates, x, 104, 152, 235, 236, 238
    multilateral aid, 63, 133, 134
    NGO funding, 218
    public information, 99, 100, 103, 104, 107
    tied aid, 19, 105, 127, 128, 134

Index　　　　　　　　　　　　　　　　　　　　　　　　　　　　　　　285

　　volume, viii, 7, 17, 19, 140, 143,
　　　　144, 148, 150, 152–3, 156,
　　　　173
　　colonies, 65, 91, 111
　　core values, 78
　　Flemish–francophone differences,
　　　　78, 85, 119, 120, 137, 150,
　　　　183
　　foreign policy, 78, 84
　　history, 78
　　international trade, 78, 140, 148,
　　　　150, 152, 153, 184, 207
　　Ministry of Foreign Trade, 127
　　national identity, 111
　　public opinion, 85
Bono (U2), 3
Bosnia-Herzegovina, 175
Botswana, 192, 193
Brandt, Willy, 12
Brazil, 182
Brinker, Hans, 124
Brundtland, Gro Harlem, 94, 161
Burundi, 153, 182, 260

Cape Verde Islands, 192
Carter, Jimmy, 219
Chile, 188, 189
cognitive science, 28
Cold War, 39, 67, 93, 96, 139,
　　　147
collinearity, 262
Colombia, 187
colonies/former colonies, 7, 16–17
　　　20, 34, 39, 42, 51, 111, 146,
　　　150, 154, 169, 171, 175, 180,
　　　182–3, 185, 188–9, 206–7,
　　　209, 214–16, 224, 233, 260
　　guilt, 13, 39
Congo/Zaire, 7, 63, 65, 79, 90–1,
　　　111–12, 115, 140, 143,
　　　150, 152–3, 180, 182–4,
　　　260
content analysis, 33, 52, 53
Cuba, 189

De Michelis, Gianni, 92, 121
debt relief, 3, 4, 9
Denmark, 7
　　aid frames
　　　humanitarianism, 220

　　aid policy, 220
　　volume, 8, 9, 20, 139, 142, 146,
　　　　159, 161
Derycke, Eric, 153
development assistance, *see* aid policy
Development Assistance Committee
　　　(DAC), *see* OECD:
　　　Development Assistance
　　　Committee
discourse, 15, 29, 31
discourse analysis, 52
Doha Conference, 3
Dominica, 173
donor states
　　DAC, 2, 8, 19
　　Europe, 18, 148, 175

Easterly, William, 4, 36, 221
Ecuador, 187
Egypt, 186, 187, 189
electoral systems, 231
　　majoritarian, 32, 225
　　presidential, 225
　　proportional representation, 32, 225
environmental issues, 43, 94, 161
Eritrea, 260
Ethiopia, 185, 186, 193, 260
Europe
　　destination for refugees, 153
　　political geography, 82, 154, 155
European Union, 19, 86
　　European Development Fund, 133
　　monetary integration, 223
export subsidies, 16

foreign aid, *see* aid policy
foreign policy
　　constraints, 36, 46
　　motives, 2
frames, 15
　　enlightened self-interest, 39, 42, 45,
　　　51, 56
　　humanitarianism, 39, 44, 46, 51
　　measurement, 33, 38, 48
　　media, 31
　　obligation, 39, 43, 45, 47
　　power/influence, 39, 41, 45, 47, 51,
　　　56
　　reputation, 39, 43, 45, 47, 50
　　security, 39, 41, 45, 56

frames (cont.)
  theory, 5, 15, 21–3, 28–32,
      34–5, 37, 39, 46–7, 76, 162,
      211
    broad vs specific frames, 224
    in monetary policy, 223
    measurement, 223, 224, 227
      legislative debates, 225
      media, 226
      public opinion, 226, 227
      quality, 225
      salience, 227, 228, 229, 230
    political parties and, 231
    prospect theory, 222
    public policy, 223
    sources, 226, 233
    specification, 223, 226, 227
    stability/change over time, 228, 230
    strategic use, 30, 31, 38, 224, 228
  wealth, 39, 42, 45, 47, 51, 54, 56
France
  aid policy
    volume, 8, 146, 147
Freedom House, 260, 261

G-8, 3
Gabon, 184
Geens, André, 100
Germany
  aid policy
    volume, 8
Gleneagles summit, 3
governance
  quality of, 44, 97, 158, 182, 190, 200
government spending, 148
  welfare, 44
Greece
  aid policy
    volume, 9
Guinea, 4
Guinea Bissau, 192

Herfkens, Eveline, 93, 131, 190, 191

ideas, 53
  causal beliefs, 126, 135, 229, 230
  causal impact of, 38
  core values, 14, 27, 37, 77, 108

frames, 14, 27, 28, 211,
    see also frames
  international norms, 13
  policy-specific, 27
identity
  national, 14, 16, 26, 27, 28, 34, 37
imperialism, 1
India, 173, 189, 191, 192, 193
Indonesia, 175, 183, 186, 188–90, 260
interests
  material, 29, 37
International Monetary Fund, 163
international organizations, 41
international relations theory, 12, 13, 14, 22, 46, 233
  constraints, 24, 27, 39
  constructivism, 26
  ideas in, 26, 44
  liberalism, 14, 25, 36
  preferences, 25
  realism, 14, 24, 36
  structural constraints in, 211
international trade, 5, 16, 39, 42, 51, 53, 56, 148, 162, 163, 166–7, 200, 206–7, 233, 259, 260, 261
Israel, 175
Israeli–Palestinian conflict, 162, 229
Italy, 4
  aid debates, 58, 59, 66, 67
  aid discourse, 154
  aid frames, viii, ix, 18, 48, 63, 68, 69, 75
    enlightened self-interest, 68, 87, 91, 93, 95–7, 101, 133, 155, 180, 186, 213
    humanitarianism, 67, 68, 92, 193
    obligation, 68, 86, 112, 169, 207
    power/influence, 80, 86, 87, 91, 155, 180, 187, 213
    reputation, 67–8, 80, 85–7, 92, 106, 112, 117, 121–4, 129, 134, 140, 154–6, 169, 180, 186, 207, 213, 230
    security, 69, 154
    wealth, 67–8, 80, 85–7, 91–2, 95, 112, 117, 121, 129, 153–5,

Index

171, 180, 187, 194, 208, 210, 213, 216
aid policy, 17, 19, 35, 102, 105, 230
  administration, 110, 112, 116, 117, 121, 122, 129, 194
  arguments for, 67
  corruption, 92, 106, 117, 123, 143, 155, 156, 169, 217
  distribution, x, 20, 176, 185, 186, 187, 206, 207, 208, 216
    dispersion, 180, 185, 186, 194
  evaluation, 106
  history, 85, 112, 115
  legal framework, 67
  legislative debates, x, 106, 121, 123, 185, 239, 240
  multilateral aid, 67, 134, 230
  NGO funding, 218
  public information, 100, 103, 106, 107, 155, 222
  public opinion, 123, 149
  tied aid, 19, 128, 129
  volume, viii, 17, 19, 134, 140, 143, 144, 148, 154, 155, 156, 173
colonies, 67
core values, 80
foreign policy, 79
history, 79
international trade, 153, 154, 186, 187
public opinion, 86

Jamaica, 189
Japan
  aid discourse, 220
  aid frames
    obligation, 220
    reputation, 220
    wealth, 220
  aid policy, 220
    distribution, 175
    volume, 8
Jordan, 187

Kenya, 191
Kipling, Rudyard, 1, 4, 6, 13, 16
Korea, 191

Latin America, 174, 175, 183
LDCs (less developed countries), 6, 8, 42, 148, 150, 154, 172, 174, 175, 182, 186–7, 190–1, 208, 216
legislature, 32
  debates, 32, 49, *see* specific countries
    Belgium, 50
    coding, 48–9, 51, 54–6, 58–9, 76
    content, 51
    nature of, 33
    Netherlands, 50
    Norway, 50
    quality of, 49, 51, 61
    representative quality, 212
    United Kingdom, 50
less developed countries, *see* LDCs
Libya, 67, 185, 260
Lie, Trygve, 89
literacy rate, 44
LLDCs (least developed countries), 186, 189, 192, 193
Luxembourg
  aid policy
    volume, 9, 146

Mali, 4
Marshall Plan, 6, 49, 67
Mediterranean, 155, 185, 187, 188
Mexico, 186
Middle East, 188, 189
military spending, 41, 147
Millennium Development Goals, 3, 4, 8, 146
missionary activities, 16, 35, 83, 84, 114
Mobutu Sese Seko, 90, 152, 184
monetary policy, 223
Monterrey Conference, 3, 4
Moreels, Réginald, 120
Morgenthau, Hans J., 1, 2, 5, 11, 13, 21
Morocco, 182, 187
mortality rate, 44
Mozambique, 175, 192, 193
multitool, 1, 2, 5, 10, 13–17, 30, 210, 222

Namibia, 192
Nansen, Fridtjof, 83
national identity, 77, 78, 83, 84, 108, 213, 220
national interest, 24, 56
  commercial, 46
  geopolitical, 46
NATO, 192
Netherlands, 4
  aid debates, 59, 81
  aid discourse, 118, 159
  aid frames, viii, ix, 18, 48, 63, 69, 70, 71, 73, 75, 118
    enlightened self-interest, 71, 93, 96, 213
    humanitarianism, 69–70, 81–2, 87–8, 93, 95–7, 125, 130, 133, 135, 140, 157–8, 172, 182, 189–91, 193, 208, 213–14, 216, 219, 229
    obligation, 70, 87, 95, 130, 140, 156, 157, 169, 213
    power/influence, 69–70, 81–2, 87, 88, 93, 96, 113, 125, 134–5, 140, 156–8, 172, 180, 189–91, 206, 208, 213–14, 216
    reputation, 70, 88, 125
    security, 88
    wealth, 71, 81, 88, 93, 118
  aid policy, 17
    administration, 19, 113, 118, 124, 125
    arguments for, 69
    distribution, x, 20, 173, 176, 180, 188–90, 193, 205, 206–8, 216
      dispersion, 182, 190, 208
    evaluation, 105, 107, 108
    history, 113
    legislative debates, x, 106, 156, 242, 243
    multilateral aid, 19, 134, 135, 229
    NGO funding, 218
    political parties and, 107, 130
    public information, 97, 98, 103, 107, 108
    tied aid, 130, 131
    volume, viii, 7, 9, 17, 20, 53, 118, 140, 142, 144–8, 156–8, 161
  core values, 81
  history, 80
  international trade, 80, 81, 189
  national identity, 80
  public opinion, 81, 102
Netherlands Antilles, 175, 188, 189, 260
Netherlands New Guinea, 188
New International Economic Order, 63, 157
New Zealand
  aid policy
    volume, 147
Nicaragua, 6
Nigeria, 189, 192
norm entrepreneurs, 77–8, 82, 84, 87–8, 96, 102, 149, 214, 220–2, 233
  NGOs, 232, 233
North Yemen, 189
Norway, 4, 7
  aid debates, 58, 59, 66, 72, 83
  aid frames, ix, 18, 48, 63, 71, 74, 75, 218
    enlightened self-interest, 73, 83, 89, 90, 94, 96, 114, 172, 182, 192, 208, 213, 216
    humanitarianism, 72, 73, 83, 89, 90, 94, 95, 97, 125, 130, 140, 160, 161, 172, 182, 192, 193, 208, 213, 216
    international influences on, 95
    obligation, 72, 73, 89, 94, 95, 114, 159, 160, 169, 182, 192, 213
    power/influence, 72, 73, 125, 131, 161, 162, 213
    reputation, 72, 73, 83, 89, 94, 125, 131, 133, 136, 140, 159, 161, 162, 169, 172, 182, 193, 208, 213, 216
    security, 72
    wealth, 73, 90
  aid policy, 17, 72, 229
    administration, 119, 124, 125
    arguments for, 72
    debates, 49

Index

distribution, x, 20, 176, 191–2, 193, 206–8, 216
  dispersion, 175, 182, 192, 193
evaluation, 107, 108
history, 114
legislative debates, x, 107, 114, 159–61, 244–5
multilateral aid, 19, 135, 136, 159
NGO funding, 218
NORAD (administration), 99, 114, 119
public information, 98, 99, 103, 107, 108
public opinion, 218
tied aid, 130
volume, viii, 9, 17, 20, 139, 142, 144, 146, 159, 160, 161, 173
core values, 82
history, 82, 83
international trade, 192
national identity, 83
public opinion, 101

OECD, 163, 174, 206
  aid donors, 9
  Development Assistance Committee, 7, 8, 110, 121, 124, 127, 129, 131, 139, 141, 144, 145, 162, 172, 175, 217, 259
official development assistance, 3, *see also* aid policy
  definition, 7, 141, 158
Oslo Accords, 162, 229
Outers, Lucien, 110

Pakistan, 189, 192, 193
Palestinian Administrative Areas, 175
Pannella, Marco, 87, 117
Pearson, Lester, 7
Philippines, 190
Polity IV dataset, 260, 262
Portugal, 192
postmodernism, 52
Pronk, Jan, 88, 124, 125, 145, 157, 158, 189, 190, 191
public opinion
  surveys
    reliability, 227

rational choice, 15, 22, 37
rationality, 15, 24
realpolitik, 11
refugees, 42, 91, 93, 96, 124, 153, 187
revealed preferences, 27
rhetorical entrapment, 31
Rhodesia, 192
role theory, 50
Rwanda, 153, 182, 260

Sachs, Jeffrey, 3
Sahel, 8
São Tomé and Principe, 6
Scheyven, Raymond, 99, 141, 182, 183
Schoo, Eegje, 93, 96, 118, 119, 157, 219
Second World War, 6, 78, 79, 81, 191
Somalia, 67, 68, 112, 123, 154, 185, 187, 260
South Africa, 192
standard of living, 44
Sudan, 187, 189
Suharto, 175
Suriname, 188, 189, 260
Sweden
  aid policy, 159
    administration, 114
    volume, 9, 20, 142, 146, 147, 159
Switzerland
  aid policy
    volume, 147

Tanzania, 175, 187, 191, 192
Third World, 6, 7, 37
Tinbergen, Jan, 87, 156
Tindemans, Leo, 153
Tobit estimator, 196
Truman, Harry, 113
Tunisia, 182, 187
Turkey, 183, 187, 189, 192

Uganda, 191
United Kingdom
  aid policy, 7
    debates, 49
    distribution, 196
    volume, 8

United Nations, 3, 4, 89–90, 94, 105, 108, 112–13, 135, 136, 160–1, 169, 187, 200, 205, 215, 260–1
  Charter, 6
  Development Decade, 7, 88, 118, 145, 146, 156
  UNCTAD, 145
United States
  aid frames, 219
    security, 219, 229
    wealth, 219
  aid policy, 220, 229
    debates, 49
    distribution, 175
    NGO funding, 218
    public information, 222
  USAID (administration), 232
  volume, 4, 8, 9, 20, 142, 143, 147, 219
  Department of Agriculture, 5
Upper Volta, 189

Van Elslande, Renaat, 152

welfare state, 140, 148, 157, 160, 168, 215
World Bank, 134–5, 145, 259–60, 261–2

Yugoslavia, 96, 186, 187

Zambia, 191

Cambridge Studies in International Relations

105 Ken Booth
Theory of world security
104 Benjamin Miller
States, nations and the great powers
The sources of regional war and peace
103 Beate Jahn *(ed.)*
Classical theory in international relations
102 Andrew Linklater *and* Hidemi Suganami
The English School of international relations
A contemporary reassessment
101 Colin Wight
Agents, structures and international relations
Politics as ontology
100 Michael C. Williams
The realist tradition and the limits of international relations
99 Ivan Arreguín-Toft
How the weak win wars
A theory of asymmetric conflict
98 Michael Barnett *and* Raymond Duvall
Power in global governance
97 Yale H. Ferguson *and* Richard W. Mansbach
Remapping global politics
History's revenge and future shock
96 Christian Reus-Smit
The politics of international law
95 Barry Buzan
From international to world society?
English School theory and the social structure of globalisation
94 K. J. Holsti
Taming the sovereigns
Institutional change in international politics
93 Bruce Cronin
Institutions for the common good
International protection regimes in international security
92 Paul Keal
European conquest and the rights of indigenous peoples
The moral backwardness of international society

91 Barry Buzan *and* Ole Wæver
    Regions and powers
    The structure of international security
90 A. Claire Cutler
    Private power and global authority
    Transnational merchant law in the global political economy
89 Patrick M. Morgan
    Deterrence now
88 Susan Sell
    Private power, public law
    The globalization of intellectual property rights
87 Nina Tannenwald
    The nuclear taboo
    The United States and the non-use of nuclear weapons since 1945
86 Linda Weiss
    States in the global economy
    Bringing domestic institutions back in
85 Rodney Bruce Hall *and* Thomas J. Biersteker *(eds.)*
    The emergence of private authority in global governance
84 Heather Rae
    State identities and the homogenisation of peoples
83 Maja Zehfuss
    Constructivism in international relations
    The politics of reality
82 Paul K. Ruth *and* Todd Allee
    The democratic peace and territorial conflict in the twentieth century
81 Neta C. Crawford
    Argument and change in world politics
    Ethics, decolonization and humanitarian intervention
80 Douglas Lemke
    Regions of war and peace
79 Richard Shapcott
    Justice, community and dialogue in international relations
78 Phil Steinberg
    The social construction of the ocean
77 Christine Sylvester
    Feminist international relations
    An unfinished journey
76 Kenneth A. Schultz
    Democracy and coercive diplomacy
75 David Houghton
    US foreign policy and the Iran hostage crisis
74 Cecilia Albin
    Justice and fairness in international negotiation

73 Martin Shaw
Theory of the global state
Globality as an unfinished revolution

72 Frank C. Zagare *and* D. Marc Kilgour
Perfect deterrence

71 Robert O'Brien, Anne Marie Goetz, Jan Aart Scholte *and* Marc Williams
Contesting global governance
Multilateral economic institutions and global social movements

70 Roland Bleiker
Popular dissent, human agency and global politics

69 Bill McSweeney
Security, identity and interests
A sociology of international relations

68 Molly Cochran
Normative theory in international relations
A pragmatic approach

67 Alexander Wendt
Social theory of international politics

66 Thomas Risse, Stephen C. Ropp *and* Kathryn Sikkink *(eds.)*
The power of human rights
International norms and domestic change

65 Daniel W. Drezner
The sanctions paradox
Economic statecraft and international relations

64 Viva Ona Bartkus
The dynamic of secession

63 John A. Vasquez
The power of power politics
From classical realism to neotraditionalism

62 Emanuel Adler *and* Michael Barnett *(eds.)*
Security communities

61 Charles Jones
E. H. Carr and international relations
A duty to lie

60 Jeffrey W. Knopf
Domestic society and international cooperation
The impact of protest on US arms control policy

59 Nicholas Greenwood Onuf
The republican legacy in international thought

58 Daniel S. Geller *and* J. David Singer
Nations at war
A scientific study of international conflict

57 Randall D. Germain
The international organization of credit
States and global finance in the world economy

56 N. Piers Ludlow
Dealing with Britain
The Six and the first UK application to the EEC

55 Andreas Hasenclever, Peter Mayer *and* Volker Rittberger
Theories of international regimes

54 Miranda A. Schreurs *and* Elizabeth C. Economy *(eds.)*
The internationalization of environmental protection

53 James N. Rosenau
Along the domestic–foreign frontier
Exploring governance in a turbulent world

52 John M. Hobson
The wealth of states
A comparative sociology of international economic and political change

51 Kalevi J. Holsti
The state, war, and the state of war

50 Christopher Clapham
Africa and the international system
The politics of state survival

49 Susan Strange
The retreat of the state
The diffusion of power in the world economy

48 William I. Robinson
Promoting polyarchy
Globalization, US intervention, and hegemony

47 Roger Spegele
Political realism in international theory

46 Thomas J. Biersteker *and* Cynthia Weber *(eds.)*
State sovereignty as social construct

45 Mervyn Frost
Ethics in international relations
A constitutive theory

44 Mark W. Zacher with Brent A. Sutton
Governing global networks
International regimes for transportation and communications

43 Mark Neufeld
The restructuring of international relations theory

42 Thomas Risse-Kappen *(ed.)*
Bringing transnational relations back in
Non-state actors, domestic structures and international institutions

41 Hayward R. Alker
Rediscoveries and reformulations
Humanistic methodologies for international studies

40 Robert W. Cox with Timothy J. Sinclair
Approaches to world order

39 Jens Bartelson
A genealogy of sovereignty
38 Mark Rupert
Producing hegemony
The politics of mass production and American global power
37 Cynthia Weber
Simulating sovereignty
Intervention, the state and symbolic exchange
36 Gary Goertz
Contexts of international politics
35 James L. Richardson
Crisis diplomacy
The Great Powers since the mid-nineteenth century
34 Bradley S. Klein
Strategic studies and world order
The global politics of deterrence
33 T. V. Paul **Asymmetric conflicts: war initiation by weaker powers**
32 Christine Sylvester
Feminist theory and international relations in a postmodern era
31 Peter J. Schraeder
US foreign policy toward Africa
Incrementalism, crisis and change
30 Graham Spinardi
From Polaris to Trident: the development of US Fleet Ballistic Missile technology
29 David A. Welch
Justice and the genesis of war
28 Russell J. Leng
Interstate crisis behavior, 1816–1980: realism versus reciprocity
27 John A. Vasquez
The war puzzle
26 Stephen Gill *(ed.)*
Gramsci, historical materialism and international relations
25 Mike Bowker *and* Robin Brown *(eds.)*
From cold war to collapse: theory and world politics in the 1980s
24 R. B. J. Walker
Inside/outside: international relations as political theory
23 Edward Reiss
The strategic defense initiative
22 Keith Krause
Arms and the state: patterns of military production and trade
21 Roger Buckley
US–Japan alliance diplomacy 1945–1990
20 James N. Rosenau *and* Ernst-Otto Czempiel *(eds.)*
Governance without government: order and change in world politics

19 Michael Nicholson
   Rationality and the analysis of international conflict
18 John Stopford *and* Susan Strange
   Rival states, rival firms
   Competition for world market shares
17 Terry Nardin *and* David R. Mapel *(eds.)*
   Traditions of international ethics
16 Charles F. Doran
   Systems in crisis
   New imperatives of high politics at century's end
15 Deon Geldenhuys
   Isolated states: a comparative analysis
14 Kalevi J. Holsti
   Peace and war: armed conflicts and international order 1648–1989
13 Saki Dockrill
   Britain's policy for West German rearmament 1950–1955
12 Robert H. Jackson
   Quasi-states: sovereignty, international relations and the third world
11 James Barber *and* John Barratt
   South Africa's foreign policy
   The search for status and security 1945–1988
10 James Mayall
   Nationalism and international society
 9 William Bloom
   Personal identity, national identity and international relations
 8 Zeev Maoz
   National choices and international processes
 7 Ian Clark
   The hierarchy of states
   Reform and resistance in the international order
 6 Hidemi Suganami
   The domestic analogy and world order proposals
 5 Stephen Gill
   American hegemony and the Trilateral Commission
 4 Michael C. Pugh
   The ANZUS crisis, nuclear visiting and deterrence
 3 Michael Nicholson
   Formal theories in international relations
 2 Friedrich V. Kratochwil
   Rules, norms, and decisions
   On the conditions of practical and legal reasoning
      in international relations and domestic affairs
 1 Myles L. C. Robertson
   Soviet policy towards Japan
   An analysis of trends in the 1970s and 1980s